God meant it for good

R.T. Kendall

MorningStar
PUBLICATIONS

Charlotte, North Carolina

Scripture quotations marked NIV are from *The
Holy Bible,* New International Version, copyright
1978, 1984 by New York International Bible
Society. Others are from the King James Version.

First North American printing, December 1988
Library of Congress Catalog Card
Number 88-51758
ISBN 1-878327-30-5
Copyright 1986 by R. T. Kendall
Printed in the United States of America

To Joseph Ton

CONTENTS

FOREWORD

Have you ever wondered why a sovereign, all powerful, loving God would allow His own precious children to suffer injustice, humiliation and persecution?

Have you ever gone through a trial and felt like the Lord was miles away and the heavens were brass?

Do you feel like you fail many of the tests which God allows to come your way?

Dr. Kendall gives the best answers to these difficult questions that I have ever heard. His solutions are not always easy, but they are given with such powerful conviction that they may forever change your life.

I am delighted to recommend *God Meant It For Good* by my dear friend Dr. R.T. Kendall. This book does not just contain another thought provoking message by a brilliant theologian and gifted expositor. It is one of the rare books that grips your heart as well as stimulates understanding like few books can except the Holy Bible.

I Samuel 16:7 says "Man looks on the outward appearance, but God looks upon the heart." When I meet a man, no matter how brilliant or successful he may be, I want to know his heart. Through the years I have come to know Dr. Kendall's heart and can say that this book successfully communicates the very essence of his heart.

I have given this book to several friends. To date, without exception, they have all said it was the most helpful book they had ever read outside the Bible. You too will find it hard to put the book down. If you, or a friend, are going through a trial or temptation right now, by all means read this book. Let the God of providence Who rescued Joseph from all of his trials change your life too as you come to better understand His ways.

Dr. Paul Cain
North Carolina
January 1994

INTRODUCTION

One of my early childhood memories was that of my father getting into bed with me just before going to sleep and telling me stories from the Old Testament. By the time I was a teenager I knew many of them backwards and forwards. My favorite was that of Joseph, possibly because it was the longest.

When my father came to the part of the story when Joseph made himself known to his eleven brothers, it would often bring me to tears. I can hardly read the early verses of Genesis 45 to this day without coming to tears. It is the undoubted climax of the story, but it was not until recent years that I felt that I understood it. For Joseph could never have behaved as he did had he not already totally forgiven the same brothers who had treated him as they did twenty-two years before.

"Total forgiveness" is the expression Joseph Ton used when he kindly warned me of a wrong attitude I had in a very sensitive situation a few years ago. Looking firmly and compassionately into my eyes Joseph said, "R. T., you must forgive them *totally*. Until you release them you will be in chains. Total forgiveness is the only way." What is more, I could see, it is the way God forgives us for the sake of Jesus Christ (Eph. 4:32).

Learning to forgive is probably the most difficult lesson for the Christian to grasp. I am convinced that our original Joseph was kept in the dungeon an extra two years because he still carried a grudge against his brothers. I think I can prove this. Any man who would say, "Make mention of me unto Pharaoh" (Gen. 40:14) is still trying to vindicate himself. Self-vindication is alien to love, for love "vaunteth not itself" (1 Cor. 13:4). When we have totally forgiven those who have mistreated us, we are at peace and feel no need to protect ourselves. The only way to achieve love is by totally forgiving others *from the heart.*

There are certain themes in this book, therefore, which will bear mention from the outset.

1. *The principle of vindication.* "Vengeance is mine; I will repay, saith the Lord" (Rom. 12:19). To vindicate means to justify or to clear from blame. When we have been misunderstood or mistreated, we want to be vindicated. Vindication is often the most fierce appetite of the mind. When one has been hurt, he longs for vindication more than anything in the world. But God comes along and says, "Vengeance is mine." Vindication is God's prerogative. It is his right. But it is also what he *wants* to do—on one condition: that we don't try to help him. As long as we put ourselves into the picture, God backs away. Once we turn this exercise utterly over to him, he is free to do things his own way. And in his own time. But he *will* vindicate! The lesson from Joseph is that we must let God do it in his own way and time.

2. *Preparation for service.* The most humbling thing in the world is to recognize that we are still being prepared. The need for preparation is often very difficult to accept. When I was at Trevecca College in Nashville, Tennessee, many years ago, I thought I should go right out into the ministry and forget further studies. I even thought I understood the Book of Revelation! I eventually saw my folly and returned to academic pursuits. But when I came to Westminster Chapel at the age of forty-one, I thought, *Surely I am ready now.* But in a matter of months I could sense that I was still in the process of being prepared. That was most humbling indeed. There is a kind of preparation that cannot be found in a university or a theological seminary. It is not even necessarily found in gaining more experience. It is that which God sovereignly ordains for a specific purpose and which drives us to our knees and to tears. The task to which we are called may be unique, therefore the preparation we need is also unique. There may be no precedents to which we can point in order to explain what is going on. The biblical word for it is *chastening* (Heb. 12:6-11).

3. *Learning to love.* I have already suggested this, but it is

12

something that cannot be overemphasized. "The heart is deceitful above all things, and desperately wicked: who can know it?" (Jer. 17:9). The heart, therefore, can play tricks on us. We think we have forgiven in one moment, but the next day we find ourselves justifying self-pity and personal hurt. "And now abideth faith, hope, charity [love], these three; but the greatest of these is charity" (1 Cor. 13:13). Love is the highest spiritual achievement there is. This is why we are always being prepared. For one does not achieve love as though by an instantaneous transaction; it is a perpetual goal. And yet it is that with which God often confronts us, as if to justify his delay in exalting us.

However, I think that Joseph was being taught to love even *after* he was vindicated. His finest hour was not forgiving his brothers when he first saw them but after their father Jacob died seventeen years later. For it might be argued that he was motivated to love so long as he needed God's blessing on his life but that after he achieved everything—and with his father now dead—he might go for his brothers after all. But no. That was precisely when he said, "Ye thought evil against me: but God meant it unto good" (Gen. 50:20). This shows that Joseph had truly learned to love.

4. *Seeing how much God loves us.* Guilt is the feeling so few will talk about, including Christians. Because a Christian knows he is no longer guilty before God (since he has confessed Jesus Christ as Lord and Savior), he often will not admit it when he *feels* guilty. He even feels guilty about feeling guilty! I suspect that guilt is one of the most common emotions for Christians, even the most advanced Christians. Jacob is a case in point. I am certain that he felt tremendous guilt as a person and as a parent, especially after he lost Joseph. But in the end he saw that God was greater than all the circumstances that suggested to him that God did not love him any more. What a relief it was to discover that God's plan had not been aborted and that *all* that happened was in God's sovereign will. God did not want Jacob to feel guilty. He did not even want Joseph's brothers to feel guilty. The height and depth of God's love to us is so staggering that we are left breathless. What a glorious God we have!

5. *The outline of the gospel.* So much that is in the Old

Testament is a "shadow of things to come" (Heb. 10:1). We will see the phrase "type of Christ" often. But Joseph was not the only one who was a type of Christ in this story. The gospel of Jesus Christ runs through the story of Joseph like a scarlet thread. When I first shared the story of Joseph at Westminster Chapel, it was done largely with the non-Christian in mind. I would like to think, therefore, that if the reader is not a Christian, this book will be the means under God to bring such a person to Christ.

ONE
A DIAMOND
IN THE ROUGH

We begin with Joseph the teenager. God began to deal with Joseph when he was only seventeen. Not everything that Joseph did was good. We are told that he brought to his father, probably regularly, an evil report of his brothers. There is nothing we can say here to make Joseph look good. This just added to his father's sorrow, and it got his brothers into trouble. Nobody likes a tattletale, and this could only make his brothers angry and cause jealousy. Two things make a person a tattletale: their self-righteousness, and their pursuit of self-vindication.

Joseph was self-righteous. We all ought to be encouraged to learn that God can use a self-righteous person, for by nature we are all like Joseph. We might have thought that the writer would leave out this part of this story—Joseph is, after all, one of the heroes of the Bible. But the Book of Genesis tells us that Joseph brought to his father this evil report because the Bible reveals the good and the bad about its heroes. It is so encouraging to know that we don't have to be perfect to be wonderfully used of God.

Joseph was his father's favorite child. This could have some advantages, but it would probably have more of the opposite. It was most certainly not a very good thing at first, and Joseph suffered a lot because of it. Being the favorite of our parents might tend to give us a lot of self-confidence, but it also alienates us from our contemporaries. Joseph had some personality and relationship problems. He was going to be used of God, yes, but he wasn't ready yet—though we probably couldn't have told him that. He thought otherwise.

Do we want to be used of God? Are we quite sure that we are ready to be used of the Lord? God knows whether we are. In the case of Joseph, there was a lot of sorting out in his personality that had to be done, and I can tell you this: God can do it. God, as he prepares us to do his work, will sort out our personality defects, many of which may have been superimposed upon us. It is easy for us to say, "I am like this because my mother was this way" or "My father did this or that." It is easy to blame our parents for the way we are. We may be shy. We may be forward. We may be reserved. We may be arrogant. But we should never think that any personality trait or hang-up (or any other blemish) rules us out as God's messengers to our generation, for God can deal with us. He certainly dealt with Joseph. All the happy trimmings that accompanied Joseph's life at this time would shortly be purged by a sovereign God.

We must remember that parents have their faults too. The reason that Joseph was the favorite child was partly because he was the son of Jacob's old age. That doesn't excuse Jacob. But we must forgive our parents and then hope that our children will forgive us. Nothing is more ridiculous than being bitter against our parents all our lives. We must sort ourselves out and let God deal with us until *we* are responsible for being *just like we are*.

Old Jacob, in order to show how much he loved Joseph, did what he thought was a good thing. He made Joseph a coat of many colors ("richly ornamented robe," NIV). But Jacob did Joseph no favor in doing this. The only thing worse than making it, though, was wearing it. Perhaps Joseph should have gone to his father and fallen down before him and said, "Please don't make me wear this." But Joseph was quite happy to put it on. He was a spoiled, arrogant teenager who was utterly insensitive to his brothers' feelings. When his brothers saw that his father loved him the most, "they hated him, and could not speak peaceably unto him" (Gen. 37:4). That was a predictable reaction, and Jacob should have thought of that. It didn't mean that they hated their father. They hated Joseph. Jacob did this to his own son that he loved so much; he turned his sons against Joseph. It is another caution to us parents that it is harmful to show any kind of favoritism to a particular child. We are doing the child no favor at all; we are not even thinking of the child but of ourselves. Joseph's coat of many colors did more for Jacob than it did for Joseph. Being partial is not a sign of love but demonstrates our own weakness, which we are also passing on to a child.

The future governor of Egypt and God's man to preserve the seed of Abraham was off to a bad start. Perhaps we feel we have had a bad break, with poor psychological or sociological beginnings. Maybe our parents are divorced. Perhaps we can look back on our childhood and say, "I have never had a good break." All we have seen above about Joseph was a blueprint that spelled trouble for the rest of his life.

But there was also something at work in Joseph's life that was wonderful and positive, a gift that God gave him. One of the keys to understanding Joseph is provided by Stephen in Acts 7:9—"God was with him." If God is with us there is no impediment, no personality difficulty, no problem about class background that can stand in the way of him making us a mighty instrument for our day. God was with Joseph and he had a gift, a gift that would shape his own life and also the life of Israel. God gave him dreams. Now that may not sound very impressive. Whoever would have thought that a gift like that could mean so much? And God has given to *you* something that nobody else can do. Because God made you different.

It is sometimes said of a particular person, "When God made so and so he threw the mold away." But wait. He threw the mold away when he made *us!* We are all different from anybody else. To affirm the gift that God has given us is a way of glorifying our Creator. Subsequent events in Joseph's life would reveal that this gift, this dreaming which apparently included an ability to interpret dreams, saved his own life and the lives of his family.

But Joseph made a mistake. He told his dream to his brothers, and they hated him all the more. He got them together when they couldn't do anything but listen to him and said, "Hear, I pray you, this dream which I have dreamed: for behold, we were binding sheaves in the field, and, lo, my sheaf arose, and also stood upright; and behold, your sheaves stood round about, and made obeisance to my sheaf" (Gen. 37:6-7). It wasn't very kind—or clever—to tell a dream like that. What Joseph did was what Jesus called "casting pearls before swine" (Matt. 7:6).

It is possible to abuse the gifts God has given us. It has some-

17

times been said that a man's genius is also his downfall. And Joseph, by abusing this gift, was only alienating his brothers all the more. At this stage Joseph had now made three mistakes. First, he was a tattletale. Second, he flaunted his coat of many colors. Third, he abused the gift God gave him. Joseph should have kept the contents of his dream to himself.

Maybe God has revealed something to us, but we have a selfish need to tell it. We should ask ourselves why we want to tell it. Is it to make people admire us? God will exalt us in due time. We don't have to tell anybody! Remember this: if we have made a mistake, and God hasn't really shown us something, we will be very glad we kept quiet about it. It will save us from being embarrassed later. Keep in mind that Paul said, "Whether there be prophecies, they shall fail" (1 Cor. 13:8). If God has revealed something to us and we tell it around indiscriminately, I predict that we may wait a long, long time to be vindicated.

The fact that we have a gift from God doesn't guarantee that we will have the wisdom or common sense to use it. Joseph told the dream, and it didn't take any "dream expert" to give the interpretation. Joseph's brothers got the message like a flash. They said, "Shalt thou indeed reign over us? or shalt thou indeed have dominion over us?" They hated him more than ever. It didn't do his brothers one bit of good to be told this dream. Flaunting a gift springs from a desire to be admired. But the result is always the opposite: it makes people positively dislike us.

Joseph just wasn't ready to be used of God. His gift was in good shape but *he* wasn't. Many of us may think we are right and ready because the gift is in operation. But God knows better. God had a plan for Joseph and for his people. Do we have a gift? Have we abused it? My counsel is to be sure that we have given ourselves completely to God. We may say, "If I give myself to God, my gift will never be known." I promise you, the only way our gift can be of value is for it to be sanctified and in the hands of our Creator and our Redeemer. When we give our lives utterly to God, even the silly mistakes we have made will turn out for good. We may even be tempted in the end to say, "That's the way I was supposed to do it." This is that wonderful truth found in Romans 8:28, "All things work together for good. . . ." The most stupid things we have done turn out right. God does that!

What Joseph needed was preparation. Polishing. "We must

through much tribulation enter into the kingdom of God" (Acts 14:22). "But the God of all grace, who hath called us unto his eternal glory by Christ Jesus, after that ye have suffered a while, make you perfect, stablish, strengthen, settle you" (1 Pet. 5:10). "The Lord will perfect that which concerneth me" (Ps. 138:8). This may well require some kind of suffering.

A sculptor was going to make a horse out of a big block of marble and somebody came along to him and said, "How are you going to do that?"

He replied, "It's simple. I just start chipping away, and I chip away anything that doesn't look like a horse!"

And so with us. God takes the big block we give him. He begins to chip away anything that is not just like his Son. We have been predestined "to be conformed to the image of his Son" (Rom. 8:29). The day will eventually come when he can begin to use us.

We might have thought that Joseph would surely have learned by now to keep his mouth shut. He was getting into all kinds of trouble. He should have learned that by telling the brothers his dream he was making matters worse. But what do we read? He dreamed yet another dream and told it to them. Why hadn't he learned? The answer is that he hadn't been truly chastened yet. The reason God lets us suffer is to chip away what isn't like Jesus, otherwise we will keep on making the same old mistakes. We may say "Why do I do that all the time?" Perhaps it is because we haven't yet submitted ourselves to God's refining fires. This is why James said, "Count it all joy when ye fall into divers temptations" (James 1:2). May I suggest this: the next time a trial comes, rather than battle it out, rather than try to be rid of it and grumble the whole time, accept it graciously. See what God does. Otherwise it may be that eventually we will have to have the kind of suffering that is almost unbearable because nothing else will work. God has to do that with us. He has had to do it with me. When I look back on my life, it's my suffering that I cherish most. Not the blessings, not the bouquets, not the compliments. But suffering.

But I want to raise this question: Why did God keep giving Joseph these dreams? We would have expected God to say, "Ah, I see you are going to abuse your gift; I am going to have to stop giving you any more dreams." But the Bible says that "the gifts and calling of God are without repentance" (Rom. 11:29). That means that they are irrevocable. God gives us a gift, and we can go on using it because he doesn't take it away. Yet the use of a gift does not imply that everything else about us is right. The gift God gives us is like the salvation that he gives us. He doesn't take it away. It is irrevocable. So here's Joseph—the gift is in operation, and he's repeating the same old mistakes.

Now see what Joseph did next. He was really getting carried away. Not only did he tell his second dream to his brothers—he told his father. His father rebuked him, "Shall I and thy mother and thy brethren indeed come to bow down ourselves to thee to the earth?" (Gen. 37:10). However, although Joseph went too far by revealing great things to those who couldn't handle them, it is still obvious that God's Spirit was at work. It is too easy to say that unless everything goes exactly right God isn't in it. Joseph went too far, but who can deny that an authentic work was set in operation in him? Joseph didn't anticipate that he would offend his father. When Joseph told his dream, he thought his father was going to like it. He thought his father would clap his hands and say, "Well done, Joseph."

Joseph was beginning the process of being emancipated from his father. Jesus said, "A man's foes shall be they of his own household. He that loveth father or mother more than me is not worthy of me: and he that loveth son or daughter more than me is not worthy of me" (Matt. 10:36-37).

Speaking personally, I too had to be set free from my father. I have already referred to him, and I thank God for him. But the time came when I had to break with him. It happened many years ago, and at the time it was a great trial. The Lord showed me certain things in the Bible, and when I came home to share them with my father I thought he would clap his hands and say, "Oh son, that's wonderful." But the opposite was the case, and it wasn't until recently that I won my father over. He now sees that God was using me.

That in part is what was going on in Joseph's life. Jacob, the doting father, had manipulated Joseph. Joseph was now having to show he wouldn't be completely controlled by his father. It wasn't pleasant for Joseph to be rebuked over what he thought would please his father. But then we read one other thing in this connection. Although Jacob rebuked him, Jacob "observed the saying"

(Gen. 37:11). As the New International Version puts it, "He kept the matter in mind." That means that Jacob somehow knew in his heart that there was indeed something to Joseph's dream.

Joseph was what we call a "type of Christ," one who makes you think of Jesus long before he ever came along. We are going to see this often. Joseph was a type of Christ, only Jesus never sinned. Jacob loved Joseph and God loved his Son. But God loved his Son perfectly and with a love with which we too are loved. "God so loved the world, that he gave his only begotten Son, that whosoever believeth in him should not perish, but have everlasting life" (John 3:16). Joseph was a product of his father, and Jesus was a product of his Father; Jesus was the perfect man. Jesus was God as though he were not man. Jesus was man as though he were not God. Jacob rebuked Joseph—what Joseph thought would please his father brought a rebuke instead. There's a parallel here. Jesus said, "My meat is to do the will of him that sent me, and to finish his work" (John 4:34). Jesus did everything right. He said, "I do always those things that please him" (John 8:29), but there came a moment in time when Jesus got far more than a rebuke from his Father. The Bible says that Jesus was "smitten of God" (Isa. 53:4). He cried out, "My God, my God, why hast thou forsaken me?" (Matt. 27:46). He "who knew no sin" was made sin for us, "that we might be made the righteousness of God in him" (2 Cor. 5:21).

We are told that Jacob gave Joseph a robe of many colors. God wants to give us a robe of righteousness, the righteousness of Jesus Christ. On the cross he was smitten of God. Not just rebuked but smitten. Put to death. All of our sins were charged to Jesus. God punished Jesus instead of us that we might be made the righteousness of God in him.

Joseph was God's diamond in the rough. He needed a lot of polishing before his time would come. But that is the way God sees each of us—diamonds that no one around us would recognize. It is what God sees that matters. When he sees us with that robe of righteousness on, he vows to stay with us to the end. "He shall bring forth thy righteousness as the light, and thy judgment as the noonday" (Ps. 37:6).

TWO
WHEN OUR DREAMS
ARE SHATTERED

Joseph was seventeen years old and chosen of God but, as we have seen, he was not exempt from mistakes. He dreamed that his eleven brothers would bow down to him and that even his parents would be dependent upon him. God gave the dream. Joseph did not have to talk about it, but he probably thought he would see it fulfilled shortly.

When God shows us that he is going to use us (and he can do that), we usually tend to think that we are going to see this happen in the next week or two. What often happens is that it is a long time before God gets around to using us as he has in mind. Take Moses. When Moses grew up, he refused to be called the son of Pharaoh's daughter, "choosing rather to suffer affliction with the people of God, than to enjoy the pleasures of sin for a season" (Heb. 11:25). Moses thought that when he left the palace and identified himself with his brethren, they would clap their hands and say, "Welcome. We've been waiting for you to come." The truth is they rejected him, and Moses needed another forty years of preparation.

It may be a good while indeed before God's greater purpose in us will be realized. It could be that you too are in a similar situation. Perhaps you are older and you have yet to see what God's greater purpose in your own life is. Perhaps you have just about given up. You thought at one time that God was going to use you. You were convinced of it, but it didn't work out. God's message to you right now is: the end is not yet. The story isn't over.

Let us return to the story of Joseph. In Genesis 37:2 Joseph was with his brothers tending the flock. But then in verse 12 we find that his brothers had separated from Joseph and were tending the flock in Shechem. What happened in the meantime? We don't know for sure, but we can deduce a few things. First, we know that Jacob had given Joseph this coat of many colors. That alone separated him from the rest. Second, Joseph had flaunted the gift God gave him—the dreams. That, too, isolated him from his brothers. It is not unlikely that the old man, Jacob, saw that there was no choice but to keep Joseph away from them.

Although Joseph's dream was of God, at a natural, psychological level, Joseph's dream could be explained in terms of a wish fulfillment. Here was a man who said, "I have dreamed a dream. Behold, the sun and the moon and the eleven stars made obeisance to me." Joseph wanted more than anything else to have everybody admire him. And his father's decision to give him the coat of many colors put him on the spot. What he wanted more than anything else was to have the admiration of his brothers. But he went at it the wrong way. It was not too unlikely that this became an obsession with Joseph. When God shows us that he will use us, there is almost always a certain appeal to our own self-esteem. God doesn't compel us against our will. He makes us willing to go. The way he makes us willing is by motivating us; he offers us something we are going to like. God does this as a kindness to accommodate our weakness.

Here is the irony. Though God speaks to us at our own level in order to motivate us, that very self-esteem to which he appeals needs radical surgery before he can in the end actually use us. Look at Joseph. Do you identify with him? Do you know what it is to have the conviction that God has a purpose for your life? Joseph had these dreams. What do you suppose was going on in his mind? I have said you could do a psychological study of Joseph. Joseph, of course, had these dreams in the days before the discipline of psychology emerged, but had he been around today, someone would no doubt have gone to him and said, "Now, Joseph, look here. You are under a lot of pressure. Your father has given you this coat of many colors. Your brothers hate you. It is quite natural for you to want them to bow down before you.

You've had this dream. Can't you see, Joseph, that the dream you had is just a wish fulfillment?"

Possibly even back then Joseph began to wonder, *Was I a fool to think that my God gave me these dreams? Perhaps I worked them up. Perhaps they are at best what I want to see happen.* Even if God does something in an undoubted way, it doesn't make us exempt from Satan's subtle temptation to suggest, "This was you. You did that. God wasn't in that at all." It can happen to a person on a Monday morning after he was converted on Sunday night. The devil pounces upon him and says, "What a fool you were last night! You did that. You worked it up. God didn't do it."

What *was* on Joseph's mind? I believe that at bottom Joseph knew that God gave him the dreams. They pandered to his ego, yes, but the fact remains, God gave them. No doubt Joseph could see that he had made a series of mistakes, and yet another lovely irony is that God kept giving him the dreams. Even though we abuse the gift God gives us, he doesn't take the gift away. The gifts and calling of God are "without repentance"; they are irrevocable (Rom. 11:29). When God gives us a gift, it is ours, just as when he saves us. He keeps us, and it is a wonderful thing to realize that when we become children of God, we can never be lost. Joseph knew that God gave these dreams. But why wasn't something happening?

I suspect that the last thing Joseph had in mind at this stage was God's greater glory or the preservation of his covenant people. The hasty conclusion most of us come to when God shows us something is that God is doing it for our own sake. We are so enamored of ourselves. If God shows us something, it often plays right into our egoistic needs, and we seldom look any farther.

Look at the disciples of Jesus. Though God had called them, they certainly had a "what's-in-it-for-me?" attitude. They had their own self-interest at heart in following Jesus for three years. Oh, how much they had to learn! Many of us start out working for God with self-interest at heart. Before we can be of any value, something must happen to us. What is that? *Whatever it takes* to bring us to the place where we see that God gives us a gift for his glory. For his greater purpose. For his church.

God is interested in the church, the kingdom, his wider witness in the world. He doesn't tell us all this at first. He leads us one step at a time. He doesn't lead us from A to Z, he leads us from A to B, B to C. Somewhere along the way we begin to realize that God did call us but that it's the same God who said, "I am the Lord: that is my name: and my glory will I not give to another" (Isa. 42:8). There comes a time when self-interest must be swallowed up by God's greater glory. Moses had to learn that, and this lesson was also in store for Joseph.

While Joseph was separated from his brothers—they were doing the work—he was, for all we know, sitting under a tree somewhere, dreaming about his dreams, hoping for something to happen. Perhaps old Jacob had become so convinced of Joseph's dreams that he thought that by separating the eleven brothers from Joseph it would make it easier for the dreams to come true.

We know that the Bible tells us in Genesis 37:11 that his father "observed the saying," and perhaps Jacob, upon reflection, said to himself, "Maybe there is something to this." Jacob kept the saying in mind. These dreams wouldn't upset him too much. After all, if the dreams were true, he himself would feel quite vindicated. He could have had some guilt feelings of his own for singling out Joseph and giving him the coat of many colors. If God had given Joseph the dreams, Jacob could feel much better. Whenever we are selective with our children we are going to feel guilty. It is guilt that often makes a parent want to relive his or her life through the child. Thus, Joseph was separated from the eleven.

One day old Jacob, deciding to make Joseph do something useful, said, "Go to your brothers in Shechem and make sure they are all right." This may have been the first thing Joseph had to do in a long time. I don't know how Joseph spent his time. Perhaps he was on a perpetual holiday. Maybe he had homework to do. Maybe he was doing the equivalent of watching television. Apparently he had nothing to do, and he himself may have been feeling guilty about the way he wasted his time.

Do you ever feel guilty about the way you use your time? If so, I want to put a proposition to you. Give yourself to God totally—100 percent. Give God your life. Mean it. But be careful. God will take you seriously, and the preparation that he will have for you will make up for the way you have wasted your time. It wouldn't be long until Joseph's holiday (or whatever it was) would be over. Joseph probably thought he had been ready for a long time. When we get the call from God to do something, our most natural feeling is that we are quite ready to go. Shortly after God called me to preach, I didn't think that I needed to stay in college, much less go to seminary. I had the message; I was ready to go. Most of us feel the same way. We don't wish for further preparation. I have since come to admire the statement of the great C. H. Spurgeon who said that if he had twenty-five years left to live, he would spend twenty of them in preparation. An extraordinary statement. Dr. Lloyd-Jones used to say that the worst thing that can happen to a person is to be successful before he's ready. Joseph wanted to be successful, but he wasn't ready. As I have said, you couldn't have told him that then. When a person isn't being chastened, it is easy for him to think that he is quite ready.

Little did Joseph know, little did his father know, that it would be the last time they would see each other for a long time. Little did Joseph know that his days of comfort, ease, and convenience were numbered. He was his father's boy, but this selfish, insensitive teenager was also God's instrument for his generation. Joseph went to the spot where his brothers could normally be found. He expected them to be in Shechem, but he learned that they were in Dothan, so he went on there.

They saw him before he saw them. It is not hard to figure out why. There was Joseph strutting along with his coat of many colors—you could see him a mile away. He loved that coat. You would have thought he would be embarrassed to wear it, especially around his brothers, but their feelings didn't put him off one bit. They saw him afar off, and the moment they saw him they knew what they wanted to do. They conspired to kill him.

It's no small thing to get rid of one's brother—so they needed a good excuse. "Let us slay him, and cast him into some pit, and we will say, Some evil beast hath devoured him: and we shall see what will become of his dreams" (Gen. 37:20). It was his dreams that bothered them. Somehow they too feared there was something right about them; if they got rid of Joseph, it was a way of challenging God. "We will see what will come of his dreams now." They continued this defiance by saying to one another: "Behold, this dreamer cometh."

Don't be surprised if the man God chooses gets a nickname, one that alludes to the way God is going to use him. The world always gives the name. It is usually derogatory. When the disciples were called "Christians" it was not considered a flattering term at all. This is why Peter in his epistle had to say, "If any man

man suffer as a Christian, let him not be ashamed" (1 Pet. 4:16). Eventually they were proud to own the name. So it was with the Puritans. It was not a happy term—it was a word of derision. Eventually they accepted it. So also with the word *Methodist.*

When God's purpose is at work, you can expect others to be jealous. We have seen that Joseph was insensitive and not without sin, and now we see the wickedness of his brothers. But in all of this, God's higher purpose was set in motion. Often we have no idea what God has in mind for us, but his purposes will be fulfilled. Where sin abounds grace does much more abound (Rom. 5:20). God's eternal purpose is at work whether we consciously feel it or not. Sometimes when we don't *feel* something, we wonder if God *is* working. But the fact that you don't feel something proves nothing. God works silently behind the scenes.

Thus, at the bottom, their motivation was: "We shall see what will become of his dreams." These brothers also knew that their father had become impressed with the dreams, so they wanted all the more to discredit the work that was going on. However, one of the brothers was conscience stricken. Reuben said, "Let us not kill him . . . but cast him into this pit that is in the wilderness, and lay no hand upon him" (Gen. 37:21-22). Reuben had the idea of going back later to get Joseph, although he didn't have the courage at the time to say what he really wanted to do. Joseph didn't know what was going on. We are told that they took him and cast him into an empty pit and that there was no water or food in it.

What do you suppose was going on in Joseph's mind now? His dreams were shattered. As far as the eye could see, as far as any human projection could be made, there was no hope. He may have hastily concluded that his dreams were delusions. In a pit, there was nothing to do but pray to his God.

THREE
FROM RICHES
TO RAGS

Throughout human history there has been the repeated phenomenon of someone going "from rags to riches." Less spectacular is
that of going from riches to rags. Moses experienced it when he
refused to be known as the son of Pharaoh's daughter, choosing
to be mistreated rather than enjoy the "pleasures of sin for a
season" (Heb. 11:24-25). Now it was to be Joseph's lot.

Joseph, as a type of Christ, like many other types in the Old
Testament, was "a shadow of good things to come, and not the
very image of the things" ("not the realities themselves," Heb.
10:1; NIV). Many Old Testament personalities may also be seen as
types of Christ. Abel was a type of Christ (Heb. 11:4). Isaac, the
son of Abraham, was a type of Christ (Heb. 11:19). Moses was a
type of Christ, as were Joshua, Samuel, David, and the prophets.

Joseph was a type of Christ in many ways, but at this point we
see it particularly in the way he became a victim of his brothers'
jealousy and cruelty. It is true that Joseph's brothers' reaction to
him was quite natural. You might even say that they couldn't help
feeling as they did.

But we must nonetheless face the fact that sin was at the
bottom of it all. Sin makes all of us want to justify what we do.
Sin is inherited from our parents and from our parents' parents,
and the most natural feeling we all have is, "I can't help feeling
like I do because I didn't even ask to be in this world." We all have

29

a way of rationalizing sin and trying to explain it away. "I didn't ask to be here. I didn't ask to be a sinner."

This leads us to an apt definition of a Christian: one who takes the responsibility for his own sins and quits blaming his troubles on his parents or upon people or upon society. When that begins to happen and we begin to see that we have got to deal with ourselves, we are close to becoming a Christian. We must see that we have sinned before God. That is where we must come before we can ever be saved.

The attitude that his brothers had toward Joseph is precisely the way men looked at Jesus. There emerged in the life of Jesus a conspiracy to set him at nought. This happened when Jesus was betrayed by Judas Iscariot. Judas went to the priests of Israel, who took Jesus to Herod, then to Pilate. The whole thing was a conspiracy. Similarly, his brothers saw Joseph coming and said among themselves, "Let us slay him" (Gen. 37:20).

But another element in the conspiracy against Joseph was that he was mocked (compare Luke 23:11). When his brothers saw him coming "they said one to another, Behold, this dreamer cometh" (Gen. 37:19). Why were they mocking? They were jealous (Acts 7:9). Even Pontius Pilate knew that the Jews had set Jesus at nought because of jealousy and envy (Matt. 27:18). They tried to come up with witnesses against Jesus, but they found none.

The next similarity to Christ in the brothers' treatment of Joseph was their cover-up. They said, "This dreamer cometh. Come now therefore, and let us slay him, and cast him into some pit, and we will say, Some evil beast hath devoured him" (Gen. 37:19-20). They wanted to cover up what they had decided to do. They would not come to their father and tell the truth. They would say, "Some beast hath devoured him."

Once you deliberately bring yourself to commit sin you will need a second sin—a lie—to cover up the first. Sin always leads to lying. This is also what happened in the case of the conspiracy against Jesus. False witnesses were brought in (Matt. 26:59ff.). They wanted to cover up their own hostility, their jealousy, and their motives; so they brought in false witnesses. But you can succeed in a cover-up process only for so long: "Be sure your sin will find you out" (Num. 32:23).

Another sin of Joseph's brothers was their attempt at self-justification. The desire to clear ourselves is a fault we all have.

They said, "We shall see what will become of his dreams" (Gen. 37:20). These brothers regarded their conspiracy to set Joseph at nought as entirely justified. Why? Because Joseph's dreams suggested predestination. If you can abort predestination, you have proved the dream was not really from God. Joseph had obviously believed his dream: "I have dreamed a dream, it will be fulfilled, therefore, you are going to bow down to me." So the brothers wanted to destroy Joseph to show that his dreams were false. This is the way they justified everything that they did. "We shall see what will become of his dreams."

And that is the way the Jews looked at Jesus when he was hanging on the cross. They said, "If thou be the Son of God, come down from the cross" (Matt. 27:39-43). They were justifying themselves. They didn't feel guilty about nailing Jesus to the cross. They said, "If Jesus is who he says he is, we don't have anything to worry about: he will just come down from the cross. We will then clap our hands and say, 'We're with you, we think you're great; now we believe.' " But when Jesus didn't do that, they were cleared then in their own eyes. This is why men today are so anxious to destroy the Bible; they want to disprove it for the same reasons. "You don't have to worry. There's no need for you to get right with God. The God of the Bible has written a book full of errors so there's no need for you to worry about a heaven or a hell." This is why men love to read an article by a minister who says that the Bible is full of errors.

But there was yet another similarity in the behavior of the brothers—"respectable neutrality." Reuben, the eldest brother, heard what the others were planning to do. They were going to kill Joseph and say that some evil beast had devoured him. And Reuben saved Joseph by pulling rank. He was not strong enough physically to stand against the others, so he used his authority as Jacob's firstborn son. Some didn't agree with Christ's death, but they remained "respectably neutral," saying nothing and doing nothing to stop it.

It appears that Reuben had a good motive. He wanted to return Joseph to his father, but all he said was, "Let us not kill him. Shed no blood, but cast him into this pit." His intention was to go back to the pit later, pull Joseph out, and deliver him to his father. But Reuben did not say what he was going to do. He was ashamed to use his authority to return Joseph then and there. He

31

might have said, "I'm the firstborn. I'm stepping in. You're not going to do that. We're going to return Joseph to our father right now." But he couldn't bring himself to do that. Here was a case of "respectable neutrality." He was convinced that what they were doing was wrong, but he wouldn't come out and stand alone.

Are you like that? In your heart of hearts do you know what is right and what you ought to do? Agrippa said to Paul, "Almost thou persuadest me to be a Christian" (Acts 26:28). But the cost was too great for Agrippa to follow Jesus Christ. He was close. Almost there. Reuben didn't agree with what his brothers were going to do, but neither did he have the integrity and courage to deliver Joseph to his father.

Now look at these brothers. They cast Joseph into a pit. Humanly speaking, Joseph could only live a day or two. But that was not all. These brothers now sat down to eat. How could they do that? They were going to have a meal. They had just left Joseph in a pit without any water. He was going to die in a day or two, and here they were about to eat! I wonder what was in their minds. How could they do it? A hardened conscience lets one do strange things. Now while they were sitting there eating they saw some Ishmaelites coming. Judah, on seeing them, had second thoughts: "Come, and let us sell him to the Ishmaelites, and let not our hand be upon him; for he is our brother and our flesh."

The brothers thought that was a good idea: "His brethren were content" (Gen. 37:27). Imagine that! They were actually able to be at peace about selling their brother into slavery! Why? The idea of selling him to the Ishmaelites was mild compared to what they had been prepared to do so that we are told they were *content!* That is another example of the deceitfulness of sin. Do we know what it is to sin so grievously that a lesser sin seems right? That is Satan's deception.

Joseph, who the day before had been in luxury, in security, with his coat of many colors, had gone from riches to rags. And that is exactly what happened with Jesus. Jesus turned his back on the glory of heaven and earth. Though he was God, he thought it not a thing to be grasped, but became man, making himself "of no reputation" (Phil. 2:5-7). "Foxes have holes, and birds of the air have nests; but the Son of man hath not where to lay his head" (Luke 9:58). He turned his back on a royal diadem for a crown of thorns. Why did Jesus do that? Why did Jesus go from riches to rags? As Paul put it, "For ye know the grace of our Lord Jesus Christ, that, though he was rich, yet for your sakes he became poor, that ye through his poverty might be rich" (2 Cor. 8:9). This Jesus became *nothing*, and it was for us. He died that your conscience and mine could be purged.

FOUR
WHEN GOD
PUTS HIS FINGER
ON ONE MAN

If God puts his finger on you, it is enough to change you, your family, your church—even a nation and the world. The highest compliment a man can ever have is to be tapped on the shoulder by God. When that happens wonderful things are at hand. Yet, when that happens it means that a time of preparation is also at hand. This can also be called God's chastening. It is God's way to get the man he has owned ready for his own use. When God puts his finger on you, things may get worse before they get better.

We don't have any evidence that Joseph ever said, "God, you can have my life. You can take my life." Have you ever prayed a prayer like that? Whether Joseph did or not, one thing is for sure: God took over Joseph's life. Be careful about saying to God, "You may have my life." He may take you seriously.

In 1956 I said something to God that I wouldn't necessarily recommend that you say. I don't know that I would do it over again. I had heard a sermon on Philippians 2:5: "Let this mind be in you, which was also in Christ Jesus." The minister showed how Jesus became the *lowest possible shame* for the glory of God. I was so moved by that sermon that I went back to my room (where I was in college) and got on my knees and said, "God make me the lowest possible shame for your glory." I actually said that! Within two months, events took place that led my closest friends and my loved ones to use almost those very words to me! They said, "You are a shame and a disgrace to the family." The only consolation I had was that I had prayed that prayer.

It is not necessary for you to pray that prayer. God has the right to do precisely that anyway because you are his property. You are not your own. You are bought with Jesus' blood. I have a theory that those who do pray a prayer like that (even if it is just saying, "God, you can have my life") have been led to pray in that way by God who has given them the prayer as a kind of merciful warning. It is a sign he is working in them already so that they won't be too surprised later. He was going to do it anyway. If it happens to you, it means he was going to take over your life. But what he did was to inspire you to pray that way so that when he took your prayer seriously, you would know *you* had prayed that way.

What often happens to us is this: we consecrate our lives to God and utterly mean it. We may say, "Lord, you can take my life. Use me as you wish." But no bright light flashes in the room. No bells ring. We are not aware that God said, "Good, I am going to take you seriously." We continue to pray about other things and for other needs, and we finish our prayer. Then, when the beginnings of God's preparation are suddenly set in motion, God is acting upon our own wish to be used.

The first thing we notice about Joseph's preparation is that it began without any advance notice. You may well prefer God to say, "I will answer in three weeks' time." Or maybe "eight months' time." Or even, "Next Tuesday afternoon about three o'clock." If only God had said to Joseph, "Be careful, next Tuesday afternoon your brothers are going to kidnap you. It is the beginning of my preparation for you." But when God hides his face, or when God begins to chasten, he doesn't give advance warning. A part of what makes chastening *chastening* is that it comes suddenly and unexpectedly. When our world is shattered and the bottom drops out, it is, in fact, the result of the most careful planning by a loving, wise, sovereign God. His ways are higher than our ways (Isa. 55:9). It is comforting to know that God has "abounded toward us in all wisdom and prudence" (Eph. 1:8). We are in his hands. He knows how to deal with us, and he alone knows how to direct our lives.

How firm a foundation, ye saints of the Lord,
Is laid for your faith in His excellent Word!
What more can He say than to you He hath said,
To you, who for refuge to Jesus have fled?

—George Keith

The second thing that God puts his finger on is our "sore spot." In Joseph's case that had to be dealt with urgently. His sore spot was that coat of many colors. His father had made it for him, but that only antagonized his brothers. The first thing that has to be dealt with is often the thing that is most dear to us but is a sore spot to everybody else. Therefore, however devoted his father was to Joseph, that coat of many colors had to go before God could use Joseph.

What in your life must go before God can truly have you and make you his instrument? It may be a gift somebody has given to you. It may be a gift that you have naturally. It may be God's very gift. I know people who are afraid that their God-given gift isn't going to be used. I remember years ago talking to a man like this. We were driving through Tennessee and he wept and said, "I am so afraid God isn't going to use my gift." I have thought about that man many times. He did have a marvelous gift, but he wasn't ready. He was so proud of it and wasn't willing to be refined, operated upon. It may be that the gift God has given must be smashed before it can be of any value. God can smash it—but he can also mend it and make it more beautiful and lovely than it ever was. Or it may be something about your personality that needs to be dealt with. It may be the area of your life about which you are most defensive or most sensitive. Maybe you have great potential, but there is something about you that makes you of little use.

In 1956, when I was at college in Nashville, Tennessee, I prayed the prayer I mentioned earlier. My grandmother had been so proud of me because I was pastor of a church. I was nineteen and the weekend pastor of a church in Palmer, Tennessee. I was the only preacher in the family. My father wasn't a preacher; his father wasn't a preacher. Nobody on either side of my family was in the ministry, and they were so proud of me. My grandmother had a little money and bought me a car, a brand new Chevrolet, with all the accessories—chrome, white sidewalls, radio! I drove that car around campus, and I am sure that it didn't look a bit different from Joseph's coat of many colors. I didn't make anybody happy with that car. It did something for me but not for anybody else. "That car has to go," God said up in heaven. When they were saying to me, "You have become a disgrace to the family, you have become a shame," my grandmother took the car away from me. She took it back! It was the best thing that could have happened to me then.

The third thing about Joseph's preparation is this: when God put his finger on him, he underwent the shock of seeing how sinful and frail other people were. Joseph knew that his brothers weren't fond of him. But little did he know that they were capable of doing what they did.

Sometimes something like this will happen to a new Christian. It is so easy for new Christians to look up to an older Christian. But it will often happen that when they begin to admire anybody too much they are in for a *very keen* disappointment. One of the greatest shocks that I had to absorb was when I saw that my godly grandmother (and she's now in heaven) didn't rejoice with me over what I had thought would thrill my family. I came home from college and I began to share with my family things God had shown me in the Bible. And I thought they would say, "Wonderful, tell us more." But they didn't react like that. It was the opposite. I had never dreamed that Christian people could be like that.

Before Joseph was ever going to be of use to God, he needed to observe people with a certain objectivity. He could hardly have expected that his own brothers would cast him into a dry pit, intending to leave him to die.

Why does God want us to see the frailty of other men? The answer is in the Psalm 118:8: "It is better to trust in the Lord than to put confidence in man." We must all learn that lesson sooner or later, but it comes hard. We want to find at least one other person we can totally trust and say, "I will believe anything you say." As soon as we begin to do that we are setting ourselves up for the greatest hurt of our lives! God shows us the frailty of other men so that we won't trust the best of men too much.

We also need to be sufficiently detached from people to help them. We must learn to see them with objectivity and discover to what extent they need us. When we do this, nothing will surprise us. God brings every man to the place, sooner or later, where he's never surprised at the depths to which man can sink. As long as we have a naive view of human nature, or a naive view of the best of Christians, we are not ready to be launched out. We need first to face the real world and discover how wicked man is.

The fourth thing God does to the man on whom he puts his finger is to bring him to a place of apparent despair. They cast Joseph into a pit—an empty pit, with no water in it, and left him to die. There was nothing for him to do but to pray.

Has that ever happened to you? God does us such a favor when he treats us like that. This is how we learn to trust him. The principle is this: God is proved through an unprecedented situation.

There was no known precedent for a true child of God being thrown into a pit to die, much less surviving! For a child of God this might even be evidence that he was out of God's will. There would be no way that Joseph could explain to anybody while in a pit that he was in God's will! The ten brothers said, "We shall see what will become of his dreams" (Gen. 37:20). They were quite sure that they had him in such a fix that nobody could conclude that he was God's man.

The way God often tests our faith is to bring us to places where there is no known precedent. We all feel rather safe with a precedent to lean on. The interesting thing about the men in the eleventh chapter of Hebrews is that every one of them had to do something different from people of the generation before. Not a single one was given the luxury of doing it exactly as it had been done before. God likes to bring us to the impossible situation when, humanly speaking, it's the end.

Finally, when God puts his finger on his man, he will bring him to the point of no return. That is what God did to Joseph. The ten brothers lifted Joseph out of the pit when they saw the Ishmaelites coming. They decided they didn't want to have his blood on their hands and that it would satisfy their own needs just to get Joseph completely out of the way. So they lifted him up from the pit and sold him to the Ishmaelites for twenty pieces of silver. Then the Ishmaelites brought Joseph into Egypt. There would be no turning back for Joseph. What is more, it was out of his hands.

Joseph was given temporary relief from his immediate ordeal when he was lifted out of the pit. He had thought that was the end. He had no water and he was thirsty. In our time of preparation God does give us definite encouragement along the way. At that particular moment, when Joseph could not have gone further, God gave him relief. He was thankful to be out of the pit, to have water, to be alive. Had you told Joseph the day before that he would be sold to the Ishmaelites and going to Egypt he wouldn't have looked forward to that trip at all, but God brought him to such an extremity that he was glad now to go to Egypt! That is the way God works.

If you knew in advance what God wanted you to do, you might say, "Oh no." But God can work things around until you would rather do that than anything in the world. An old song put it, "He doesn't compel us against our will; he just makes us willing to go." God has a way of bringing us through a horrible ordeal with joy, even though a new trial is on the horizon. It will seem mild compared to what we just went through. Why does God do that? One answer is that we will see his intervention and know that he is never too late, never too early, always just on time. God brought Joseph to the place where he would be thankful just to be delivered out of that pit.

Joseph would always remember how he was lifted out of that pit. He knew God was with him. He had seen God act, and he could never forget that.

> *Through many dangers, toils and snares,*
> *I have already come;*
> *'Tis grace hath brought me safe thus far,*
> *And grace will lead me home.*

—John Newton

Joseph's new home was Egypt. A lot had happened in the last twenty-four hours for Joseph. God can accomplish a lot in a very short period of time. What was accomplished now was the impossibility of turning back. Perhaps the single most important thing that happens to the man God puts his finger on is to bring him to the place where there is no turning back. It was still painful. He didn't even get to say good-bye to his father. He could only say in his heart, "Good-bye, Father. Good-bye, Canaan. Good-bye, coat of many colors." But he could also say good-bye to that pit that he was thrown in! Now he would have to wait and see what God would do next.

FIVE
STARTING
A NEW LIFE

Joseph had suddenly been put in a strange new country. He was forced to cope with unwanted new beginnings. Born with a silver spoon in his mouth, Joseph was now a slave. The Ishmaelites owned him for a while but later sold him to a man called Potiphar. Potiphar was an Egyptian, a high ranking officer in Pharaoh's army, a man of class and prestige. He had wealth but also perception.

St. Augustine said a long time ago that God loves every man as though there were no one else to love. God also prepares every man as though there were no one else. Joseph never asked for this preparation. He was forced to start a new life as a way of being prepared for future service. A great upheaval had taken place. Perhaps a few people have to undergo the shock of change as Joseph underwent it in those swiftly moving days. Everything was happening so rapidly. Now we find him in Egypt, cut off from all the people and surroundings he had ever known.

Do you know what it is to start a new life when that isn't what you wanted to do, when it was thrust upon you? It may have come because of sudden illness. It may have been the consequence of losing a loved one, so that nothing was ever to be the same again. It could be a change of job. It could be a marriage breakdown. Or getting fired. Financial reverse. Illness. Being lied about. Betrayed. You had to start *all over.*

Has it occurred to you that all this is nothing more than a

blueprint that is being carefully conceived and carried out by your Creator and your Redeemer? In Joseph's case it was an irrevocable emancipation from his past. He couldn't go back. It wouldn't do any good even to daydream about returning. Do you know what it is to daydream? To sit and wish? Most of us daydream at some time or other, but we normally dream about what is at least remotely possible. We don't usually dream about what we know *couldn't* happen. Joseph couldn't dream about going back to Canaan.

God does us an enormous favor when he makes us see we simply cannot return. Sometimes we are at a standstill because we are still hoping somehow to go back to things as they once were. We can waste days and months—possibly years trying to go back. Joseph could not because God prevented him.

Now Joseph was in phase two of his preparation. Phase one had been falling into the pit and being rescued in time and kept alive. Phase two could almost be called the "fun part." When God makes us break from the past, he puts something in its place to make things not only bearable but even pleasant.

Moses underwent a similar change. He broke with his past. He left the palace of Pharaoh and thought that when he identified himself with his brethren they would be glad to see him. But it didn't work out that way. He had to wait another forty years before he could really be used, but those next forty years were happy years for Moses. He was given a wife, a change, a respite from the pattern of life he knew. God did that for him. God doesn't want us to be unhappy. He wants us to get joy from him, but also from the provisions that he gives us. And God does this to encourage us to go on.

There were three ways in which God made things bearable for Joseph. First, Joseph had rest from his enemies. He had a rough time. He had brought a lot of it on himself, yes, but he had become a victim of cruel hatred. There came a time when God said, "Enough is enough." God knows how much we can bear. There comes a time when he looks down from heaven and lets us know he sees what we are going through. It may be persecution. It may be somebody constantly annoying us. It could be a threat. It could be a severe kind of pressure under which, were it to last, we would crack up.

Paul said, "There hath no temptation [or trial] taken you but such as is common to man" (1 Cor. 10:13). That means that others have been through it before. It could be that what we are going through seems unique in the history of man. We all tend to think that about ourselves. But Paul said that that's not true. God will not put us through any temptation that hasn't been experienced by others. "But God is faithful, who will not suffer you to be tempted above that ye are able; but will with the temptation also make a way to escape, that ye may be able to bear it."

Now Joseph was given rest from his enemies. He was able to live free from the kind of terror and jealousy and hatred that he had known. He wasn't overjoyed about being in Egypt, but at least he didn't have that terror.

The second thing that made all this bearable—and this is the main thing—Joseph had the presence of the Lord. "And the Lord was with Joseph" (Gen. 39:2). Now this had been true before. Joseph had had the presence of the Lord before. But perhaps he hadn't *felt* it all that much. And there is a sense in which he hadn't needed it before now. He had his father to whom he could always turn. If he ever got into trouble, he didn't turn to the Lord. Many of us have never been brought to the place where we have needed God alone. The only way we sometimes come to feel the presence of God is when God himself pulls the rug out from under us and we begin to fall. Then we cry to him, and possibly for the first time we *feel* him.

God does that not because he is mad at us, not because he wants to see us cry, but because he wants us to feel him. As long as there is a mother or father, or a brother or a sister, or a good friend, or money, or that job or that house—or whatever means so much to us that we don't need the Lord—we probably won't depend on God. When God selects a man for a mission, high on God's agenda will be this: God alone must become precious. This is why he makes us break with our past. This is why he cuts us off from father, mother, brother, sister, homeland—so that for the first time we will really know what God is like!

There was a third thing that made things bearable, even pleasant for Joseph. He prospered in his new career. There is only one explanation for this: God did it to encourage him. If God wanted to, he could have brought Joseph to Egypt and let him live in the dust. There was a dungeon not far away that Joseph would eventually inhabit, but he couldn't take that yet. God knew that.

God knew that Joseph needed a time to be encouraged, otherwise he might have been demoralized. God never demoralizes us.

Joseph would be tested, however, to see if he would put his most cherished gift in suspension. God put it on the shelf for a while. Joseph was an expert in dreams, but he couldn't very well say to Potiphar, "Don't make me start at the bottom. Don't you know about my gift? I'm overqualified to do jobs like that. Have you had any dreams lately?"

But God knew that Joseph had other gifts. Joseph's other abilities would never have emerged if he hadn't had a new job like this. Perhaps you have a gift you haven't discovered yet, simply because you think that what you are chiefly qualified to do is the only thing you can do. Joseph had other gifts, and they had to come out. Do not forget, we are talking about a man who was destined to be the future governor of Egypt. But although he didn't know that, God did. Joseph didn't know that starting at the bottom of Potiphar's household was preparing him to be governor of Egypt. We don't know what God is preparing us for. We may be a future president of the United States. One of us may be another C. H. Spurgeon. Who knows what God will do with us? It may be that we will use a gift we didn't know we had. We will never discover it as long as we are concentrating on the only thing we think we are good at.

Joseph needed to learn the graces of his new culture in his new country, and Potiphar would be his model. Potiphar was a man of class and prestige, a man of wealth who had the sort of skills and qualities that would be required of a governor. Joseph merely said to himself, "I am going to obey this man. I will do what he says." Joseph couldn't help noticing Potiphar's mannerisms. Potiphar would be his mode,l and Joseph, no doubt, vowed early on he would make the most of everything in this new situation.

It is important to remember that Joseph started at the bottom. Genesis 39:2 shows that Joseph was elevated to live in the house of his master. Imagine living in the house itself! There were quarters for the slaves far from the master's own house.

Moreover, Potiphar *saw* that "the Lord was with him" (Gen. 39:3). I find this very interesting. Verse 2 says that the Lord was with Joseph. Verse 3 says, "His master saw that the Lord was with him." We are talking about a godless Egyptian who saw that the Lord was with Joseph. There are two Hebrew words for Lord.

One is *Yahweh* and the other is *Adonai*. *Yahweh* was God's special revelation of his name to his people only. In Egypt they would know nothing of *Yahweh*. They had never heard of a God like that. But we are told that Potiphar, this godless Egyptian, knew that *Yahweh* was with Joseph. How could that be? Well, there is only one way. Joseph told him. Now I don't know how it came about that Joseph would witness to Potiphar. It may have come out in an interview, or when Potiphar began to notice that this Joseph was excelling. Perhaps Potiphar called him alongside and said, "Tell me more about yourself." But at some point Joseph *talked about his God.*

That could have put Potiphar right off, but it didn't because Potiphar recognized in Joseph something so unusual that it commanded his attention. He may or may not have liked what he heard, but he thought, *Well, I am interested in this.* Joseph, except for perhaps his great-grandfather Abraham who had visited Egypt earlier, was the first worshiper of the true God to live in Egypt. This meant that Joseph would be watched by Potiphar to see what came of a man who made a profession like that.

I should say here that there's a right way and a wrong way to witness on the job. When the time comes for our Christian faith to emerge, then watch out! A careless, lazy Christian, one without industry or without integrity, can be fatal to the testimony of the Christian faith. When it is known that we are Christians and also that we are the best workers there—this is marvelous. Will they find out that we are the easiest ones to get along with? That we are not only likable and lovable and sweet but hard-working and conscientious? If so, should our employer hear that we are a Christian, he's going to say, "I would like ten Christians in this place." That's the kind of man Joseph was.

One indication that the Lord was with Joseph was the way in which he adjusted to his new surroundings. Potiphar must have known that this way of life hadn't been easy for Joseph, that he had never had to work. Potiphar could merely look at Joseph and tell. He could feel his hands—they weren't rough. He could look at his face—it wasn't weather-beaten. Clearly Joseph hadn't lived a rough life. But look at Joseph now—he had to start at the bottom and work his way up.

I think it is also fair to say that another explanation for Joseph's prosperity was that he excelled partly because this new life meant comparatively little to him. He was quite detached from what he was doing. First, he was attached to the Lord. Secondly, his heart and his ambition were elsewhere. People who are *too* attached to their own surroundings sometimes aren't as effective as they could be. Egypt meant nothing to Joseph. Therefore he didn't get so personally or emotionally involved that his struggles were counter-productive.

I have a friend who lives in the Florida Keys—Pastor Bruce Porter, a fine, godly young man. He started a church there in a house with twelve people. At the time of this writing, the congregation numbers more than three hundred. I spent a few weeks there one summer, and when it was time to leave, I said, "You lucky man. I've got to return to England, and you get to live in the balmy breezes with the palm trees and the ocean and fishing."

He calmly said, "This is not where I would like to live. I would rather be in the mountains of North Carolina." And he couldn't have been more serious.

Then I went up to Fort Lauderdale. I said to O. S. Hawkins, "You lucky man, you get to live in sunny Fort Lauderdale."

He said, "We would rather be in Texas!"

My point here is that God doesn't want us to like our surroundings too much. I fear that if I were living in Florida I wouldn't be worth anything. I would want to go out and bonefish and swim and things like that. Those servants around Joseph would have given anything in the world to be living in Potiphar's house. It didn't mean that much to Joseph, though. Partly because he was in this strange country, Joseph didn't take himself all that seriously. After all, there wasn't anybody there that knew him. There is little delight in being exalted if nobody knows us and recognizes us. Now if he could have shared it with his eleven brothers, that would have done something for him.

What *was* Joseph's ambition? More than anything else in the world, he wanted vindication before his brothers. But that appeared to be an unreachable goal. Sometimes I think that God gives some of us an unreachable aspiration so that what we do attain doesn't go to our heads. Perhaps Potiphar also could see this in Joseph.

SIX
A NEW KIND
OF TRIAL

Little did Joseph know that some day he would look on his eleven brothers and say, "You meant it for evil, but God meant it for good." If he had known, he might well have endured these trials with a feeling of lightness. He could have just said, "This is part of the training." But here he was in an alien country with, humanly speaking, no hope of ever seeing any good come of what had happened to him. The glory is that he kept his faith in God through it all. But now a new kind of trial was looming up before him.

He was faced with sexual temptation. What is remarkable about his reaction to this temptation is that he didn't know that God was testing his mettle to see if he could be trusted with truly great responsibility. We are not talking now about a man in public life—like a minister or a deacon or some godly man who has so much to lose. Many people maintain a moral standard for the sole reason that they know what they would lose. And so they resist temptation, managing somehow to go on without falling into this kind of sin.

But look at Joseph. Here was a servant, a slave in a foreign country, with little to lose. Even if he did give in to the temptation and was subsequently found out, he had no family nearby to be hurt, no reputation to defend. And yet what we find is that when this man Joseph was put to a most severe test, he passed it, with flying colors—and nobody knew! He was accused of sinning as though he had done it. What is more, he was punished for it.

It was said of Hezekiah, "God left him, to try him, that he might know all that was in his heart" (2 Chron. 32:31). That means God hid his face for a moment. When God shows his face, it is the most wonderful feeling in the whole world. When God lets us feel his presence, we feel joy in our hearts. We read the Bible and want to read for hours. When we pray, we talk to the Lord as though he is right there. We sometimes think that if we open our eyes we will see Jesus right before us. That is how real the Lord can be. And when things are like that we can go along and sing; we can whistle; we feel really good, wherever we are— on the subway or in a train or bus. There is nothing to compare with the feeling of God's presence.

When God withdraws the light of 'his countenance, we pray and we feel that God isn't even listening to us. We read the Bible and our eyes stare at the same verse for thirty minutes and we think, "I'm not getting anywhere." We pray again, and the Lord apparently isn't there at all. And that is how we discover what we are really like—for example, whether we will *go on* and pray, as Paul put it, being instant "in season, out of season" (2 Tim. 4:2). "In season" is when the Lord shows his face; "out of season" is when he hides it.

Yet another principle that emerges from this part of the story is that we should not expect a new kind of trial to come our way unless we have made it through the old one with dignity. If we are experiencing a kind of trial such as we have never had before, God has paid us a high compliment. I fear there are Christians who never have a truly new trial—it is the same old kind. That is partly because God in his kindness continues to allow another chance to dignify the old trial, by working through it without murmuring and without complaining. The purpose is to come through tried as gold. If we do, then we are able to move on to a new vista or a new horizon. It means we have passed the test in the old one.

When God does allow a new kind of trial, remember that he notices everything about it—every thought and move we make. Most of all, remember that the trial is never without significance. No matter how senseless it may seem to be—God is watching every move we make. Remember also that if God allows a new kind of trial to come along, it means he has definite plans for us.

Joseph had been faithful in Potiphar's house. Furthermore, God had blessed Potiphar because of Joseph (Gen. 39:5). Everything good was happening to Potiphar just because Joseph was on the premises. One day the wife of Potiphar cast her eyes on Joseph, "well-built and handsome" (Gen. 39:6; NIV). She made a move toward him for which he wasn't prepared. Normally it is the man who is attracted by sight—not the woman. Normally it is the man who sets something in motion, not the woman. But here is young Joseph, having been put in charge of Potiphar's household and living right there in the house, becoming the target, not the instigator, of sexual overtures. So one day Potiphar's wife thought, *I've got to have Joseph.*

As for Potiphar himself, the man who is likely to be forgotten in this episode, we would think he had it made. He was a very prosperous man, with nothing to concern himself with except to come to breakfast, lunch, dinner. Joseph had taken over, and everything was going well. Never once did it seem to enter Potiphar's mind that young Joseph was a potential threat to his marriage. Potiphar trusted Joseph, if only because Potiphar knew how much Joseph loved God.

We don't know a lot about Potiphar's wife, so we have to be careful not to speculate. It is possible she was a fashionable woman. As an officer's wife, she moved in circles that made it likely she would normally have little to do with a servant or a foreigner like Joseph. But she came directly to Joseph: "Come to bed with me" (Gen. 39:7, NIV). Joseph refused her and gave as the final explanation for his refusal, "How then can I do this great wickedness, and sin against God?" (v. 9).

It will be our love for God alone that will—in the end—keep us from falling into sexual sin, assuming very acute temptation. For when it is a case where we have nothing to lose and we are unlikely to be caught, only our relationship with God will stop it. Many people are able to maintain a certain moral standard only because they have so much to lose or they are afraid they might get caught—or perhaps because they haven't met Potiphar's wife! If we are ever in a situation (no doubt we have been or will be) where it would appear that we could do it, and nobody would ever find out, one thing and one thing alone will keep us pure: our love for God. Nobody is exempt from the temptation, but if we do not have a love for God that is greater than the intensity of

51

that temptation, we will give in. It is *then* we discover what we are really like.

The beauty of this story is that Joseph gave as the bottom line reason for refusing, "How can I sin against God?" This is the level of devotion that God wants from every Christian. For if we have a love for Jesus Christ that is so powerful and so real that we could go around the world and not sin against God, we show we can be trusted with great things for God. The fear of offending him must be the worst thing that we can imagine.

Potiphar trusted Joseph utterly and he was certainly justified in this trust. He was sitting on top of the world—no cares, no worries. Yet when we are sitting on top of the world, we are in a rather dangerous position; we have no place to go but down. When we are on top of the world, the devil can take advantage of that situation.

The point is made by some interpreters that Potiphar neglected his wife, that if Potiphar himself had been the kind of husband he ought to have been, Potiphar's wife wouldn't have come to Joseph like that. That is sheer speculation. Whereas in some cases this may serve as a small part of the explanation, there are many cases (my pastoral experience would suggest most cases) where the husband or wife have absolutely no excuse. Most adulterous situations come because someone thinks the grass is greener on the other side of the fence. And there is one reason for this: it is sin. We may come up with a psychological explanation for it. We may say, "It is due to the way I was brought up—my father was like this, my mother was like this, or this situation happened to me." There's almost always a psychological (or sociological) explanation for sin. We may call it immaturity. We may say a person suffered from an arrested emotional development at this or that age or lived under adverse conditions. But the reason is still ultimately sin. No amount of understanding of our background will guarantee help to control sexual sin. We can go to a psychologist, even spend five years in psychotherapy or psychoanalysis, and be no closer to mastering ourselves. The only thing that will ultimately keep a person from falling into sin is his love for God.

If God has a work for us to do and he wants to use us, we should not be surprised if at some stage we are confronted with the kind of temptation that we are talking about here. It is to see whether God can trust us with other things he has in mind for us.

"We did this because we were in love" it is often said. Some even go so far as to say that Potiphar's wife really loved Joseph. Love is often the excuse for sin, as if to say, "If it's love, it is all right." Remember this: any sexual involvement outside marriage is sin, and it is not real love that motivates it. It is never love—it is *lust*. It will appear as love at the time, but it is not that. The proof that Potiphar's wife didn't love Joseph is the way she turned on him when he rejected her. If she had really loved him, she would never have lied about him. It was her own lustful nature that had to have him. The devil is so crafty. He will make us think that something is rather noble so that we will go on and do it. Any sexual involvement outside of marriage is sin.

But what about a person who is neglected or lonely? What compensation is there? Ultimately there is only one answer: our love for God. God can give us a love for himself that is so real and so great that the love of God is actually greater than the temptation or loneliness that plagues us at the moment.

> *When through fiery trials thy pathway shall lie,*
> *My grace all sufficient shall be thy supply,*
> *The flame shall not hurt thee; I only design*
> *Thy dross to consume, and thy gold to refine.*
> —George Keith

Joseph, faced with this new trial, resisted the temptation. He would never be sorry. What is more, he qualified for greater trials that promised incalculable blessing.

SEVEN
FALSELY ACCUSED
AND HELPLESS

Victor Hugo said, "Hell hath no fury like a woman scorned." Perhaps it was Potiphar's wife who gave Hugo his cue for this famous statement. She resented Joseph for not acquiescing to her evil desire and accused him of trying to seduce her. When he ran from her, she grabbed his cloak. He kept on going. She used that garment left behind as evidence against him. Immediately she began to spread her poison to the other slaves who were nearby. When her husband came home, she showed him the same garment and claimed that the Hebrew came to "make sport of me" (Gen. 39:17, NIV).

Potiphar, the Egyptian officer, was enraged. Joseph had no way of defending himself. He was a foreigner in a strange land and a slave with no status. There were no witnesses. The only one that could tell the truth—Potiphar's wife herself—certainly wasn't going to. The evidence was stacked against Joseph on the side of Potiphar's wife. She was the one everybody was going to believe. She had his cloak as evidence. So before Joseph had time to pack a suitcase, he was slammed into prison where he had no voice—not even a lawyer.

Yet God did Joseph a special favor. If Joseph had had an opportunity to defend himself, that is probably what he would have tried to do. But he was rendered absolutely helpless; all he could do was keep his mouth shut. He might as well; nobody would believe him. He would look like a fool if he tried to say a word. God did it with good reason—that he and we might see what God can do when we take our hands off a situation.

If you are a child of God and you have been hurt by being falsely accused, God feels more deeply about it than you do, but if you try to defend yourself, he will back off and say, "Oh, *you* want to do it. That is what I wanted to do. So are you going to do it? Get on with it." I promise you, you will find yourself in the biggest mess and in the deepest trouble! If anything, it will be worse than ever. You will look like a fool.

But if you will only be quiet, say nothing, and do not try to manipulate the situation, God will be moved and he will act. He will say, "I'm going to step in." God loves to do that. But he wants to do it all by himself.

This is why I say that God did Joseph a favor by putting him in a position where he couldn't speak. If God does that to you, be thankful. God knows that if he lets you become unhandcuffed or puts you in a position to speak, then you are probably going to do it, and you will simply be competing with what he wants to do.

It is a singular blessing when God shuts us up. God wanted to show that what is utterly impossible with man is absolutely possible with God. So God put Joseph into an impossible situation.

Consider the method Joseph followed when he refused to sleep with Potiphar's wife. First, when Potiphar's wife came to Joseph initially and said, "Come to bed with me," he refused, saying, "My master does not concern himself with anything in the house; everything he owns he has entrusted to my care" (Gen. 39:8, NIV). He valued Potiphar's trust in him. He also considered Potiphar's feelings.

The second thing was that he looked at his own position. "There is none greater in this house than I; neither hath he kept back anything from me" (v. 9). Joseph had self-respect.

Third, he respected Potiphar's wife. "Thou art his wife." Here *was* an example of true love in operation. Whenever you begin to look at another man's wife or another woman's husband and you say, "It is love that is compelling me," it is lust not love. Lust has a way of camouflaging itself as love. I can tell you how you would behave if it were really love. You would behave exactly like Joseph, who said, "You are his wife." That showed unselfish love and proved that he respected himself and her.

The fourth method Joseph used was to remember that he would be sinning against God. "How then can I do this great wickedness, and sin against God?" This is the New Testament teaching of righteousness of the law without the law. Have you ever heard of that? Joseph was carrying out the righteousness of the law, and the law hadn't even come! The law was to come hundreds of years later and yet Joseph said, "How can I do this wickedness and sin against God?" The seventh commandment, "Thou shalt not commit adultery," came years later, and yet here was Joseph, speaking as though the law were in existence.

And that is how it is with the Christian. The law has been fulfilled in Christ. It is over and done with, and yet, by walking in the Spirit, the Christian has fulfilled the righteousness of the law (compare Rom. 8:4). He doesn't have to have the law inside him to tell him how to live. The Christian knows how to live. The Spirit of God has purged his conscience (Heb. 9:14). That is what was true of Joseph.

Look also at Joseph's approach when he was again confronted with this temptation. It is a case of persisting with a right principle. When Potiphar's wife first came to him and he refused, Joseph might have said smugly, "Well, I've paid my dues. She came to me and made a pass at me and I said no." If she were to come again he might say, "Well, I refused her once. I did the right thing, but if she comes again, I am not responsible this time."

A lot of us are like that. We feel so good about ourselves if on one occasion we avoid doing something wrong, and we want to talk about it all the time. But then the next time the temptation comes we fall. Joseph refused her the first time, but what about the second time? "It came to pass, and she spake to Joseph *day by day,* that he hearkened not unto her." This is what is truly pleasing to God. It is not simply that you can say once, "I can't do that," but that you are so absolutely committed to Christ that when the temptation comes back again and again and again, you say, "No, no, no!" That was Joseph.

But that wasn't all. He began avoiding Potiphar's wife altogether. "He hearkened not unto her, to lie by her, *or to be with her*" (v. 10). Paul said, "Make not provision for the flesh, to fulfill the lusts thereof" (Rom. 13:14). That means that if you have any idea where temptation will be, you won't go there. You may think you are strong because you can be with this person or that without

57

being influenced. You may say, "I'm strong enough to rub shoulders with this situation without it bothering me." But Joseph fought this so hard that he finally wouldn't even be around where she was. He had already shown how strong he was, and then he shows more strength. He doesn't even go where temptation is. Strength is not merely an ability to resist temptation; true strength lies in refusing to go where you know temptation will be.

Despite all this, he went to prison. One might be tempted to say, "That's the thanks he got for being true to Potiphar, to himself, to Potiphar's wife, and to God!" Joseph at the time of temptation might have said, "If God were really with me, he would remove this temptation." This is the way the devil comes alongside to tempt us. The devil says, "If God were really with you, and you were doing the right thing, by this time the temptation would have left." The Apostle Paul told the story of how he was given a particular temptation which he called "a thorn in the flesh." We will never know until we get to heaven what that was. Under the inspiration of the Holy Spirit, Paul used a phrase that would be an umbrella term covering almost anything! Whatever your situation may be you may therefore identify with Paul. Paul said, "I've prayed three times for this to depart and it didn't, and all I could get back from God was, 'My grace is sufficient' " (2 Cor. 12:7-9).

God allowed Potiphar's wife to secure evidence that resulted in Joseph's imprisonment. Joseph's cloak was left there, and Potiphar's wife used it as evidence and played it to the hilt. She had the "goods."

They did this to Jesus. Jesus made a statement rather early in his ministry: "Destroy this temple, and in three days I will raise it up" (John 2:19). That is what Jesus actually said. One may have thought at the time that nobody took any notice of it. Sometimes we wonder if people are listening to us or if anything is being heard. But if we have enemies, they are going to seize upon our every word and are waiting for the slightest thing we might say that they can use against us. Here was something Jesus said early on, but when it came to the trial of Jesus (if you can call it a trial), they used it against him (Matt. 26:61). God allows this to happen to his own people. He let it happen to Jesus, and if he let it happen to Jesus, he could let it happen to us. Why? Because God allows others to take advantage of us in order to carry out his secret will for us. Others may seem to have the "goods" on us, and were we to speak before God's time, we would look like fools. So God has boxed us in!

An interesting thing to me is that if Potiphar's wife had been upright and her case truly sound, she wouldn't have needed to make a big fuss about all this. Yet she used this "evidence," Joseph's cloak, with people to whom she would not normally give the time of day. We are talking about an officer's wife who had servants. She wouldn't normally invite them in for coffee or tea. She would just say, "Do this. Do that." Why would she need servants to help her case? They should believe her anyway. After all, they wanted to keep their jobs. They were probably jealous of Joseph in any case because this foreigner had come in out of the blue and gotten to live in Potiphar's house. She had nothing at all in common with these servants, yet she shared with them what was none of their business. She revealed her insecurity when she spoke so candidly to those to whom she normally would not speak. She actually blamed her husband before these servants!

"See, he [Potiphar] hath brought in an Hebrew unto us to mock us" (Gen.39:14). Imagine that! This woman stooped so low as to talk about her husband to her servants. When a vengeful person is filled with rage and hate, he says and does crazy things that betray the weakness of his case. Uncontrolled sin will lead one to say and do bizarre things. Potiphar's wife felt she had to defend her honor to people who had nothing to do with the matter. If she had been truly honorable, all she would have had to do was talk to her husband quietly when he got home and say, "You're going to have to get rid of this Hebrew. Here's what happened today." Her calm word would have been sufficient. But no. She had to shout and scream and tell everybody. "The lady doth protest too much," wrote Shakespeare, in *Hamlet.*

God did Joseph a great favor when he couldn't defend himself. It meant God himself would take over. That is what God does when he seeks out the next person he is going to save. He brings him to the place where he has no defense. He realizes he cannot boast. "Nothing in my hand I bring." John Cotton, the old Puritan, used to say, "As long as there is a wiggle left in you, you are not ready." Thus, when you realize you have no defense (you just shut up—your mouth has been stopped) it is at that moment that God will justify you.

EIGHT
LOSING THE BATTLE
TO WIN THE WAR

The most important test that a person may have to pass before he is ever greatly used of God is to be punished for well doing and then to keep quiet about it.

That is exactly what happened to Joseph. He was put into prison because he did everything right. When we follow Joseph's example, or as Peter put it, follow in the steps of Jesus (1 Pet. 2:21), we are then reaching heights of glory. For Peter went on to say, "The Spirit of glory . . . resteth upon you" (1 Pet. 4:14). He raised the question, "What glory is it, if, when ye be buffeted for your faults, ye shall take it patiently? But if, when ye do well, and suffer for it, ye take it patiently, this is acceptable with God" (1 Pet. 2:20).

Joseph was punished because he did everything right. It is not going too far to say that he was chastened by God because he did everything right.

When God chastens us, he is not getting even with us for our sin. There is hardly a pastor in the world who hasn't come across someone who, having experienced some tragedy, calamity, or adversity, has hastily concluded, "I know why this has happened to me. God is angry for something I once did." The Bible says that God "hath not dealt with us after our sins; nor rewarded us according to our iniquities. . . . As far as the east is from the west, so far hath he removed our trangressions from us" (Ps. 103:10,

12). God's chastening is not God's way of getting even: *God got even at the cross.*

It does not follow that God will not sometimes chasten a disobedient Christian. That is obviously true (see 2 Sam. 12:1-23). But the chastening isn't God getting even; it is preparing that person for something better, more valuable and worthwhile. God chastens us "for our profit, that we might be partakers of his holiness" (Heb. 12:10). Often God chastens the very one who, as far as anybody could tell, didn't apparently need it or deserve it. Job "was perfect and upright" (Job 1:1). God put him through a trial that was extreme, but not because Job had sinned. "For whom the Lord loveth he chasteneth, and scourgeth *every* son whom he receiveth" (Heb. 12:6, italics mine). You don't have to do anything wrong for God to decide to chasten you. The promise is already there. You can be living the most godly kind of Christian life and quite suddenly be tapped on the shoulder by God saying, "I have got a little trial for you."

D. L. Moody was seated on a platform when he heard the man preaching make this statement: "The world has yet to see what God can do with one man who is utterly committed to him." Mr. Moody said in his heart, "I propose to be that person." We might think that anybody who would want to be used of God like that would get the applause of the angels—that everything would start going right. Within days his church burned down. His own house burned down. It is through much tribulation that we enter the kingdom of God (Acts 14:22).

When God chastens you because you have done right—and you take it well—then you can be trusted. God had a plan for Joseph that was greater than anything that could be seen at the time. Not everyone who is chastened can find an immediate reason why. Living a godly life does not guarantee that you are going to be *recognized* as being godly. People may say the very opposite about you, and many will believe them. Potiphar's wife came out shouting to everybody, "I've been mistreated; I've been molested," and Joseph's reputation was ruined.

God could have vindicated Joseph right on the spot. God can do anything. Why didn't God vindicate this falsely accused righteous man then and there? The answer is that it is better to lose the battle in order to win the war. God had a lot more in mind for the kingdom of God than Joseph's personal vindication. Are you suffering right now because somebody has said something about you that is not very nice? Has somebody done something to you that is not very kind? Do you yearn for the moment of vengeance, for the moment when everybody will see the truth? Of course you do. But if you can't keep quiet about it, and you begin instead to act as a busybody, trying to protect yourself and your self-esteem, God will back off from the whole situation. He will let you handle it, and you will lose the war. The wisest thing one can ever do when mistreated is to be quiet about it. As I have already said, there is nothing he wants to do more than vindicate an abused child of his. Joseph kept quiet. God wanted him to lose the battle so that he might win the war.

Joseph was never cleared of the charge made by Potiphar's wife. There is no mention in Scripture that everybody eventually saw that Joseph was innocent. Later on he became governor of Egypt. I suppose Potiphar's wife felt a bit odd when Joseph became her husband's boss. Potiphar himself may have kept quiet, even though he probably knew in his heart that his wife's story was not true. (If Potiphar had really believed his wife, Joseph would never have gotten off with just a prison sentence.) Potiphar had been utterly convinced of Joseph's integrity. I suspect that one look at Joseph's face told Potiphar all that he needed to know, but to protect his own household, his dignity, his wife's reputation, and his marriage, Joseph had to be punished—but only with a prison sentence. Potiphar probably knew the kind of wife he had married. Yet Joseph seems never to have been cleared. The only ones to clear Joseph are those who read the Bible. Moses (who wrote Genesis) said that Joseph was innocent; therefore the only people who have arisen to clear Joseph's name are believers.

In this way, also, Joseph is a type of Christ. Jesus was never vindicated by those who sent him to the cross. When Jesus was raised from the dead, did he go straight to Herod and say, "What do you think now?" Or did he go to Pontius Pilate? To the chief priests? No. Jesus didn't go to anybody to clear his name. He went to those who loved him. It was only the believers who saw the resurrected Christ. At the Crucifixion Jesus could have so easily won that battle. At any moment he could have stopped them or struck them dead. Even when they were driving in the nails or while he was hanging on the cross and the mobs were shouting, "Come down if you are the Son of God," Jesus could have vindicated himself. He could have "won" that battle, but he would have lost the war. He could have called ten thousand angels. God could have dispatched the angels and delivered Jesus from all that. But Jesus didn't want personal vindication. He had a greater love for the kingdom of God. That is why he died—"the just for the unjust" (1 Pet. 3:18).

Jesus lost the battle to win the war. As for Joseph, vindication on the spot might have done something for him at that moment; but it wouldn't have done anything for the kingdom of God. When we are being mistreated in any way, we must realize that our suffering has profound and vast implications for the greater kingdom of God. There are unseen reasons for continued suffering. Who knows what God will do with your life if you can take mistreatment with dignity? What probably means so much to you—to be cleared right now—could well lose the war should you get your immediate wish. Jesus could have come down from the cross. Thank God he didn't. Joseph could have been vindicated, but he wasn't. His eleven brothers would later be thankful that everything worked out just as it did.

God had more preparation for Joseph. Hadn't he had enough? How much more did Joseph have to be put through? "How long wilt thou hide thy face from me?" (Ps. 13:1). You may say, "I can't take any more." Look at Joseph. He was betrayed by his brothers. He became a slave in a strange land. Then he was falsely accused and slapped into prison. How much more can a person take? The Christian life can be explained as one kind of preparation after another. If there were a way to be prepared other than through trial or testing, God would do it that way. But he knows best.

Joseph had something more to learn. He needed to learn that God could do exactly the same thing twice under different circumstances. What did God do the first time? Genesis 39:2 says, "The Lord was with Joseph, and he was a prosperous man." That was when Joseph first came to Egypt. In Genesis 39:21, when Joseph was in prison, we read, "The Lord was with Joseph, and showed him mercy, and gave him favour in the sight of the keeper of the prison." God did it again. God did exactly the same thing again but in an opposite kind of situation. Joseph needed to see that it *really was God* who had done it the first time. When he saw such prosperity in Potiphar's house, he may have been tempted to say, "I've just hit it lucky. Everything is going right for me. If only I could believe that God is in this. If I could believe God is really blessing me like this, then I would know that all those dreams he gave me in Canaan are going to be fulfilled." Joseph needed to know that it was really God and not an accident. So there he was in prison, not a very likely place to succeed and prosper. But he did. God did it a second time, exactly as before.

The keeper of the prison was impressed with Joseph. He saw in Joseph an unusual man. There's an old saying, "You can't keep a good man down." It is also true that you can't keep a godly man down. "Touch not mine anointed, and do my prophets no harm" (Ps. 105:15). And yet it is to the credit of the keeper of the prison that he recognized true goodness in Joseph. Moreover, because the keeper of the prison was good to Joseph, everything in the prison now went well for the keeper. He did not want to lose Joseph if he could help it.

Joseph was thus prospering again, though in the most unlikely place. He never wanted to be there, and the keeper of the prison was not on his list of people to get to know. I don't suppose there was any kind of pamphlet describing life in Egypt and the different people you should meet while you are there. But if there had been, nobody would have thought to say, "You want to get to know the keeper of the prison. That will come in handy." The keeper turned out to be his best friend.

Perhaps God has you in a place that is apparently unredeemable. You feel nothing good can come out of it. Are you in a place where your own gift could not possibly be recognized, a place the opposite of your personal choosing? Perhaps you have a boss you don't like or a teacher that you don't get along with. And you've got to stay there. Your first reaction may be, "I'll have to stick it out and wait until it's all over. Nothing good is going to happen here." But not only can you make the most of a situation; God can bless you where you are. These can be some of the sweetest days you will ever know. Who knows what will happen to you particularly and the kingdom of God generally if you take it well?

Joseph was put in charge of all the prisoners—not the type of people he normally mixed with. But whatever they did, Joseph was the ringleader. God may have put you beside somebody you don't get on with naturally. Perhaps you are in an office or school where there are not the sort of people you like. Who knows what God can do with you right there in that situation? Don't be too hasty to change things. It is better to win the war.

NINE
VINDICATION
DELAYED

Preparation is not so painful when you consciously choose it, but what makes it hard is when you don't recognize it for what it is. If God were to say to us, "I am behind all of this; what is happening to you right now is my way of refining you," the whole ordeal would be more bearable. But as a rule God doesn't do it that way. He just puts us through test after test, refining us and shaping us. Only later do we see that what happened to us was his own planning.

God had an extraordinary plan for Joseph, one which called for extraordinary preparation. When God puts us through an extraordinary trial, nothing should be more encouraging, for God doesn't mock us. He treats us with dignity and prepares us according to the task ahead. He doesn't hurl us from A to Z but leads us from A to B, B to C, and so forth, following his own design for us.

The butler and the baker of the king committed a crime, so they joined Joseph in prison. Who would have thought that this could have anything to do with a child of God? But it did. It provided an essential link between Joseph and his eleven brothers back in Canaan, whom God had not forgotten. One night the baker and the butler each had a dream. Their dreams troubled them so much that, had they not been in prison, they would have sought an interpreter. In Egypt there were many astrologers and sooth-sayers who interpreted dreams. It was a lively occupation in those days; if anybody had a strange dream, he could make his way to the nearest interpreter the next day. But here they were having dreams in prison with nobody to explain them.

Now anything that involved dreams was up Joseph's alley. Joseph was gifted along this line. God communicated to him through dreams. Up to now he had been called on to do nothing in Egypt that required him to use his chief gift. He had had to learn new things. He had had to start a new career. His real gift had been laid aside.

Perhaps you have a gift. God gave it to you, but it is not being used. You may wonder why God gave it to you when you have had no opportunity to use it. Possibly the outlook is worse than ever because you are now in a particular place, so it would seem, where there is no chance of your gift being used. Perhaps you are having to do things quite beneath your capabilities; you are over-trained or you have ability far beyond what is required of you to do. It is all so humbling, having to do what you are now doing!

Joseph was in prison. Who would have thought that his best gift could be used there? But here came the butler and the baker. Joseph and these two men got to know each other fairly well. Some Bible commentators speculate that they were together about a year. At any rate, Joseph was able to look at their faces and say, "Why are you so sad? What's wrong?" He knew that something was wrong.

They said, "We have each had a dream, and there is nobody to interpret it."

Joseph replied, "Do not interpretations belong to God?" (Gen. 40:8). Joseph's moment was at hand. He could use his gift, the very gift he may have thought God had forgotten about.

"Who hath despised the day of small things?" (Zech. 4:10). The promising things that God brings about often seem so insignificant at first. For example, a lackluster event may eventually be treasured. Nothing about it signaled, "Ah, this is going to be significant." This is the way God frequently operates. The person who turns out to be of immense importance to you may not have impressed you at first sight. No lights flashed, no bells rang, no voice uttered, "That person will be very special to you." "Be not forgetful to entertain strangers: for thereby some have entertained angels unawares" (Heb. 13:2).

So, Joseph got to know the butler and the baker very well and was able to say to them, "You look sad." Imagine that! Joseph was the one who ought to be sad. He was the one who had been falsely accused and put in prison. Yet there he was, cheering up somebody else! Even though we may be in adverse conditions we can still encourage a person who is in even greater trouble than we are. When we are waiting for somebody to encourage us, it may be that we can be encouraging somebody else. "As the sufferings of Christ abound in us, so our consolation also aboundeth by Christ. And whether we be afflicted, it is for your consolation and salvation, which is effectual in the enduring of the same sufferings which we also suffer: or whether we be comforted, it is for your consolation and salvation" (2 Cor. 1:5-6). Therefore we can comfort others by the same comfort that we have been "comforted of God" (v. 4).

Joseph had the right to be sad if anybody did. But now he was bringing comfort to these two men. At this stage Joseph was not thinking of himself at all but only of how he might encourage these two men. It is a great leap forward for us when we begin to get our eyes off ourselves. Many of God's preparations for us are simply aimed to get our eyes off ourselves, to lead us out from our self-pity.

When Joseph saw that the two men were troubled and heard that each had a dream, it was his cue to bring God into the picture. There are many of us who think we have little opportunity to witness, but if we open our eyes and our ears, we will be amazed at how many opportunities come to us—more, perhaps, than we may wish for. Joseph brought God in: "Do not interpretations belong to God?" Joseph reasoned that if two men were badly troubled by dreams in the same night, this must be more than a coincidence. God could well be at work.

When it comes to this matter of interpreting dreams it ought to be said that in those days God often communicated through dreams. We now have the Scriptures. That doesn't mean God can't give a dream that has significance today, but it is probably something that doesn't happen very often. I think we must not take our dreams very seriously, if only because the devil can give dreams. I have known Christians who began to take their dreams so seriously that the devil got in and was controlling their whole day or immediate future by a dream they thought was from God. For example, they would have a dream that suggested something bad was going to happen, and they would be downcast all day long. It was the devil.

There can be many causes for dreams. Modern psychology takes dreams seriously. Ever since Freud it has been argued that dreams expose some inner wish or fear. But what you eat can even determine what you dream. The devil can come in and make you think that it has godly significance.

But Joseph in a flash saw the meaning of these two dreams. The Spirit of God told him something. The three branches in the butler's dream meant three days. Had he said three years there would have been a lot of time to wait and see. Many today will give a prophecy that is vague. Those also who take their astrology charts seriously will find something to fit their situation; the devil inevitably works through this. The devil will always bring a person into bondage by reading an astrology chart. Always.

However, so convinced was Joseph that the interpretation of the dream was of the Holy Spirit that he put himself on the line: "Within three days Pharaoh will lift up your head and restore you to your former position" (Gen. 40:13 NIV). He was not only right, he was exactly right. He *knew* that he was exactly right. At this stage we can again see how flawless his gift was.

We have seen Joseph as a type of Christ. We have seen how he handled everything perfectly, behaving himself before Potiphar's wife in the most decent and honorable way. We stand back and thank God for a man who had such courage, integrity, and fidelity. Many of us would say, "Here surely is a man ready to be used of God." He has passed the test that shows that he can resist sexual temptation.

By the way, it is a test that must be passed. Sexual temptation is the downfall of many people. Some cannot be trusted with a lofty position or with the secret things of God because at the level of natural, sensual, sexual temptation they cannot pass a test like Joseph's. God can never put them in a strategic place where they can be used. There are many people who seem so impervious and above any kind of taint, but maybe that is only because the right circumstances have not brought out the evil that is there. Many people have never fallen into sin because they haven't yet met Potiphar's wife! That ought to stop many of us from being critical of others. Our immediate reaction is often to be self-righteous and say, "How could they do that? That's awful." But have you been brought to the same situation? How do you know what your reaction would be in the same circumstances?

Yet Joseph still wasn't ready. He had a particular malady that nobody would have believed. Outwardly he was flawless. He certainly appeared ready. Why then couldn't he be exalted right now and get the eleven brothers into Egypt? Why couldn't God get on with it? Because Joseph still wasn't ready. This should be the key to understanding every trial God gives us. Every trial is designed to show you something about yourself that you didn't know.

Take Job, for example. Job was famous for his patience (James 5:11), he was "perfect and upright" (Job. 1:1), but God saw a gross imperfection in Job. Nobody else could see it, for as we have already said, it wasn't because Job had outwardly sinned that God allowed him to be tested. God put him through the kind of trial that forced that imperfection to surface. No ordinary trial would have caused this. It had to be the kind of trial in which his best friends would ruthlessly accuse him. Job eventually got very self-righteous. In the end, however, Job saw himself as he was. He repented in sackcloth and ashes, and he saw that he was a great sinner (Job 42:6).

A very important part of Joseph's preparation was for him to be delivered from self-pity, self-righteousness, and from any need to manipulate his future. God gave a dream to the butler and to the baker that Joseph might in fact see himself. How do you suppose it happened? He rightly interpreted the butler's dream: "You are going to be restored," but in an unguarded moment Joseph went too far. He said, "But think on me when it shall be well with thee, and shew kindness, I pray thee, unto me" (Gen. 40:14). He was trying to manipulate his future: "Make mention of me unto Pharaoh, and bring me out of this house." Joseph thought that it was his duty to call attention to himself that he might be exalted. Now God *could* have let that be the very way Joseph got out of prison. But God wanted to teach Joseph a deeper lesson: that God could do it utterly without Joseph's help.

The butler was restored to his job but completely forgot about Joseph. Joseph was to be in prison for two more years. God was determined to show Joseph that he could be exalted by God's power alone. How many of us really believe that? If God wants to put us in a particular place, he can do it; but if all the time we are pulling the strings and trying to manipulate things, he may have to keep us in chastening a while longer.

That is not all. Having said, "Remember me to Pharaoh," Joseph continued, "I was stolen away out of the land of the Hebrews: and *here also have I done nothing* that they should put me into the dungeon" (Gen. 40:15, italics mine). He insisted on defending himself. "I'm innocent. I don't deserve to be here." You wouldn't think it is the same Joseph, and yet, alas, it sounds like the spoiled, arrogant teenager that once treated his brothers in a selfish, insensitive manner. The "old" Joseph still survived.

What God was doing with Joseph is what he has to do with all of us. God wants to bring us to the place described in 1 Corinthians 4:4 when Paul said, "I know nothing by myself; yet am I not hereby justified: but he that judgeth me is the Lord." The kind of work that God had in mind for Joseph meant that Joseph had to be devoid of any defensiveness, any kind of self-pity, or any tendency to manipulate.

And so God said, "Well now, Joseph, you need another two years." That was the sentence. Another two years. We may think we can't take any more; the trial is intensified, and we may say, "God, stop. I can't go on. I cannot take any more." God says, "You can and you must." It is his way of bringing to the surface what no simple trial would cause to emerge. It took Job a long time to see how self-righteous he was.

Joseph had been trying to nudge the arm of Providence. He still wasn't ready.

TEN
THE TRUTH ABOUT
PREDESTINATION

It is not every day one gets an interpretation of an event or Scripture that is absolutely and undoubtedly from God. The worst thing that can happen to a nation is not famine or earth-quake or even the awful problem of unemployment. The worst thing that can happen to any nation was forecast a long time ago by the prophet Amos: "Behold, the days come, saith the Lord God, that I will send a famine in the land, not a famine of bread, nor a thirst for water, but *of hearing the words of the Lord*" (Amos 8:11, italics mine).

The man of the hour was Joseph. He had God's word and knew he had it. It was actually going to be heard. The butler and the baker could at first have had no way of truly appreciating the man with whom they were brought into contact in prison. We are all like this. In any case, when a man of God has a word that is undoubtedly from heaven, it is a most wonderful thing. Should God reveal truth to one of his servants, it is marvelous. The worst thing in the world is a famine of the Word of God.

On the other hand, the butler and the baker had no choice but to listen. They were shut up in prison. Keep in mind that the butler and baker of Pharaoh would not normally give someone like Joseph the time of day. Go to Buckingham Palace now and request to talk to somebody there who is in daily contact with the queen. You would get nowhere! Furthermore, he was a foreigner and a Hebrew. Perhaps he was even the equivalent of a fundamentalist today; he believed God's word totally. The public generally wouldn't listen to anybody like that. What a kindness God gave to the butler and the baker; they were boxed in and were even eager to listen to Joseph. It is a mercy when God makes us listen to somebody whom we would normally ignore. The most unexpected person will sometimes speak words of pure gold. Even after we become Christians, God often still speaks to us like this. He has a way of boxing us in to make us see something that we didn't want to see and listen to someone we would not have chosen to hear.

There was once a man of Ethiopia, a man of great authority under a queen. He was riding in his chariot one day and happened to be reading from the Scriptures. (We never know who might be reading the Bible at a particular time.) Philip, a deacon, saw this Ethiopian, and the Spirit said, "Go to that chariot." He went. How many of us would do that? Has the Holy Spirit impressed you lately with the need to witness in this manner? Or are we so outside of God's wavelength that we wouldn't even hear the voice of the Spirit?

But Philip heard the voice and obeyed. And we find that this Ethiopian of great authority had been boxed in. He was reading from the Book of Isaiah but didn't understand what he was reading. God now prepared him to listen to anyone who had the Word. Do you know what it is to be boxed in like that? It may be illness, trouble, or financial reverse that makes you seek the Lord. God can do that. It may be a keen disappointment or the loss of a friend that drives you to your knees.

When we were in America during the summer, we watched a TV program called "Praise the Lord" with Paul and Jan Crouch. On one program they had as a guest Efrem Zimbalist, Jr., the Hollywood movie star. He told this story: One night he couldn't go to sleep, so he turned on his television set. He said he didn't like anything he was watching and kept changing channels till he came across channel 40 in Los Angeles. He got interested. He had a guest who was staying in his home, and Zimbalist got him out of bed to watch this religious show. They both thought it was hilarious at first and assumed it must be some kind of joke, but they stayed up and watched it all the way through. He watched it the next night and the night after that. A telephone number was flashed on the screen that viewers could call. Efrem Zimbalist, Jr. dialed this number, and when he said who he was, the person at the switchboard thought it was a joke. They gave the phone to Jan Crouch who recognized his voice. He said, "I want to confess Jesus Christ as my Savior." He came out of hiding in that manner and let the whole world know he had just been converted.

Now here he was on this television show—an unashamed evangelical. What brought it about? He had been boxed in. He listened to something and someone because he was in no mood to do anything else. And the word of God reached him.

The butler and the baker were boxed in. They could not have known at the time the kind of man placed in their paths. Had they known that they were talking to the future governor of Egypt, not only would they have shown the deepest respect, but the butler would not have been so quick to forget Joseph. However, the most important fact about the man in front of them was not that he would be the future governor of Egypt, but that he had the word of God for them.

As a rule of thumb (there are exceptions to this), I dare say that a man of God is seldom recognized as that at first. It is usually realized later as we look back. Take the two men on the road to Emmaus (Luke 24). They were not able to recognize who Jesus was. After he vanished they said, "Did not our heart burn within us?" We know that Jesus' own brothers didn't believe him. As for the chief priests who had Jesus crucified, they thought he was an imposter—the very opposite of what he claimed. Peter, preaching boldly, later said, "This is the stone which was set at nought of you builders which is become the head of the corner" (Acts 4:11). "Who hath despised the day of small things?" (Zech. 4:10).

Joseph listened carefully to their dreams. He was no respecter of persons. He was impartial in his interpretation. Joseph didn't love the butler more because the butler was going to live longer. He didn't dislike the baker because he gave an interpretation that said he would die in three days. So with Jesus. He is no respecter of persons. Even his enemies knew that (Matt. 22:16). God is no respecter of persons. If you have an ordeal heavier than someone else, it is no sign that God loves you less.

Joseph was not responsible for the outcome of either the butler's or the baker's dreams. He emerged again as a type of

Christ—one very like Jesus before Jesus ever came. Joseph's word was not the cause of the butler being restored or of the baker being hanged. Joseph was simply *there,* and as a result, these two men were given advance notice of what would happen—all because Joseph was true to God.

So it is with Jesus. Never forget this. It is not the coming of Jesus that sends anybody to hell. He said it himself: "For God sent not his Son into the world to condemn the world; but that the world through him might be saved" (John 3:17). It is the coming of Jesus that saves people. Jesus is the only one who can help us. Moreover, Jesus never says no. "All the promises of God in him are yea, and in him Amen" (2 Cor. 1:20). The only time Jesus will ever say no will be at the final judgment when all stand before him. He may have to say to you, "I never knew you: depart from me, ye that work iniquity" (Matt. 7:23). You may cry out to him then. Jesus will give the orders, "Bind him hand and foot, and take him away, and cast him into outer darkness" (Matt. 22:13).

But while you are alive remember this: Jesus never says no. While on earth, Jesus did what he was sent to do. What is more, anybody who saw him knew that he could go to Jesus and be accepted. It did not matter what that person was like—whether a tramp, a beggar, a blind person, or a sophisticated Jew. Nicodemus knew that if he came to Jesus, he would receive him. And he did (John 3:1ff.). When he died, he tasted death for every man (Heb. 2:9), then ascended to heaven where he also carries out God's secret will. Joseph actually administered the secret will of God in the prison. He was constrained to reveal the baker's imminent death. He did it in love, for what a kindness it was that the baker had advance warning.

As it happened, Pharaoh's birthday was at hand. Nobody thought that on his birthday Pharaoh was going to do anything unusual or spectacular, but in the secret will of God the butler and the baker were given dreams—three days in advance of that date. Joseph interpreted the dreams, thus revealing the secret will of God. Doing this did not make Joseph the cause of what happened three days later. In the same way, you can never blame Jesus if you go to hell. The decree concerning the butler and the baker was fixed, unchangeable and unalterable. You may call it predestination. Joseph said in the case of the butler, "The three branches are three days." In the case of the baker, "The three baskets are three days." Nothing would change this. After three days the butler was restored and the baker hanged.

And so with Jesus. What did he say? "I came down from heaven, not to do mine own will, but the will of him that sent me" (John 6:38). God knows from the beginning who will be saved. I don't know. You don't know. Nobody knows. But I can tell you that God knows. He knows what is going to happen five minutes from now. I don't. You don't. He does. He knows what is going to happen two days from now, two years from now. He knows the exact day when Jesus is going to come again (Mark 13:32). He knows the day on which you are going to die. He knows whether you are going to go to heaven or hell. God knows the end from the beginning (Isa. 46:10).

Nothing is hidden from God. *How* God determines the end from the beginning is absolutely secret. You can try to get behind God, you can speculate, you may try to find out what makes him "tick." But when it comes to the way God knows the future and how he knows it, *that is hidden.* "For my thoughts are not your thoughts, neither are your ways my ways, saith the Lord. For as the heavens are higher than the earth, so are my ways higher than your ways, and my thoughts than your thoughts" (Isa. 55:8-9).

We don't know God's mind, but I will tell you what we *do* know: we know what most certainly does *not* lie behind his choice of who is to be saved: good works. God has "saved us and called us with an holy calling, not according to our works, but according to his own purpose and grace, which was given us in Christ Jesus before the world began" (2 Tim. 1:9). We don't know how it was determined. We only know how it *wasn't* determined. It wasn't by our works.

Is this bad news to you? If you stop and think about it a moment, it is good news. Very good news. Are you actually hoping to be saved by your works? This ought to be the happiest news you could ever get in your life—it is not your works that will determine heaven or hell for you. If you wanted God to judge you by your works, have you any idea what you would be asking for? God's eyes are too pure to look on sin (Hab. 1:13). "God is angry with the wicked every day" (Ps. 7:11). Moreover, the perfection God demands from those who stand before him is far, far out of the reach of any of us. John looked in heaven, on earth, and under the earth and found nobody who was worthy (Rev. 5:2-4). So it is not our works. And that is the best news we can ever have.

But if God does not save us by our works, how does he save us? He sent his Son, who tasted death for every man (Heb. 2:9). That means we all have an equal claim to Jesus' death. It is level ground at the foot of the cross. You can come to God and say, "God, your Son actually died for me." What happened when Jesus died? It was God punishing him instead of you. God punished Jesus, who knew no sin (2 Cor. 5:21). All of your sins were transferred to Jesus, and God punished him. We are saved with a holy calling, but not according to our works.

As Joseph administered the secret will of God, so did Jesus. "I have not come to do mine own will." Jesus did everything that the Father ordered. He actually prayed, "I thank thee, O Father, Lord of heaven and earth, because thou hast hid these things from the wise and prudent, and hast revealed them unto babes. Even so, Father: for so it seemed good in thy sight" (Matt. 11:25-26). In his high priestly prayer Jesus said, "I pray not for the world, but for them which thou hast given me" (John 17:9). He was simply carrying out the secret will of God. Jesus gave us words, which Martin Luther called the Bible in a nutshell: "For God so loved the world that he gave his only begotten Son, that whosoever believeth in him should not perish, but have everlasting life" (John 3:16). "He that believeth on me hath everlasting life" (John 6:47).

This matter of predestination is probably the greatest mystery of the Bible. I can tell you this much without the slightest fear of contradiction—if you go to heaven, it won't be because of your works, and if you go to hell, it *will* be because of your works. For your works at best are vile in his sight: "Filthy rags," said Isaiah (Isa. 64:6).

Everything that Joseph forecast was literally true. The butler was restored; the baker was hanged. In the case of Jesus, he gave specific prophecies and put time limits on them. On one occasion, when they were talking about the temple and its beauty, Jesus said to his disciples, "See ye not all these things? Verily I say unto you, There shall not be left here one stone upon another, that shall not be thrown down" (Matt. 24:2). He also said, "This generation shall not pass, till all these things be fulfilled" (Matt. 24:34). Now that was putting his integrity on the line! He said that in approximately A.D. 29. Do you know what happened in A.D. 69, at the close of that generation? Caesar's army marched on Jerusalem and began ravaging everything, and when it came to the temple, Josephus the Jewish historian tells us that because of the gold that was in some of the stones, they literally turned every stone of some parts of the temple to get the gold.

Jesus said to Simon Peter, "You are going to deny me." He gave a time limit. "This night, before the cock crow, thou shalt deny me thrice" (Matt. 26:34). He said that Judas Iscariot would betray him. In his high priestly prayer, Jesus said, "Those that thou gavest me I have kept, and none of them is lost, but the son of perdition; that the scripture might be fulfilled" (John 17:12). Jesus' word was exactly right. As the butler and the baker were hearing a word from Joseph that was exactly right, so everything that Jesus said was utterly true. "Heaven and earth shall pass away, but my words shall not pass away" (Matt. 24:35). We may ask whether the baker was saved. What did he do during those three days in which to prepare to meet God? We won't know until we get to heaven. We just know he had three days to prepare for death he wouldn't otherwise have had because God sent a man to talk to both the butler and the baker.

God knows the end from the beginning. He comes to you in this moment to warn you to make your calling and election sure. Nothing is more merciful than such a warning.

ELEVEN
WHEN GOD'S TIME
HAS COME

"Like the trampling of a mighty army, so is the force of an idea whose time has come," wrote Victor Hugo. The greatest idea that ever was is simply called the Word. "In the beginning was the Word, and the Word was with God, and the Word was God. . . . And the Word was made flesh, and dwelt among us, (and we beheld his glory, the glory as of the only begotten of the Father,) full of grace and truth" (John 1:1, 14). Paul said, "When the fulness of the time was come, God sent forth his Son, made of a woman, made under the law, to redeem them that were under the law" (Gal. 4:4-5). Jesus, following John the Baptist, began his ministry with these words, "The time is fulfilled, and the kingdom of God is at hand" (Mark 1:15).

"He hath made everything beautiful in his time" (Eccles. 3:11). As God made the seed that becomes an oak tree, but which takes time, so God has allowed himself to be bound by time. Truly extraordinary is this, that God has allowed himself to be *bound by time*, although a day with the Lord is "as a thousand years, and a thousand years as one day" (2 Pet. 3:8). There is one thing that God cannot do and that is to make things happen any sooner than we may wish or even than he may wish. For he has bound himself in this way by his own wisdom. He chose to be bound by time, with the result that he himself waits for some things to happen.

81

"He hath made everything beautiful in his time" so that when God's time has come, he delights in it as much or more than we do. Happy—very happy indeed—is the man who learns to wait for God's time to come. God himself waits for it—and surely there is no greater folly than for us to get ahead of the Lord. Happy is the man who waits on him. Eye has not seen, nor ear heard, neither have entered into the heart of man, the things which God has prepared for them that wait for him (see Isa. 64:4; 1 Cor. 2:9). But if God waits, how much more must we? And yet how wonderful when the moment comes that we can look into the face of our heavenly Father and say, "Lo, this is our God; we have waited for him" (Isa. 25:9).

One of the happiest things I ever get to do is to have a part in a marriage ceremony. The ultimate moment is looking at the bride and groom and pronouncing that they are husband and wife. Perhaps the peak moment, really, is when the bride comes down the aisle and the groom looks at her. What a moment, though it lasts for seconds; the moment each of them has waited for. God's time. How wonderful when it comes.

But now for this important principle: when God's time has come, our time has come. And it is conversely true: if God's time has not come, our time has not come.

It was precisely this very principle that Joseph had to learn. God selected Joseph as a chief instrument for a work that would live for generations. God chose Joseph to do something that would later be recognized and revered in history. But Joseph had to wait for his time to come because he had to wait for God's time. He had to learn this lesson, and he didn't learn it easily or quickly. None of us do. The Psalmist said, "How long wilt thou forget me, O Lord? for ever?" (Ps. 13:1). Again and again we have all cried to God: How long must this go on? I am sure that is exactly the way Joseph felt. Here was a man who had been given a witness by the Lord years before that he was going to be used. But nothing was going right. He was being severely chastened—but not because of any particular sin, for chastening is not God getting even but only his way of refining us. Much of God's chastening is geared to teach us something of God's timing. It is as though God says to us, "Look, I too have to wait. Why don't you learn to wait?"

Joseph was thus a man in preparation. Most of his life up to then had been nothing but God's preparation of him. You couldn't have told him that he needed more preparation; and this is the way all of us are. We all think we are quite ready just as we are. One of the chief things that Joseph had to learn was to wait for God's time to come. Joseph correctly interpreted the butler's dream, and he knew it. And as soon as he interpreted the dream he said, "You are going to be restored to your former position, you are going to get out of this dungeon. Remember me, Joseph— *Joseph*—you won't forget me, will you?" He couldn't resist getting himself into the act.

God looked down from heaven about that time and probably said, "Ahem. My instrument Joseph needs a little more refining. I think two more years in the dungeon might do." God wanted to turn Joseph the manipulator into Joseph the man. Paul said, "When I became a man, I put away childish things" (1 Cor. 13:11). That is what old Hugh Latimer had to shout back to young Ridley in the Balliol ditch at Oxford when they were being burned for the truth. In those days Queen Mary was killing Protestants right and left. Ridley was trembling. The fires were about to come sweeping over their bodies. Latimer, tied back to back with Ridley, shouted over his shoulder, "Be of good comfort, Master Ridley, and play the man. We shall this day light such a candle by God's grace in England, as I trust shall never be put out."

Play the man! This is what God wants. Men. I fear they are a scarce commodity in this generation. But that was what God wanted to do with Joseph—to make him a man.

How do we know God's time has come? There are various ways. First, we know that God's time has arrived when we have come utterly to the end of our own strength. We may say, "Well, that's not me, I'm doing fine thank you." That means God's time hasn't come for us. But if we have come to the end of our own strength, God's time has come for us. This is something that comes hard to us. We don't like to think that we are utterly helpless. Joseph wasn't helpless yet. He saw an opportunity. He didn't know the day before that the butler would have a dream and he would be interpreting it. But as soon as he interpreted it, he got personally involved. "You will be restored. Remember me."

Now we can't help but identify with Joseph for doing that. We are all like that. Once we see an opportunity to nudge the arm of Providence—to advance ourselves the slightest bit—we do it, don't we? It shows Joseph was human. It shows that he was naturally ambitious, that he was assertive. There is nothing terribly bad about being like that. But God didn't want Joseph to be exalted that way.

I must say, however, that God does let a lot of people get exalted that way. There are many people who get to the top simply because they exalted themselves. But it is a special person of whom it is said by God, "That is not the way *you* are going to be exalted." If God has kept you down and you have been laid aside, it may be that you are one of the special ones. God is saying, "I am going to be the one to exalt you." The worldly way is pushing yourself. You pull the strings and you advance yourself. You advertise yourself. You do everything you can to promote yourself.

Joseph was trying that. If you have tried and you have failed at it, it is a good sign, a sign that God wants to do it his way, and then he does it so well it dazzles the mind. He works things in such a manner that the only thing you can say is, as Cowper put it, "God moves in a mysterious way his wonders to perform."

So the butler forgot. Probably the last word Joseph said to the butler was, "Remember me, now. Please don't forget. I'll be sitting here waiting." But the butler did not remember. Joseph couldn't have known this, and probably every day he was thinking, *Any day now.* Every moment he expected the jailer to rap on the door and jangle the keys, saying, "Come on out, Joseph, your time has come, you're getting out." The days went by. Weeks went by. Months went by. It was now two years.

But had that rap on the door come, it would have meant that Joseph did it entirely by his own efforts. After two years perhaps Joseph began to get the hint that God wanted to do it his way. "Humble yourselves therefore under the mighty hand of God, that he may exalt you in due time" (1 Pet. 5:6). What a compliment it is that God wants to get utterly involved with us! He kindly says to us, "Let me do it. I want to do it." When God enters into our lives like that it is absolutely the most wonderful thing that can ever happen. How can I know that God wants to get into my life like that? When I have come to the end of my own strength, I may be sure that God's time is at hand.

Here is another sign: God's time has come when he does a work utterly outside ourselves. At the end of the two years Pharaoh had a dream. Who would have thought that Pharaoh, the king, would have a dream that would relate to a Hebrew prisoner? Pharaoh, of all people, had a dream. Who gave it to him? God. What did Joseph have to do with Pharaoh's dream? Absolutely nothing. Joseph could never say, "I'm the one who put a seed in Pharaoh's mind." What happened was utterly detached from anything that was apparently connected to Joseph. God's time had come when a phenomenon appeared for which there was no natural explanation.

Pharaoh, in fact, had two dreams. He had the first dream (Gen. 41:1-4), then fell asleep and dreamed the second time. When he woke up, he was very upset. But that is what astrologers are for; that is why we have magicians and interpreters of dreams. Pharaoh, being king, had access to all the so-called wisdom of Egypt. And so he started calling in his wise men, one by one. His first choice was probably the man with whom he had so far had the best results. But the interpreter of the dream said, "I haven't a clue." So another magician came, then another and another and another.

When has God's time come? When all human resources fail. When has God's time come? When the wisdom of men comes to nothing. When has God's time come? When something appears for which there is no natural explanation—Pharaoh's dreams. We are told that all the wise men came, and *none* of them could interpret the dream. God delights to show the world that for which there is no known explanation. When the common explanation fails, God's time has come. As long as there is a natural or traditional explanation to something, men may well debate it. But when all explanations fail, God's time has come.

Another indication that God's time is at hand is when God works successfully at the precise point we have failed. Joseph pinned all his hopes on the butler. He got nowhere. Then the king dreamed things the greatest occultists in Egypt could not explain. Now listen to the same butler. He had been working in Pharaoh's house, and he knew something was going on. He saw one astrologer after another going into the presence of Pharaoh and coming out dejected. After so long, the butler began to wonder what it was all about. He asked someone, "What's going on with

His Majesty of late? These magicians—I recognize them, they've all been here before—but this time they're coming in full of confidence and leaving dejected."

"Oh, you haven't heard?" says someone. "His Majesty has had a dream and he's sent for everybody. We don't know what's going to happen. Everybody who knows anything about dreams has been here, but not a soul has had the first clue as to the meaning."

Then the butler remembered Joseph. "I do remember my faults this day" (Gen. 41:9). Surprise, surprise! The butler went off to ask for an audience with the king. He told Pharaoh about Joseph. God did what Joseph couldn't do.

Why couldn't Joseph succeed? Simply because he was God's special man and had taken vindication into his own hands. I repeat that many people take vindication into their own hands and succeed. It is therefore a high compliment God pays you when you try and you fail. For God is saying to you, "That is what *I* want to do." That is the way God deals with his special ambassadors. "For whom the Lord loveth he chasteneth, and scourgeth every son whom he receiveth" (Heb. 12:6).

Joseph had worked on the butler and failed because he had tried to anticipate God's timing. God wants to make everything beautiful in *his* time.

There is another sign that God's time has come: when someone pleads your case (and knows all the facts) without your opening your mouth. Who interceded for Joseph? The butler. You may say that what Joseph had done in trying to get the butler to remember him was finally vindicated. No, not at all. The butler remembered everything that Joseph did that had been worthwhile. The butler remembered Joseph's gift. Joseph hadn't needed to say to the butler, "Remember me." The butler remembered—not because Joseph had begged him to remember, but because the facts spoke for themselves.

So there went the butler to the king: "I dreamed this dream when in prison, and there was with us a young man, a Hebrew, servant to the captain of the guard. The baker and I told him our dreams, and he interpreted them perfectly. All came to pass just as he interpreted them. You restored me to my office, and the baker was hanged, just as the Hebrew said." God has a way of bringing out the details of things so that your gift will be noticed.

He has a way of bringing out that which you are so afraid nobody will recognize. The butler gave the king of Egypt all the details. It was out of Joseph's hands. God was at work.

There is yet another proof that God's time has come: when God reaches us where we are without any effort on our part. Two years went by. No doubt months before Joseph had given up hope. But one day right out of the blue came the rap on the door. It happened suddenly. Where was Joseph? In the dungeon. They knew where he was. God knows where we are. Are we afraid nobody will remember where we are? God's time has come when he reaches us where we are without any effort on our part. God reached for Joseph. "Pharaoh sent and called Joseph, and they brought him *hastily* out of the dungeon" (Gen. 41:14, italics mine).

Do you see all the implications of this beautiful story? The outline of the gospel of Christ is clearly seen. The gospel is the good news that you may be saved when you come to the end of your own strength. "For when we were yet without strength, in due time Christ died for the ungodly" (Rom. 5:6). Have you been going about the business of trying to reform yourself? Have you really tried to be a better person by good works? You may be improving in your ways. But this might be the worst thing that could happen to you. For you could take that improvement to be the sign that you are ready. You are not ready. As long as you have strength within, you aren't ready. Christ died for those who see in themselves no ability to do anything right. The good news is that God has done a work at the precise point where you have failed. Joseph failed with the butler, but God succeeded with him.

God succeeded. How? He provided a substitute, one who stood in your place, one who did everything exactly right. It was Jesus, God's Son, who died on the cross and in his body took all the punishment for your sin. But you have to give up any idea of competing with what Jesus did. Jesus was your substitute. He did it all by himself, and he did it perfectly. Furthermore, he knows all about you, and he will plead your case. God's time has come when he reaches you where you are without any effort on your part. Are you in the equivalent of a dungeon at this moment? Are you afraid that God doesn't see you? He does see you and he's come right now. All is in God's timing.

Just as I am, without one plea,
But that Thy blood was shed for me,
And that Thou bidd'st me come to Thee,
O Lamb of God, I come! I come!

—Charlotte Elliott

One more thing. When God's time has come, he makes you fit to stand before a king. "Get ready, Joseph. You are going to go into the presence of His Majesty, the Pharaoh of Egypt." The first thing Joseph did was shave himself. Then he put on different clothes. When God saves you, he cleans you up, changes your countenance, and puts a smile on that face—a shine. Others will ask, "What has happened to you?" But the most important thing of all is that God will give you new raiment—new clothes. They are provided for you. God doesn't ask you to get clean from the inside out. He doesn't say, "Get worthy." He says, "Let me clothe you with my Son's robe of righteousness." From this day forward, God will see to it that you are fit to stand before the King of kings.

TWELVE
THE UNLIKELY
CONVERT

It is not often that you hear of a head of state, a prime minister, a president, or a king who is converted to Jesus Christ. Once in a while this happens. Most of us know about Jimmy Carter, the former U.S. president, who claimed to be born again. This is unusual, however. Paul said, "Ye see your calling, brethren, how that not many wise men after the flesh, not many mighty, not many noble, are called" (1 Cor. 1:26). He didn't say not *any*, he said not "many," for once in a while the professor, the philosopher, the very rich, or the very famous man is converted.

If God can save you, he can save anybody. It takes no more grace to save a Saul of Tarsus than to convert you or me. In this chapter we see how God can reach the one you would have thought was unreachable.

We have looked at the story of Joseph largely through Joseph's own eyes. Now I want us to look at the story of Joseph through the eyes of Pharaoh, the king of Egypt. We are talking about the most powerful and "unreachable" man of his day; but a man who had a soul. We may get into his skin and see how a most powerful man was brought to such a state of desperation that he sought help from a source he would never normally have considered.

Pharaoh had two dreams in one night, and they left him in a traumatic state of mind. Waking up in the morning in great anxiety, he knew they had deep significance. He immediately turned to the "wise" men, the men who were the professionals in the interpretation of dreams.

We may observe here that the most powerful man can be reached when a very personal matter brings him to a state of anxiety. He must have that particular need resolved. The most powerful men are beset with personal concerns and needs that show how utterly frail and human they are. The best of men are men at best, and the greatest and the most powerful of men *are* reachable. "God moves in a mysterious way his wonders to perform." That should encourage us to believe that God can save anybody.

Do you have particular unsaved people on your prayer list? I pray for a number of world figures every night before I retire. I call them by name, that God will save them. This is something all Christians ought to do.

The Pharaoh could not have known that a Hebrew slave in prison would be the answer to all of his problems. Pharaoh probably didn't even know that Joseph existed. But when a man is desperate, he will do anything to find real help. If a man is stranded—whether it be in a desert or a snow storm—he will take help wherever he can get it. When God is working his plans out, he brings together the circumstances and the timing. This is a process otherwise known as *providence;* God alone can make it possible to reach the "unreachable."

By the way, are you one of those who has been unreachable? Perhaps not because you are a world figure, famous, or rich. But there is, nonetheless, an invisible wall around you that nobody can penetrate. When it comes to this simple gospel of Jesus Christ, you have never been interested. Nobody has had any success in reaching you with this gospel. You, humanly speaking, are unreachable.

When a person is in trouble, he usually turns to those he knows best. Pharaoh turned to all the wise men and magicians of Egypt, possibly one by one. He sent for the men who probably earned their living in things pertaining to the supernatural. This sort of thing was right up their alley. I don't doubt that some of these magicians said, "Well, here's what it means," and gave their interpretation. But Pharaoh wasn't satisfied. I wouldn't be at all surprised if many interpretations were given to the Pharaoh. But one proof that the Spirit of God is at work is when you know the answer that you are receiving is not the right answer. Now if the Spirit is not at work, you may well accept the wrong answer. The proof that God was at work in the heart of the Pharaoh is that he did not settle for an inferior interpretation of his dreams.

Are you looking for an answer to a problem that has you troubled? Have you started at the "top"? Have you turned to those who have always helped you in the past? Perhaps you have consulted this book, or that group of people, or this particular man. Education is often defined as knowing where to find the answer. Perhaps in the past, with your learning and experience, you have always known where to go to find the answers. But maybe this time, like the Pharaoh, you are bewildered. Perhaps you are disillusioned. Has it occurred to you that you have been looking in the wrong place? If the present problem seems different and nobody can help you through it, I can tell you this: it means that God is the one who has created the problem. Only God, then, has the answer, and it is likely that you will have to go to the most unexpected place to find it.

Enter the butler. Now the butler (or cupbearer) was a very important court official, but he knew his place. This particular butler most certainly knew his place because he had been in trouble once before. He had already been put in prison once. We don't know why, but you can mark it down that this butler was going to watch every word he said. He didn't want any trouble again. But he knew in his heart that he, and he alone, had the answer to Pharaoh's problem. This butler was willing to risk his own position by asking for an audience with the king to tell him about Joseph.

This is what a good witness for Christ will do. He seizes upon an opportunity to speak, for he knows that nobody else around him has the answer. He may do it with fear and trembling but, as Esther put it, "If I perish, I perish" (Esther 4:16); and as he begins he may feel like the butler who said, "I do remember my faults." When it comes to witnessing, most of us feel much shame that we haven't done it more or that we haven't done it better. There is probably not a one of us but feels like crawling in the dust; we have all failed. The butler began with confession: "I do remember my faults this day." This is important. When we feel convicted about witnessing, we will usually do one of two things: defend ourselves or accuse ourselves. There are those who bristle and justify themselves. That is one way to look at it. Then there are those who say, "O God, help me. I am not what I ought to be."

Is there the equivalent of the butler in your life? Has somebody been talking to you about Jesus Christ but you have said, "I don't want to hear any more of that"? Perhaps you are going around the world looking for happiness and joy, and here is this person right next to you who says, "You need the Lord; you need the gospel." But you have not been ready to listen.

The butler gives us the clue to good witnessing. He begins by admitting he hadn't done as well as he should have, and I think that is where all of us can begin. But what did the butler do next? Are we talking about an eloquent man or a man who has had a lot of experience? No. The butler simply *told what he knew.* That is all. He had met a Hebrew in prison who had done something for him. He believed that this Joseph was real, that he was authentic. The butler knew that he wouldn't go wrong if he told the Pharaoh about Joseph. That is all witnessing ultimately is. Why would anybody want to become a Christian? Because of what Jesus has done for us.

The butler said, "There is a man who interpreted my dream exactly right." And so the Pharaoh, having listened to the wise men, to the magicians, and to all of those skilled professionals, said to himself, "All else has failed." It may have been humbling to have to go into a dungeon and bring out a foreigner—a Hebrew—who had been thrown into prison because of an alleged indiscretion with the wife of one of the king's officers. What a shame that Pharaoh had to stoop so low. But all else had failed.

And yet Pharaoh believed the butler. When God is at work, you listen to a man you normally would pay no attention to. And so the Pharaoh called for the man the butler had been so keen about. Pharaoh took the butler's advice, the best thing he ever did.

When Pharaoh called on Joseph, it was done by faith alone. The Pharaoh simply took the word of the butler. There was nothing else he could do. The Pharaoh might have said, "Well now, wait a minute. I can't do a thing like this. We must do more research on Joseph. We need to find out more. Can all this be substantiated?" No, he simply took the word of the butler.

And when you call upon Jesus you are going to be doing it in faith alone. You are taking the word of somebody who has talked to you about Jesus. You may say, "I want to investigate this more." There are those who want to check the religions out. They want to examine Buddhism, the teaching of Confucius, Islam, or perhaps Hinduism. One is never saved like that. Never. That is not the way it is done. Rather it is this: "The word is nigh thee, even in thy mouth, and in thy heart: that is, the word of faith, which we preach" (Rom. 10:8). It is by *faith alone*. It is taking the word of the one who has met Jesus. "Whosoever shall call upon the name of the Lord shall be saved. How then shall they call on him in whom they have not believed? and how shall they believe in him of whom they have not heard? and how shall they hear without a preacher?" (Rom. 10:13-14).

It may seem ridiculous to you that the way you are saved is that you take the word of another person. But that is the scandal, that is the offense; that is why Christianity is often scoffed at. And yet the wonder is, when you call on Jesus, he comes in right then.

Pharaoh told Joseph everything that was on his heart. "I have dreamed a dream. Nobody can help me. All else has failed. I am told that you can help." Do you know what Joseph said? Joseph answered, "It is not in me: God shall give Pharaoh an answer of peace" (Gen. 41:16). Jesus said almost these very words. "Verily, verily I say unto you, The Son can do nothing of himself, but what he seeth the Father do: for what things soever he doeth, these also doeth the Son likewise" (John 5:19). "I can of mine own self do nothing" (John 5:30). That's what Jesus said. "The answer is not in me, God will do it, and it will be an answer of peace."

Pharaoh believed the butler. He would also believe Joseph.

THIRTEEN
RECOGNIZING THE
SPIRIT'S WITNESS

A troubled, desperate king sent for a Hebrew prisoner. The Pharaoh decided to tell Joseph his dream—a dream nobody could interpret. And now Joseph, a man Pharaoh had never met (and had only heard of briefly), gave the king hope. The king related the dream. Joseph listened, then gave Pharaoh his interpretation, after which he gave the king explicit advice. The result of this conversation was that Pharaoh said, "Can we find such a one as this is, a man *in whom the Spirit of God is?*" (Gen. 41:38, italics mine).

Pharaoh ended up putting all of his eggs into one basket. He heard Joseph's interpretation of the dream—and believed it. He not only believed it but made a decision on the spot that would affect his future and the life of a whole nation. This is because he believed with all his heart what Joseph had said. He believed and acted upon it, although it would take fourteen years before Joseph's word could be proved absolutely right. Pharaoh believed Joseph's interpretation for one reason: in Joseph there was the Spirit of God.

Now all this is relevant to us because what is at stake here is how a person is converted to Jesus Christ. A person is converted by hearing the word of another person, often a man he has never met before.

Perhaps we have never met. You are reading this book, written by a man who is going to tell you plainly to put all of your eggs

95

into one basket. I am going to ask you to believe that what I am saying is absolutely true. I shall ask you to make a decision right now that will shape your life, and who knows how many other lives.

The essential thing, the thing you need to be sure of, is whether the Spirit of God is at work. That is all you need to know. You don't need to know anything about me. It wouldn't particularly help you to know details of my life or of my family. It might be of some interest, but it would not bear any relevance on your future. What you need to know is whether what I'm saying is trustworthy. If what I'm saying is the result of the Spirit of God leading me to say these things, you don't have anything to be afraid of. You can put your total trust in it, not because of who I am, but because it is the Spirit of God dealing with you.

The Holy Spirit is the Spirit of truth (John 14:17). When the Spirit of truth speaks, you can tell by the way he speaks that you are not ever going to be deceived. If you had to prove to somebody how you know this, you couldn't do it.

There was no way that Joseph could be proved right on the spot. Or, I should say, there was no way that Pharaoh could prove that he had made the right decision when he trusted completely in Joseph's interpretation of his dream. It would take fourteen years to prove whether Joseph was right. And yet Pharaoh somehow knew he wasn't going to make a mistake. He *knew* this, and that was a proof that the Spirit was at work.

Paul put it like this: "For what man knoweth the things of a man, save the spirit of man which is in him? even so the things of God knoweth no man, but the Spirit of God. Now we have received, not the spirit of the world, but the spirit which is of God; that we might know the things that are freely given to us of God. . . . But the natural man receiveth not the things of the Spirit of God: for they are foolishness unto him: neither can he know them, because they are spiritually discerned" (1 Cor. 2:11-14). When the Spirit bears witness, you know at once that you will be safe following him.

The first thing to know about recognizing the Spirit's witness is that he gives peace. Joseph said, "God shall give Pharaoh an answer of peace" (Gen. 41:16). Now it ought to be said that when the Spirit *begins* to work the first evidence may be the opposite of peace. When Pharaoh first had this dream, he woke up and his spirit was troubled (Gen. 41:8). Pharaoh didn't have any peace at all. The first thing the Spirit often does is to bring a person to a state of being troubled. But there is only one way to get peace and that is to believe God's word.

Another evidence of the Spirit's witness is an unhesitant authority. Joseph listened as Pharaoh related the dream—which turned out to be two dreams. Pharaoh was afraid that Joseph wasn't going to be able to interpret them. For after relating the two dreams he added, "I have told this to the magicians but none could help me." When Pharaoh finally quit talking, Joseph calmly said, "The dream of Pharaoh is one" (Gen. 41:25). He started right in, and as soon as Pharaoh heard him speak, he knew Joseph was on to something. Joseph began speaking with an unhesitant authority, thus demonstrating the work of the Spirit of God.

A calm authority. This always reminds me of the three Hebrew children: Shadrach, Meshach, and Abednego. They were told they would be thrown into a fiery furnace if they did not worship the golden image that Nebuchadnezzar had set up. When asked, "Who is this God who will deliver you?" they replied, "We are not careful to answer you" (Dan. 3:16). An unhesitant authority. That is the authority of the Spirit. It's what Peter had on the Day of Pentecost.

Another evidence of the Spirit's witness is that he provides coherence. Things come together. What did Joseph say? "The dream is one." Pharaoh had two dreams. But Joseph said, "The dream is one." It was one coherent whole. The Spirit always does this; he causes everything to "fit." The Bible even talks about the unity of the Spirit. The Spirit even gives a unity to life itself.

Do you know that it will be through the Spirit alone that you will, for the first time, know why you are here? Why have you been created? Why do you have "existence" (to use the existential phrase)? You haven't known why you are here. Perhaps you have said that you didn't ask to be born—you are just here. The Spirit will show you that there is meaning and purpose to your own life. When the Spirit witnesses, you will see a coherent unity to life.

It is the Holy Spirit alone that gives unity to the Bible. Pharaoh had two dreams. But it was "one" dream. In the Bible we have two covenants, two testaments: The Old Testament and the New Testament. It is really one covenant. There is a coherent whole to the Bible. Paul called this "comparing spiritual things with spiritual" (1 Cor. 2:13). God in his Word shows a perfect, coherent unity. The Bible does not contradict itself. It is when you see how one scripture triggers off another, and yet another triggers off still another—as you compare spiritual things with spiritual—then you know the Bible is true. John Calvin called it "the analogy of faith." It is the ultimate proof of the infallibility of Scripture. Though some forty different men wrote the Bible, they all were tuned into the same network.

And so here were two dreams, and they indicate different things. But Joseph said, "The dream is one." And so with God's Word. This Word will also give you unity as a person. Until you become a Christian you are divided within—torn between. This is why Jesus went about making men "whole." Perhaps you have tried to get every kind of pleasure at one level. I sometimes call it the level of nature. You can see, you can taste, you can hear, you can feel and smell. Sense perception it is called. It is the natural level. But you are not only that; you are a spiritual being. You have a soul. And you become whole when that part of you that has lain dormant is touched. Then you become a new person.

Another evidence that the Spirit is at work is that the witness of the Spirit is always personal. Joseph said unto Pharaoh, "The dream of *Pharaoh* is one: God hath shewed *Pharaoh* what he is about to do" (Gen. 41:25, italics mine). God was interested in Pharaoh as a person. Why do you suppose the Spirit is at work? Why do you suppose I am writing at the moment like this? It is because the Spirit of God is interested in you. God wants you. He is interested in your own future. He wants to show *you* what he is about to do. Not only for the next seven years or the next fourteen years, he is concerned about your final destiny. God's Spirit doesn't dwell in trees, plants, animals, or buildings. God wants to dwell in man. Furthermore, when you become a Christian, you become the temple of the Holy Spirit (1 Cor. 6:19).

Joseph said unto Pharaoh, "God hath shewed Pharaoh what he is about to do. The seven good kine are seven years; and the seven good ears are seven years: the dream is one" (Gen. 41:25-26). The Spirit of God was revealing God's mind for the future. God knows the future perfectly. That God knows the future is the only explanation for prophecy and its fulfillment. In the Old Testament there were basically two kinds of prophecies. Sometimes the prophets would reveal what the Lord was thinking in the present. At other times their words would have a meaning that might not be fulfilled for a thousand years. But the prophecy would be fulfilled—perfectly.

Joseph proceeded to unfold the meaning of Pharaoh's dream. He did so in detail. For seven years there would be prosperity, followed by seven years of famine. The details were given to Pharaoh that he might prepare for the future.

One further thing about the Spirit's witness is that it always has a confirming element. The Spirit's witness is not given in isolation; it always relates to something that has gone before—it confirms what you previously had been assured of. For Joseph continued, "The dream was doubled unto Pharaoh twice" ("in two forms" Gen. 41:32, NIV). In this way, the prophecy was "established" by God. The Book of Hebrews speaks of "two immutable things"— the promise and the oath—which were both given to Abraham (Heb. 6:18). It is a wonderful thing that God always *confirms* his witness. There is no contradiction. So there were two different dreams providing a perfect unity and a mutual confirmation that the Spirit's witness was trustworthy.

The final proof of the Spirit's witness is that the correct interpretation is utterly simple and self-authenticating. The two dreams made no sense until Joseph spoke. But when he gave the interpretation, the whole matter was so obvious that one wonders how anybody could have missed it! It was so clear. Those magicians who made their money interpreting dreams couldn't handle this one, yet when you read it now you could almost say, "I could have predicted that." Of course it is easy for us to say that because we have the interpretation and it is so obvious.

But the point is that this is the way God always works; once the breakthrough comes it is all so simple that you wonder how you ever missed it. It was so obvious to Pharaoh that he immediately put it into action. Pharaoh said to his servants, "Can we find such a one as this is, a man in whom the Spirit of God is?" (Gen. 41:38). The king knew that he was not deceived and would never regret putting all his eggs into one basket.

FOURTEEN
PUTTING
YOURSELF
ON THE LINE

How does one become a Christian? What is involved? This chapter has particular relevance to these questions, especially with regard to the nature of "saving" faith—the kind of faith that determines whether a person is truly a Christian.

Joseph interpreted the king's dream, and the king accepted the interpretation. Joseph put himself on the line not merely by interpreting the dream but by giving some unsolicited advice to Pharaoh. He gave an interpretation that not only applied to the distant future but to the immediate future. He was also specific. Anybody would know within a year or so whether Joseph had really got it right. He would quickly look like a fool if there wasn't an abundance of rain, of sun, and vast vegetation in good soil. If great prosperity did not emerge in a very short period of time, it would mean that Joseph had got it wrong. Back to prison he would probably go. He would live in disgrace for the rest of his life if the interpretation of his dream wasn't verified.

Now we come to the one who risked more than Joseph. Joseph isn't ultimately the one who put himself on the line. It was the king. Pharaoh put himself on the line in a most extraordinary manner. He had even rejected the experts. Pharaoh knew they hadn't got it right. But as soon as he heard Joseph give his interpretation of the dream, Pharaoh immediately said, "That's it!" It was "good in the eyes of Pharaoh, and in the eyes of all his servants" (Gen. 41:37).

Pharaoh affirmed Joseph right on the spot. He accepted everything that Joseph said, including some unsolicited advice. Consider this: the Pharaoh, the monarch of the most powerful nation in the world, putting himself on the line before everybody! And yet in a very short period of time—in months, all would know whether the Pharaoh had made a fool of himself in taking the counsel of this Hebrew slave.

Imagine Pharaoh taking a man like that seriously! Anybody might well say to the king, "Do you realize what you are doing? Do you realize who you are listening to? This man is a foreigner. He's a slave. We don't know anything about his background. He's an accused rapist. Are you really going to listen to him and take him seriously?" That is exactly what Pharaoh had to face when he took Joseph seriously. Pharaoh had much to lose. His reputation was at stake. He was a wise and powerful monarch. But a monarch can only continue as long as he has the respect of the people.

But Joseph did more than just explain the dream. This is very interesting to me. He slipped in something about the way of God. It was a great testimony. Joseph took note that there were two dreams (making one complete whole), and commented: "The dream was doubled unto Pharaoh twice." And Joseph added, "It is because the thing is established by God, and God will shortly bring it to pass" (v. 32). Very soon.

Now how could Joseph say that? How could he know? It is because Joseph knew something of the ways of God. As we saw in the last chapter, the "doubling" of the dream was tantamount to what is called the "promise" and the "oath." What is the difference? Whenever there is a promise in the Bible, it is always a conditional thing. A promise will be kept "if." It is always given upon the condition of faith and obedience. But what about an oath? An oath is unconditional: it will be done, no matter what. There are no conditions attached to an oath because it is settled— it will happen. If God swears in his wrath, something bad will happen. If God swears in his mercy, something good will happen. Nothing can change it. Once the oath is disclosed, that is it.

Now in the case of the Pharaoh, God in his sovereign mercy disclosed both the promise and the oath at the same time. Two things at once. Joseph knew therefore that the dream would be fulfilled and that it was going to happen very soon. Joseph hadn't spent an extra two years in the dungeon for nothing. He had learned in greater depths the ways of God. Therefore, when Joseph saw this "double confirmation," it gave him all the boldness in the world. You may have wondered how he could get away with talking like this—even telling Pharaoh what to do! It was no small thing to have Pharaoh, the king of Egypt, accept his interpretation, and I don't doubt that humanly speaking Joseph went into the presence of the king shaking like a leaf. So how could he speak with authority and certainty? It was not that he was arrogant or cocky; it was simply that he knew something of the ways of God and had no fear whatever of being contradicted. Joseph knew that God wouldn't have given the dream twice—this double confirmation—if there was any doubt as to the outcome. He also knew in the Spirit that Pharaoh was going to believe him.

Joseph not only gave an interpretation of the dream, he gave an application. Having explained that the second set of seven years would bring a great famine in the land, Joseph gave this sensible advice: "Let Pharaoh look out a man discreet and wise, and set him over the land of Egypt." The king should appoint officers over the land and take a fifth of the harvest during the seven plenteous years. They should collect all the food of those good years and store up the grain under the authority of Pharaoh. In this way, despite those seven years of famine, the people of Egypt would still eat. They would not only have food, but all this would make Pharaoh very rich for he alone would have food, and the word would get out all over the world that there was plenty in Egypt. Everyone would come to Pharaoh to buy grain. So Joseph showed Pharaoh how he could make a lot of money.

Without this application, there would have been no purpose and no value in the dream. It wasn't enough merely to know what the future was. The question was, what are you going to do about it? Now we know that Pharaoh was very upset because he hadn't been able to get the dream interpreted. He had sleepless nights over it and wanted more than anything in the world to have it interpreted. Therefore, Pharaoh might have stopped Joseph and said, "Look here, you've explained it. That's enough. Thanks very much. You've solved it. Now go on your way." He could have said to his servants, "Give this man a reward, let him be free. I now have this dream off my chest. I knew there was a riddle to this. I just needed to know what it was."

But Joseph knew that the powerful Pharaoh needed more than

the mere interpretation of the dream. He needed to be told what to do. And so Joseph told him. Like good preaching, the exposition needed to be followed by application.

It is not enough to know who Jesus is, why he came, why he died, and where he is today. All that Jesus is and did for us must be applied. It is not enough to know that Jesus died for all—or even that he died for you. The question is, do you trust him? Will you transfer all hope you have in your good works to what Jesus did for you? In other words, will you *apply* Jesus' death to your own life?

The Bible says that you must confess him. If you do, you will be saved. This is the promise, you see. I said that a promise in the Bible is always given with a condition. Here it is: "That if thou shalt confess with thy mouth the Lord Jesus, and shalt believe in thine heart that God hath raised him from the dead, thou shalt be saved" (Rom. 10:9). Jesus said, "Whosoever therefore shall confess me before men, him will I confess also before my Father which is in heaven. But whosoever shall deny me before men, him will I also deny before my Father which is in heaven" (Matt. 10:32-33). It is not enough just to believe in your heart; you must do something about it.

The Pharaoh, when he heard the interpretation, knew it was right. But now he had to put himself on the line. Pharaoh openly said that Joseph was right. He affirmed Joseph in front of everybody.

Jesus put himself on the line for you. I must ask you to put yourself on the line for him. Right now. On the spot, just like Pharaoh. He knew when he heard it that it was right. If you, in your heart of hearts, know that this is right, you too must put yourself on the line. I don't know what it will cost you. Perhaps the embarrassment to confess Jesus before a lot of people. Does that embarrass you? Are you actually ashamed of what has gone on in your own heart? I hope not.

Pharaoh actually made his confession before his servants! "Pharaoh said unto his servants, Can we find such a one as this is, a man in whom the Spirit of God is?" (Gen. 41:38). Think of this—the great Pharaoh before his servants affirming the word of a slave! What a humbling thing it was for him to do.

The Christian is a person who has put himself on the line, even though there is no way he can prove to another he has got it right with regard to the message of Jesus. To become a Christian one must act on the basis of the message, or word, alone. "But what saith it? The word is nigh thee, even in thy mouth, and in thy heart: that is, the word of faith, which we preach" (Rom. 10:8).

You either believe the word that is "preached" (whether by a pastor, minister, or any believer) or you don't. If you do, do not fall into the temptation to wait for a bit of "proof" that you're right in advance of the Judgment (when everyone will get the proof); act now. Otherwise faith ceases to be faith. Faith to be faith is being persuaded without the empirical evidence (Heb. 11:1). Therefore, when you act without the possibility of immediate vindication, it shows a valid confession based upon faith alone. That is saving faith.

FIFTEEN
HUMILIATION
TODAY—
EXALTATION
TOMORROW

At long last, we have reached the time in Joseph's life when pain gives way to pleasure. It is the pleasure God wanted Joseph to experience.

God wants every one of us to have pleasure—his pleasure, his joy. God wants us to be happy. It is equally true that God wants us to be holy. But if we are not happy, there is good reason to question whether we are holy. Holiness is genuine happiness.

God doesn't want us to be under a cloud all the time. "For his anger endureth but a moment . . . weeping may endure for a night, but joy cometh in the morning" (Ps. 30:5). There comes a moment when God says, "It is enough." That moment came for Joseph.

It is basic to human nature to want to be exalted. We may say, "I don't want to be exalted." But we do. That term implies something other than merely being openly exalted. It can simply mean to be lifted up; to be encouraged; to be relieved; to be set free. All of us want that.

Indeed, far more than some dare admit, we want to be vindicated. Nobody likes it when his reputation has been harmed, if he has been lied about, or something unfair has taken place. It is basic to the way we are made to want to have our name cleared. Such an expectation is not abnormal. There is nothing wrong at all with wanting to have our name cleared. Otherwise, why should we have so many promises concerning vindication in the

Bible? Jesus said, "He that humbleth himself shall be exalted" (Luke 14:11). It must mean that being exalted is right, providing we get there the right way. Everything in the Bible points toward vindication and exaltation. That is the way it all ends. But before the crown there is the cross, and he who exalts himself shall be abased.

Exaltation is what God wants for us. But in his way and time. "Humble yourselves therefore under the mighty hand of God, that *he* may exalt you in due time" (1 Pet. 5:6, italics mine). Jesus gave this word to the church at Philadelphia: "Behold, I will make them of the synagogue of Satan, which say they are Jews, and are not, but do lie; behold, I will make them to come and worship before thy feet, and to know that I have loved thee" (Rev. 3:9). The ultimate exaltation is described like this. "And God shall wipe away all tears from their eyes; and there shall be no more death, neither sorrow, nor crying, neither shall there be any more pain: for the former things are passed away" (Rev. 21:4).

Joseph was a man who looked forward to being exalted. But if ever a man apparently lost hope, it would seem it was Joseph. For here was a man who had everything going for him at the beginning but everything going against him soon afterwards. We would never have predicted that the man chosen by his father (and given a coat of many colors) could be soon right on the bottom. But he was. We have seen him humiliated, abased, hurt, lied about. At one stage anybody would say, "That man has no future whatever."

It all began when God gave a promise to Joseph through a dream. "The sun and the moon and the eleven stars made obeisance to me," said Joseph (Gen. 37:9). Joseph's grave mistake was telling that dream to his eleven brothers. It didn't take a lot of imagination to figure out that interpretation! The brothers got the message. Surprise, surprise, they didn't like it. And though Joseph didn't handle things very well, the fact remains that God gave the dreams to him. What Joseph didn't know was that exaltation was a long time off.

It is now thirteen years later. Joseph still wants that dream fulfilled. He lives for the moment when he can be vindicated. But God wasn't going to do that yet. God had an exaltation in mind for Joseph far greater than any personal vindication. That's what we must see in this chapter. Exaltation has come. But it is not his eleven brothers bowing down to him. Rather it is the king of the greatest nation in the world, affirming and exalting him. Joseph's dream would be fulfilled eventually, yes, but that day would have to wait a while longer. What God had in mind now was something far greater than mere personal vengeance.

When the time did come for God to fulfill Joseph's dreams, Joseph himself had virtually no interest at all in it. Jesus said, "For whosoever will save his life shall lose it: but whosoever will lose his life for my sake, the same shall save it" (Luke 9:24). God wants to teach us a different set of values so that the kind of thing we start out wanting becomes secondary. God has something in mind for us far greater than the interest we began with.

Joseph's day of exaltation had arrived. And yet, through it all, a very real humiliation had to take place. He experienced an unexpected trauma, for in a real sense he had to kiss his own life good-bye. We know about the humiliation Joseph had experienced thirteen years before—sold by his brothers into slavery, then taken to Egypt. We know how he was falsely accused and cast into prison. But painful though it was, Joseph was his own man. At least he was himself.

But then came a different situation. Joseph had had a triumph and been given an exaltation, but the kind he really never asked for. He did not appear to be all that interested in what was about to happen. He watched as the Pharaoh took his ring off his finger and put it on Joseph's finger. Joseph never asked for that. All he wanted was to go home. He longed to go back to Canaan, to see his father, and to have his dreams fulfilled.

And so here we find an extraordinary incongruity: a humiliation in the heart of vindication. A triumph that was the opposite of everything he himself could have envisaged. Joseph wanted to go home, but a one way ticket to Canaan wasn't on. Before he knew it, he had Egypt in his hip pocket. He was *the* man in Egypt. He had never prayed for that. But God wanted Egypt. What God wanted is what Joseph got.

Joseph was given something that he could be trusted with because it didn't mean that much to him. It was actually more important to him to have his eleven brothers bow down to him than to be prime minister of Egypt. But being prime minister of Egypt was what he got.

When it comes to seeking happiness, we must stay open to

what God wants to do. As long as we try to force God to fit into our little mold, we will never find him—or his will. We must be open and accept what he is doing. Joseph had the odd experience of becoming what many people dream of but what he had not dreamed of or desired. The exaltation, dazzling though it was, was still short of Joseph's dreams. The glory of being prime minister did little for Joseph's ego when he remembered the original dream he really lived for.

On the other hand, Joseph knew that God had been behind all that had been happening. When he had been lied about by Potiphar's wife, he could now see plainly that God had overruled. No one could have told him that at the time. But now he could see. A stupendous moment had come. He was standing before the Pharaoh. How could *he* have engineered that? God had done it. God had been behind it all so that he could actually say that the worst thing that had ever happened to him had been done by God. God will bring us to that place also.

What was the nature of Joseph's exaltation? It really was vindication, even though his ultimate wish was to remain unfulfilled for a while. But three things were nonetheless true—we could call them spiritual, moral, and intellectual. First, Joseph's own spirituality was affirmed. It was affirmed by Pharaoh who said, "Can we find such a one as this, a man in whom the Spirit of God is?" (41:38). It came from an unexpected quarter. The one who affirmed his spirituality was not the covenant people of God but the king of Egypt. What a disappointment when our spirituality isn't affirmed by those we want most to reach!

Second, it was a moral vindication. Joseph's character was affirmed in this moment. Accused of immorality, Joseph had been put in prison, but look at Genesis 41:39: "Pharaoh said unto Joseph, Forasmuch as God hath showed thee all this, there is *none so discreet* and wise as thou art" (italics mine). Potiphar's wife had accused Joseph of, to put it mildly, an indiscretion. Then Pharaoh came along and said, "There's none so discreet as you."

If you have been lied about on a large scale or a lesser scale and you are at work trying to vindicate yourself, remember that "he that saveth his life shall lose it, but he that loseth his life shall find it." Let God do it. He will do it in the most unexpected way.

Third, it was an intellectual vindication. His own gift was affirmed. Pharaoh said, "None is so discreet and *wise* as thou art."

Joseph was so anxious for this! He had wanted his gift to be recognized. He had said to the butler, "Don't forget me; don't forget me." His brothers had made fun of his gift. But the day came when his gift was affirmed by the Pharaoh. It came at an unexpected time in an unexpected place by an unexpected person. But it came God's way.

I may have a gift that I am so afraid won't be recognized. If I go about exalting myself—pulling strings and doing anything like that, I am going to find that it will elude me. Success will always be outside my grasp. But once we get right with God and are willing for God to use us as he wills, "Eye hath not seen, nor ear heard, neither have entered into the heart of man" what God will do.

Humiliation today, exaltation tomorrow. Pharaoh said to Joseph, "I've set you over the land of Egypt." Pharaoh took off his ring from his hand and put it on Joseph's hand and "arrayed him in vestures of fine linen, and put a gold chain about his neck; and he made him to ride in the second chariot which he had; and they cried before him, Bow the knee." Pharaoh said to Joseph, "I am Pharaoh, and without thee shall no man lift up his hand or foot in all the land of Egypt" (Gen. 41:42-44).

What is the humiliation that is required? Two things: First, be open, for you don't know the way God wants to do it. Second, affirm him. Don't question his judgment. His ways are higher than our ways (Isa. 55:9). You may ask: what will my exaltation be? I don't know. There was no way to calculate what God would do through Joseph. But I can tell you this: no cross, no crown.

SIXTEEN
WHEN GOD CLEARS
HIS NAME

If God is in control and all-powerful; if he is a God of justice, of love, and can do anything or stop anything, why does he permit evil? Why does he allow famine? Earthquakes? Why are people starving in a world that he made? Why is there war? Why is there crime? Why do we read in the newspaper of the birth of Siamese twins? Or, as it was a few years ago, why were so many Thalidomide babies born deformed with physical and mental handicaps? How can anybody believe in a God who has the power to stop it and doesn't, and yet sets himself forth in his own Word as a God of love?

I know a minister who came to doubt the Bible, although he had started out as an evangelical—believing in the full inspiration of the Bible. But he changed his mind. One day he actually went to the pulpit and made a statement that was as close to blasphemy as anything you could hear. He said, "God has a lot to answer for." Here was a minister who posed as a Christian man but was repeating what unregenerate men feel in their hearts.

May I ask you a question? If I may use this expression, would you *bet* that God can clear his name? Would you be among those who would say there is no way he can? Many say, "If he is all powerful and just and loving, there is no way God can clear his name." And yet the same Bible that says that God is all-wise, all-powerful, and loving also says that someday he will clear his name. He promises to do so. Romans 14:11 says, "Every knee

113

shall bow to me, and every tongue shall confess to God." John said:

> I beheld when he had opened the sixth seal, and, lo, there was a great earthquake; and the sun became black as sack-cloth of hair, and the moon became as blood; and the stars of heaven fell unto the earth, even as a fig tree casteth her untimely figs, when she is shaken of a mighty wind. And the heaven departed as a scroll when it is rolled together; and every mountain and island were moved out of their places. And the kings of the earth, and the great men, and the rich men, and the chief captains, and the mighty men, and every bondman, and every free man, hid themselves in the dens and in the rocks of the mountains; and said to the mountains and to the rocks, Fall on us, and hide us from the face of him that sitteth on the throne, and from the wrath of the Lamb: for the great day of his wrath is come; and who shall be able to stand? (Rev. 6:12-17)

You find this theme running right through the Book of Ezekiel, for example, "They shall know that I am the Lord." "I the Lord love justice." God says that.

We are talking now about God's claim that a day of vindication is coming—a date in history. The Bible calls it "the last day." It is when God will clear his name. Vindication—it means "to be proved right when one has been right all along." Vindication means that your name is cleared, that the accusations were false and ill-posed; that what they said about you wasn't true, and your name is completely cleared.

Now let me just use this expression again. I wonder how many would be willing to bet or lay a wager that God is able to do this? How many are willing to say, "Some day God will clear his name; he was right, he was just and loving all along?" Let's suppose that somebody had started a company called "God's Reputation Limit-ed." They were selling the shares at $100 per share. I wonder how many would be willing to buy? If you knew you could buy stock in "God's Reputation Limited" or "God's Vindication Limited" at $100 a share would you buy? I know this, that if there were such a company I would sell all I had and buy. It's like that parable of Jesus: "The kingdom of heaven is like unto a merchant man, seeking goodly pearls: who, when he had found one pearl of great price, went and sold all that he had, and bought it" (Matt. 13:45). This God who gave us this word will one day clearly, unmistakably, and convincingly clear his name—so manifestly that everybody will know that he was right all the time. That is why they will cry for the rocks to fall on them. They will cry to the mountains, "Hide us, fall on us, crush us; hide us from his wrath—from him that is on the throne."

How does one become a Christian? By agreeing with God now. God calls on you to confess that he is just, holy, and righteous. You may ask how you can know that this is true. You know because you become inwardly persuaded of the integrity of God by his Word. The difference between a Christian and a non-Christian can be simply stated. The non-Christian will clear God's name some day—at the last day, on the day of judgment. The Christian does it now.

Joseph had been summoned by the Pharaoh to stand before him. He heard the dream that Pharaoh had dreamed. He interpreted it and gave an application. Before that moment, how many then living would have been willing to bet that some day Joseph would be vindicated? Look at his life. Here was a man who had no hope at all of being vindicated. But he was. So was God. How can God clear his name when he has allowed such evil to go on in the world? Most people say, "There's no way God can clear his name. It's too late. It's not possible. Even if he would change, there's no way. Millions have already suffered. It's too late."

You could say exactly that about Joseph. How many living then would have invested $100 per share in a stock company called "Joseph's Reputation Limited" or "Joseph's Vindication Limited"? Who would invest $100 a share? Who would give $10 a share? Or $1? Would anybody? There was no hope. Why should anybody want to come to the rescue of Joseph? What impresario then living would interview Joseph and say, "I want to be your agent. You have got a brilliant future. I just want you to sign this contract here." We can only say, humanly speaking, that there was no way this man Joseph could ever be vindicated. The only person who might have vindicated Joseph after he was in Egypt was Potiphar's wife. But she wasn't talking. And as for his brothers back in Canaan, they were not ever planning to say what had happened.

Joseph was absolutely alone. It was said of the disciples, when Jesus was being led away to be crucified, that they "all forsook him, and fled" (Matt. 25:56). And there was an occasion when the Apostle Paul explained it, "At my first answer no man stood with me, but all men forsook me: I pray God that it may not be laid to their charge" (2 Tim. 4:16). God delights in putting a chosen instrument through the kind of tribulation where he has to stand absolutely alone or be utterly rejected by everybody: to test him. It was said of Hezekiah in the Old Testament, "God left him, to try him, that he might know all that was in his heart" (2 Chron. 32:31).

Look at Joseph. Here was a man who was tested. He had nobody who believed in him. But then none other than the king, the head of the mightiest nation of that time, said to Joseph, "Forasmuch as God hath shewed thee all this, there is none so discreet and wise as thou art: Thou shalt be over my house, and according unto thy word shall all my people be ruled: only in the throne will I be greater than thou. . . . See, I have set thee over all the land of Egypt" (Gen. 41:39-41). Pharaoh took off his ring from his hand and put it upon Joseph's hand, arrayed him in vestures of fine linen, put a gold chain around his neck, and made him to ride in the second chariot. All cried out before him, "Bow the knee." Pharaoh made him ruler over all the land of Egypt and said to Joseph, "I am Pharaoh, and without thee shall no man lift up his hand or foot in all the land of Egypt" (v. 44).

I call that vindication. That is having your name cleared indeed. Who was it that cleared Joseph's name? The Pharaoh, a man whose eyes God opened, a man who actually put his own reputation on the line. Who else affirmed Joseph? Pharaoh's servants did. Did anybody else vindicate Joseph? Yes. The people. The people of Egypt cried, "Bow the knee."

We may want to question Pharaoh's wisdom and verdict on Joseph. We may also question the Father's verdict on Jesus. For the voice came from heaven at Jesus' baptism, "This is my beloved Son, in whom I am well pleased" (Matt. 3:17). But as the people of Egypt accepted the Pharaoh's verdict concerning Joseph, so those who are drawn by the Father (John 6:44) affirm what the Father said about Jesus.

One main thing needs to be kept in mind. The verdict that was pronounced concerning Joseph was done before there was the remotest visible sign that Joseph had got it right. There very well may have been cynics in Egypt who thought, *Shouldn't the king wait and see what's going to happen first? Has Pharaoh gone clean off his head?* And that is the way the world will look at you if they ever hear you have become a Christian, if they find out that you have accepted God's verdict about Jesus. The Christian says, "Jesus is the Son of God. He's my Lord. I worship him. I believe that he died on the cross for my sins, that God raised him from the dead. I declare that he is God in the flesh. He's my Lord and I'm not ashamed." There will be people who will say to you, "Have you gone right off your head? How can you say that? How can you vindicate God? Look at the evil in the world. Look at the famine that's taking place at the moment in Africa where people are dying every day. You claim that there's a just God, but you cannot know this."

There are two ways of looking at vindication. Vindication may be either hidden or open; secret or revealed. By "hidden" I simply mean that not everybody affirms what is nonetheless true. Perhaps only a few see it. In some cases nobody but you may see it. You may be tested like the Apostle Paul, who wrote, "No man stood with me—they all forsook me." You know what is right but have no way of clearing your name. It is an enormous honor to have a trial like that. But you will blow it if *you* try to clear your name. Trying to win the battle, you will lose the war. But if you let God do it? "Eye hath not seen, nor ear heard, neither have entered into the heart of man, the things which God hath prepared for them that love him" (1 Cor. 2:9). Let God do it.

For vindication may be open. To anybody living in Egypt at a moment such as that, it was obvious that Joseph's name was cleared. Open vindication is when everybody sees it and when you are not alone. It is also possible that the ones you want most to see it (who couldn't or wouldn't see it before) now do see it. Therefore, Joseph's vindication was open in a way, but it still did not satisfy the longings of his heart. Those he wanted most to bow to him were not the people of Egypt but his brothers in Canaan. A million people shouting "Bow the knee!" before Joseph would not do for him nearly as much as eleven brothers in Canaan doing it. Thus Joseph's open vindication was still limited.

But the lesson here is that we must let our vindication come through those God has affirmed. We must affirm God's *way* of vindicating us by accepting the *people* he chooses to work through. The people he raises up to vindicate us may not be the ones we would have chosen, much less the ones that massage our ego.

The early church faced this. Paul wanted so very much to teach the Jews (Rom. 9:1-4; 10:1). But he gave up and went to the Gentiles. The call "Come over into Macedonia and help us" (Acts 16:9) has been repeated in various ways many times. The open vindication we may want at the natural level must stay subservient to the open manner God chooses. His people may well not be our first choice; it is enough that they are his. At the end of the day, the clearing of our own name is of little importance. The Judgment will be sweet, however long we wait for it. Paul was willing to wait for this (1 Cor. 4:4).

How will God clear his name in the Last Day? I don't know. We can't figure it out, can we? It is like reading a detective story. We can't work out in advance "who did it." But when we come to the last page, we read it and we say, "Why didn't I think of that?"

God will clear his name and will do it more spectacularly and more perfectly than Pharaoh ever did it with Joseph. If we wait until the "seven years of plenty" and the "seven years of famine" have passed by before we affirm his integrity, we will be fools. The Bible says that God will laugh at our calamity. It will then be too late to enjoy his vindication. For those that affirm him must do it on *faith*—faith in his Word. Will you?

SEVENTEEN
FINDING YOURSELF

Joseph had finally come home. This may seem surprising. One may say that Joseph wasn't home, because home for Joseph was in Canaan. Here he was living in Egypt, a place where he never wanted to be. But it is nonetheless true: Joseph had finally come home.

Home is not a *where* but a *when*. It is when you find yourself, no matter where you are on this earth. One can be somewhere that is normally thought of as home but be utterly lost. On the other hand, you can be in a place that is hardly regarded as home and yet be completely and utterly at home.

Consider the parable of the Prodigal Son (Luke 15:11-32). There is an analogy between Joseph and the prodigal son. A young man prematurely got his inheritance and went into a far country. He was determined to live it up and to have a good time. Perhaps he did have a good time for a while. But then all that pleasure came to an end. When the prodigal "came to himself" (v. 17), he was at home. In that moment he was already home though he was physically in a far country. He was at home the moment he came to himself.

Where is home? Home is God's will for your life. Home is where you are happy. At ease. It is where you can put your feet up, where you feel secure, where you are at rest. It is an internal condition. It has something to do with conscience and the heart. It is true success. Dr. O. S. Hawkins defines success as finding the will of God and doing it. Then you are at peace with yourself.

Joseph finally found his niche in life. You could never have told him in advance that his niche in life was to be the governor of Egypt. Who would ever have thought that? And yet all that had gone on before in Joseph's life was God's preparation for this very position. What his brothers did by throwing him into a pit, then rescuing him from the pit, and selling him to the Ishmaelites was preparing Joseph for his real home. His brothers meant it for evil, but God meant it for good. When Potiphar's wife accused Joseph of making a pass at her, she meant it for evil, but God meant it for good. Egypt in general, and the governor's job in particular, were things God had in mind all along for Joseph.

> God moves in a mysterious way
> His wonders to perform;
> He plants His footsteps in the sea,
> And rides upon the storm.

—W. Cowper

God has more in mind for you than even your wildest fancy can grasp. God has a plan for your life. He has a plan for you greater than anything you could conceive. Get out a piece of paper and write down your wildest fancy. I promise it, what God has in mind is greater and better.

But in the process certain things have to be dealt with, and these things take time. We may well wish that God could do it much sooner, that he could get everything over with. My favorite line in Dickens's A Christmas Carol comes when Scrooge looks out the window and sees the little boy walking down the street. Scrooge asks, "What day is it?"

The boy replies, "Why it's Christmas, sir."

Scrooge exclaims, "Ah, the spirits did it all in one night!"

What a happy thought. That is the way we all want it to be, that God will get it over with all at once.

But what God had in mind for Joseph took thirteen years, and that was the preparation. One reason it took so long was not because God was so slow but that Joseph had to be taught. All of us think we are teachable. We say, "Lord, I will do what you want me to do." I suppose 99 percent of most Christians would quite gladly sing the hymn, "Take my life, and let it be consecrated,

Lord, to Thee." We really mean that. What we don't usually realize about ourselves is that when we are told to do something by the Lord we say, "Well now, just a minute; do I really have to do that?" and we back off. This is why it takes years. All of us have to be chastened.

I know what it is to be a Jonah. God says, "Go to Nineveh." But I say, "No, Lord, please, please."

I tell myself that God replies, "Well, all right. I am sorry I put it like that. You don't have to go to Nineveh after all."

So I say, "Thanks, Lord. That was good of you to let me out of that."

That is the game I have played. I fancy that I am released. And then a year or two later it hits me—God meant it. I have got to do what he said! I suspect many of us are like this. We are at bottom unteachable, though we think we mean it when we say, "Lord, I will do what you say."

Certain misconceptions had to be dealt with in Joseph's life. So with us, before we can ever find ourselves. In the case of Joseph, his first misconception was that he overestimated the satisfaction he would feel if he got his own way. (The prodigal made the same mistake. He went to his father and said, "Divide to me my living, I want it now. Give me what's coming to me.") He said to the butler, "Remember me," but the butler forgot. It was God's will that the butler should forget. God overruled Joseph's request. It is always a singular favor when God doesn't let us have our own way. There is that curious verse in the Psalms, "He gave them their request; but sent leanness into their soul" (Ps. 106:15). If there is something we want and can't have, it is because God in his kindness is withholding it from us.

Joseph's second misconception was in underestimating the power of the Holy Spirit, who was responsible for Joseph's gift. First, he had the gift of having dreams. The Holy Spirit was behind all that. But Joseph got panicky and thought, *Will anybody ever recognize my gift?* He didn't realize that if God gives the gift, he is the one who will make it available to be used—in his way and his time.

God's time came. Pharaoh said to Joseph, "Forasmuch as God hath shewed thee all this, there is none so discreet and wise as thou art." The time came. His gift was recognized.

Joseph's third misconception was in underestimating the security that God had in mind for him. This can happen to anybody who has had a series of bad experiences. Perhaps so many bad things have happened to us that it has affected us psychologically. I know the feeling. *There's just nothing for me,* we think.

Joseph was a man who was beginning to feel very insecure. He lost his home, was thrown into a pit, then sold to Ishmaelites. Then he got a second chance, as it were, working in Potiphar's household. Things went well for a while. Then Potiphar's wife falsely accused him, and he ended up in the dungeon. Joseph began to wonder, *Will I ever have a home? Will I ever know security again?* When we have had so many people let us down, push us down, disappoint us, and turn their backs on us, we become very insecure. We feel we can't trust anybody!

But look at what happened. Pharaoh said to Joseph, "Forasmuch as God hath shewed thee all this; there is none so discreet and wise as thou art: thou shalt be over my house." Not only was he going to have security, he was going to be in control. "I have set thee over all the land of Egypt." That is the security Joseph got by waiting.

Not only that. God even provided for him at another level, something Joseph probably never dreamed could happen—God gave Joseph a wife in Egypt. "It is not good that a man should be alone" (Gen. 2:18). Most of us need a husband or a wife. We must wait on God; if it is what we want and really need, we will get the wife or the husband of God's choice.

Joseph came home—in Egypt, not Canaan. "Eye hath not seen, nor ear heard, neither have entered into the heart of man, the things which God hath prepared for them that love him" (1 Cor. 2:9).

EIGHTEEN
MERCY SET FORTH

We have already observed that Joseph may be seen as a type of Jesus Christ in the Old Testament. He was a person that makes us think of Jesus before Jesus himself came along. "Joseph was thirty years old when he stood before Pharaoh" (Gen. 41:46), reminding us of Jesus who was thirty when he began his public ministry (Luke 3:23).

We won't know until we get to heaven what all our Lord's own preparation consisted of before he reached the age of thirty. We know something of his temptation after his baptism. But Jesus equally was being prepared and was tempted before he was thirty. Hebrews 4:15 says that he was "in all points tempted like as we are, yet without sin." It would be a mistake to think that all Jesus' temptations took place only after his baptism. He must have endured temptation throughout his lifetime.

We don't know everything that Joseph went through. We really know just a little bit. When we get to heaven I look forward to meeting Joseph and asking him more about it. What were his thoughts when he was in the dungeon? What was it like? I am absolutely sure of this: Joseph had to learn to love. He had to reach the place where he could forgive his brothers. I don't merely mean that he could say, "I forgive you for what you did." He had to come to the place where it didn't even bother him any more. He had to reach the place where he could forgive the butler who forgot him.

I am absolutely sure that what Joseph had to learn, then, was to love. God will not greatly use any man who harbors a grudge. Learning to love is the chief part of God's preparation for us.

We now enter into the next phase of Joseph's life, the fulfillment of all that he prophesied to Pharaoh. He had put himself on the line when he put a time limit on his prophecy. He might have given a general kind of interpretation of Pharaoh's dream. But he didn't do that. He gave a time limit so that everybody would know if he got it wrong. But we have seen that the one who really put himself on the line was Pharaoh. Time would tell whether Joseph had got it right or Pharaoh had lost his head.

What actually happened? During the first seven years "the earth brought forth by handfuls" (Gen. 41:47). Joseph gathered up the food of the seven years and stored it in the cities. He gathered so much corn—"as the sand of the sea"—that he stopped keeping records. It was beyond measure.

Then came the end of the first seven years. The seven years of abundance ended. Now there was famine in the land, and the seven years of dearth began, "according as Joseph had said" (v. 54). Moreover, the dearth was in *all* lands; "but in all the land of Egypt there was bread."

It turned out just as God had said. If you are a Christian, you have discovered this about the Lord—he keeps his word. Nobody will ever be able to point a finger at God and say, "You let me down." For if there is anything that God esteems above all else it is his own word. "Thou has magnified thy word above all thy name" (Ps. 138:2). When you touch God's word you are touching his heart; for his integrity is at stake.

When Joseph gave the interpretation of the dream, it was the Spirit of God speaking through Joseph. Joseph could never have come up with an interpretation like that. He hadn't done it in his own wisdom or strength. Jesus said, "Ye shall be brought before governors and kings for my sake, for a testimony against them and the Gentiles. But when they deliver you up, take no thought how or what ye shall speak: for it shall be given you in that same hour what ye shall speak. For it is not ye that speak, but the Spirit of your Father which speaketh in you" (Matt. 10:18-20).

God will surely vindicate his Word. Jesus said, "Heaven and earth shall pass away, but my words shall not pass away" (Matt.

24:35). God has appointed a day "in which he shall judge the world in righteousness by that man whom he hath ordained" (Acts 17:31). That man was his Son, Jesus Christ, who said, "He that rejecteth me, and receiveth not my words, hath one that judgeth him: the word that I have spoken, the same shall judge him in the last day" (John 12:48). The words of Jesus will be the basis of judgment when all stand before God. They are even called the "books" (Matthew, Mark, Luke, John) at the Great White Throne (Rev. 20:11-12).

It gives God the highest pleasure to vindicate his own Word. He does it so that all see it was exactly like God said. When the Spirit of God comes down in power, the most immediate reaction is, "God is real. His Word is true. It's exactly like the Bible says." For the Bible leaps out in gold letters and you see it is literally true. Nothing gives God greater pleasure than vindicating his own Word. He loves to have his people rediscover how real he is.

On one occasion in the early church there was a prayer meeting and the "place was shaken." The power of God was felt physically. Moreover, "They were all filled with the Holy Ghost, and they spake the word of God with boldness. . . . And with great power gave the apostles witness of the resurrection of the Lord Jesus: and great grace was upon them all" (Acts 4:31, 33). The Spirit of God was there with such presence that Jesus was absolutely real. He was so real that his physical presence would not have made anyone more convinced that he was raised from the dead. Now all we have is his Word. But when the Spirit comes in power, we see clearly that it is exactly like the Bible says.

This is a good reason for believing that hell is literal. I fear that ours is a generation that has seen less preaching of the message of hell than any generation in the history of the Christian church. It seems to be something we want to apologize for. Jesus told the story of a rich man who went to hell. Jesus said, "In hell he lifted up his eyes, being in torments . . . and said, 'Father Abraham, have mercy on me, and send Lazarus, that he may dip the tip of his finger in water, and cool my tongue; for I am tormented in this flame'" (Luke 16:23-24). One will discover in hell that it is exactly like God said.

We have before us in this section of Genesis an account of God's great mercy but also an account of his great wrath. God can give or withhold mercy and be just either way. When God saves, it will be because he does it with justice. When God condemns, it will be because of his justice.

The seven years of plenty show the wonderful mercy of God. It even gives a picture of the sovereign rule of Jesus Christ. Pharaoh said to Joseph, "Without thee shall no man lift up his hand or foot in all the land of Egypt" (Gen. 41:44). That is exactly the way Jesus has been given authority in the world. Just before he ascended to heaven, he announced to his disciples, "All power [authority] is given unto me in heaven and in earth" (Matt. 28:18). The father gave all authority to Jesus and said, "Sit thou at my right hand, until I make thine enemies thy footstool" (Ps. 110:1; Acts 2:33-35).

Anyone who defied Joseph in Egypt did so at their peril. So the word went out, "Bow the knee." Wherever they saw Joseph they bowed the knee. Psalm 2 says, "Kiss the Son, lest he be angry" (v. 12). That means you must bow the knee to Christ and make your peace with God.

It is also a picture of the sovereign rule of Christ over all the nations. Four times we are told about Joseph's authority. Pharaoh said to Joseph, "I have set thee over all the land of Egypt" (Gen. 41:41). Later we read, "He made him ruler over all the land of Egypt" (v. 43); and Joseph "went throughout all the land of Egypt" (v. 46). Joseph was given absolute control over the nation.

It is even a picture of how Jesus Christ has control over this world. He is not only the Head of the Church but the Head of every nation. Happy is the nation that recognizes this. "Blessed is the nation whose God is the Lord" (Ps. 33:12). Historians can verify that those nations that have honored the gospel have been blessed even at a material level. It is an extraordinary thing that wherever the gospel has gone into a nation it has elevated that nation's standard of living. That has not been the missionaries' primary goal. They have wanted only to preach the gospel, to see people saved from the flames of hell. But an offshoot of this has been that wherever the gospel has gone, people have been blessed at other levels as well. Why was all Egypt prospering? It was for Joseph's sake. When Joseph was working in Potiphar's household, we are told that the whole house was blessed for Joseph's sake (Gen. 39:5). It is the same thing here. For Joseph's sake everything was going right. Just as he had prophesied.

This also provides a picture of Christ's sovereign administration in his Church. We even have an analogy to revival, when the Spirit of God comes in great power. Mind you, this doesn't happen every day. It may bypass a whole generation. But when it does happen, everybody is aware of it. Joseph gave this instruction to Pharaoh: during those seven years of plenty they must store up for the future. For when the seven years were over, the dearth was going to come over the whole world. If you store up now, you will have something to live on when the dearth comes. And that is one of the functions of revival. Revival not only blesses the immediate generation, but it leaves a legacy for future generations should a great dearth follow.

For example, the apostles forecast that there was to be a great falling away. That very thing happened around the turn of the first century. But what did the apostles do while there was time? They were moved by the Spirit to begin writing the New Testament. During the era of great blessing, in the providence of God, Matthew began to collect the different things that Jesus had said and wrote a Gospel. Mark, one of the early followers, did the same thing. So did John.

Afterwards Luke, though not one of the twelve apostles, felt led to write about what was going on in the Church. He gave us the Book of Acts, the first church history. When there were problems in various churches, God moved Paul to write letters. Also Peter, James, John, and Jude. And so we have the Bible. This Bible was born during a time of extraordinary power. It is infallible. It is perfect and inerrant. It is God's own Word. And so when there is a famine of God's Word, we can read the Bible and thank him that he gave it to us. Are you glad you have a Bible? Do you appreciate that Bible that is in your house? Do you realize it is the one book you have that can change your life and will give you hope?

Therefore, revival is not only for the present but also for the future. One forgotten reason why the Great Awakening in the eighteenth century had such lasting fruit was because there were men like Jonathan Edwards. He started churning out books as fast as he could—while the revival was going on. He began to report everything, writing it down, leaving a legacy for the church. One reason why there is a "Bible Belt" in America today is because of Jonathan Edwards. It was his legacy. Dr. Lloyd-Jones often used to say to me that the great pity of the Welsh Revival of 1904 was that when it was over, it was over. There was no great theological legacy as such. And yet it still stands as a twentieth century reminder of what God can do!

Joseph gathered corn as the sand of the sea. So great was the harvest that they quit keeping records. But they stored the food for future years. How blessed they were for those first seven years! But God said it first.

NINETEEN
MERCY WITHHELD

God always keeps his word. But he does more than that. He does it so abundantly and so perfectly and with such a flourish that we never could have dreamed in advance how wonderful it would be. There is nothing that gives God greater pleasure than keeping his word. He loves to say to us, "Didn't I tell you it would be like that?" If you will surrender completely to him, God will do things for you that you couldn't have imagined. How great is his mercy!

We now look at the other side of the coin. It is equally true that when God *withholds* mercy, it will be just like he said. As his mercy is better and greater than anything we could have dreamed of, so is the withholding of mercy worse than anything that we could dream of. Cain, the world's first murderer, was quoted later as saying, "My punishment is greater than I can bear" (Gen. 4:13). The seven years of plenty were an unveiling of God's mercy, but the seven years of famine were an unveiling of God's wrath.

Why must God show both sides of his nature? I don't know. The best answer I can give is that he must be true to himself. I certainly don't have all the answers. I don't know why I was born in 1935 and not 1835, why I was brought up in a Christian home rather than a pagan home. I don't know why I was born in Kentucky and not China, in the twentieth century not the fourth century B.C.

I don't know why God made hell. We know that it was for the devil and his angels (Matt. 25:41). But I don't know why God chose to demonstrate his wrath.

You may ask, "How can you serve a God like that?" I can answer that. It is because Jesus, who is God in the flesh, knew all about these problems. I believe in him and I trust him utterly. He knew about these theoretical and philosophical problems. He knew about the problem of suffering in the world. In the end Jesus himself suffered. He died on the cross and knew a rejection such as we will never know. And it was Jesus who said, "I am the way, the truth, and the life: no man cometh unto the Father, but by me" (John 14:6). Jesus himself has shown me so much that is of purest integrity and love that what I *don't* know about God does not frighten me. I accept that there will be a time when God will clarify everything.

There is as much meaning and purpose in his justice as there is in his mercy.

> There's a wideness in God's mercy,
> Like the wideness of the sea;
> There's a kindness in His justice,
> Which is more than liberty.

—F. W. Faber

Nothing illustrates this better than the story before us. In the inscrutable purpose of God, the seven years of plenty in the land of Egypt ended. It was all over. Why seven years? Why not fourteen? Why not fifty? Why did it have to end? I don't know. But this is what God said would happen. And that is what did happen. The seven years of scarcity began to come exactly as Joseph had said. Moreover, the famine was in all lands. "But in all the land of Egypt only there was bread" (Gen. 41:54).

What we have before us is not the reason why God shows his wrath but rather a pattern of it. For when he shows his wrath, there is mercy in it that can still be seen. And yet the main thing is that whether the prophecy is about God's mercy or his justice and his wrath, it turns out exactly as God said. For all that is laid down in the Bible regarding God's wrath will be demonstrated as perfectly and astonishingly as his mercy.

Joseph prophesied that the seven years of plenty would end. But when things are going well, it is hard to imagine anything else. It is somewhat like the weather. When it is lovely and sunny, we tend to forget that it could all change by the next day. In fact, my friend Dr. Barrie White often says, "Praise the good day at night." And then when it is bad, and you hear from somebody elsewhere that the weather is magnificent, that is hard to believe. God said that the good times would end; there would be seven years of famine. That is exactly what happened. This ought to be a sufficient lesson for all of us to take seriously every word of God—every word. "He that being often reproved hardeneth his neck, shall suddenly be destroyed, and that without remedy" (Prov. 29:1).

God has told us in advance that some day he will unveil his wrath and that it will be universal. All men will experience it. As I have said, Martin Luther called John 3:16 the Bible in a nutshell; "For God so loved the world, that he gave his only begotten Son, that whosoever believeth in him *should not perish*, but have everlasting life" (italics mine). These are the words of Jesus. This gospel alone will keep us from *perishing*. The assumption is, therefore, that all men are perishing anyway and that the gospel is the only thing that can help. I fear that this is a missing note in modern preaching. But wouldn't you agree that if it is true, that warning of hell is the kindest thing we can do? Paul said, "Much more then, being now justified by his blood, we shall be saved from wrath through him" (Rom. 5:9). Jesus has delivered us "from the wrath to come" (1 Thess. 1:10).

The story of Joseph is a demonstration of the universality and the totality of God's wrath. "The dearth was in all lands" (Gen. 41:54). Nobody escaped it. As the mercy of God is universal, so is his wrath. Jesus tasted death for every man that he might have mercy on all; but those who reject this gospel have nothing but the wrath of God awaiting them.

And yet God declares his justice that he might reveal his mercy. There is a "kindness in his justice." "The dearth was in all the lands; but *in all the land of Egypt there was bread.*" In the prophecy of Habakkuk we have these words: "O Lord, I have heard thy speech, and was afraid: O Lord, revive thy work in the midst of the years, in the midst of the years make known; in wrath remember mercy" (Hab. 3:2). This is what God did here. God remembered mercy. The whole world was affected by the famine, but in Egypt there was bread.

The gospel is disclosed in the context of God's purest justice, for when God saves us, although it demonstrates his mercy, it equally demonstrates his justice. The Bible basically says two things about God: he is merciful and he is just. When the Bible says God is just, it means that God must punish sin. His nature demands it. I am a sinner, therefore God must punish me. But the Bible also says that God is merciful. That means he doesn't want to punish me. The question that the world ought to be asking is this: How can God be just and merciful at the same time? If we can truly understand how he can be both simultaneously, we will grasp the essence of the gospel.

The answer is this: God sent his Son into the world—Jesus Christ, who was God in the flesh. The Bible says, "In the beginning was the Word, and the Word was with God, and the Word was God. . . . The Word was made flesh, and dwelt among us" (John 1:1, 14). When Jesus died on the cross, it was actually God punishing him. That doesn't seem fair, does it? But that is what happened. "The Lord hath laid on him the iniquity of us all" (Isa. 53:6). When Jesus was hanging on the cross, at some time between noon and three o'clock on Good Friday, all of our sins were transferred to Jesus. Literally transferred to Jesus, as though he had committed them. He took our guilt. God smote his only begotten Son. He poured out all his wrath on Jesus. In this way his justice was carried out. That is why he can be merciful to me. His justice was satisfied. God can be just and merciful at the same time because his Son paid our debt.

We feel no need of the Savior as long as we are enjoying plenty. As long as we are sitting on top of the world and things are going right for us, we will not be likely to feel the need of this gospel. In all the land of Egypt there was bread. But when all the land of Egypt was famished, the people "cried." Are you at the end of your plenty? Consider the story of Jonah. Jonah ran from God. God said, "Go" and Jonah said, "No." God prepared a fish that swallowed up Jonah. What happened then: "Then Jonah prayed" (Jonah 2:1). In much the same way, when all the land of Egypt was famished the people *cried*.

Until we are broken, God isn't really on speaking terms with us. For the proud heart God despises; but "a broken and contrite heart, O God, thou wilt not despise" (Ps. 51:17). We must be ready to say, "God, you win. But thank you that you brought me to this place. If you hadn't done it, I would have never called on your name." There is a kindness in his justice.

God saves those who cry to him for mercy. Mercy may be given or withheld, and justice will be done in either case. If God doesn't give us mercy, he is simply giving us what we deserve and we can't complain. Therefore, it must never be a matter of snapping our finger at God. It is sheer kindness on his part that he brings us to the place where we ask for mercy. For if God sends us to hell, it will be to demonstrate his justice. And if he saves us, it will be to demonstrate his justice. He could do either and be true to himself. But only because he accepted what Jesus did on the cross.

TWENTY
FOUND OUT

The idea of God "discovering" our sin has deep biblical roots, but I suspect it is largely an unexplored teaching. "The punishment of thine iniquity is accomplished, O daughter of Zion; he will no more carry thee away into captivity: he will visit thine iniquity, O daughter of Edom; he will discover thy sins" (Lam. 4:22). In this chapter we will examine a case of being found out—Joseph's brothers.

Jonah was found out. He thought he would get away with disobedience, and he did for a while. God said, "Go"; Jonah said, "No." God said, "All right, go on." For a while things were going right. But the time came when God discovered—that is, uncovered—Jonah's sin.

It is a most blessed thing if God discovers our sin. I would also agree that it is most painful, for the last thing we naturally want to happen is to get caught for having done wrong. We think it is a wonderful thing not to get caught. We may feel good about it. But the worst thing in the world is *not* to get caught. "Who can stand before his cold?" (Ps. 147:17); who can bear God's cold shoulder? It is horrible if God lets us go and doesn't do a thing about it. We may fancy that we are having a great time and have even been given a blank check to sin—as if God says, "It's all right in your case." So we go on in our rebellion—until the Judgment when all secrets will be laid bare.

For it is not a question of *whether* we are going to be found out.

135

It is only a question of *when*. We may win the battle, but God will win the war.

Now the wonderful thing is that sometimes God discovers a person's sin before the Judgment. It is the best thing that can happen to us. It is far better that God should discover it now. For if he points it out now, there is time to repent and get things right so we can go to the Judgment and not be ashamed before him. "Wherefore doth a *living* man complain, a man for the punishment of his sins?" (Lam. 3:39, italics mine). If God discovers our sin now, we should be thankful. The peace and joy that follow are worth it all.

Joseph was at long last entering the era of vindication, which he wanted more than anything else in the world. He had waited a long time for it—twenty-two years to be exact. During those twenty-two years, Joseph had to get right himself. He had to get over his personal grudges. He had to learn to forgive, especially to forgive his brothers. He, of course, also had to learn to forgive Potiphar and Potiphar's wife, and even the butler that forgot him. But finally Joseph was ready.

For twenty-two years, ten of his brothers appeared to get away with a most cowardly, awful act. They had sold their own brother into slavery. They had gotten away with it—for a while, that is. They had dipped Joseph's coat in blood and brought it to their father. Old Jacob had drawn the conclusion that a wild beast had killed him. The brothers made no comment. Jacob had said, "I will go to my grave in mourning." I suspect the ten brothers looked at each other and breathed a sigh of relief. Jacob would never know. They were prepared to live happily ever after. And they did—for twenty-two years.

But then they said to one another, "We are very guilty concerning our brother, in that we saw the anguish of his soul, when he besought us, and we would not hear; therefore is this distress come upon us" (Gen. 42:21). For years their sin had gone unpunished, unconfessed, and unnoticed. But then it was brought to the surface. These ten brothers knew why ominous things were happening to them. It was clear to them. "He that covereth his sins shall not prosper: but whoso confesseth and forsaketh them shall have mercy" (Prov. 28:13). Here is the good news. If we confess and forsake our sins, they will be put completely behind us and will never be held against us again.

In this chapter I want to show nine graduated stages by which we can tell whether God is about to discover our sin. The first sign is when we become conscious that God is dealing "roughly" with us. Joseph saw his brethren, knew them, but made himself "strange" to them and spoke "roughly" with them (Gen. 42:7). Martin Luther's famous observation is applicable here—you must know God as an enemy before you can know him as a friend. When God begins treating us not as a friend but as an enemy, it is a sign he is at work.

The second sign is when we realize afresh that sonship in God's family is a thing to be esteemed above all else; that being a child of God is the most important thing in the whole world. The brothers said, "We are all one man's sons" (Gen. 42:11). They knew that alone could vindicate them; that they were true sons of Jacob and that they were brothers. This was preeminent, if only because this had to be proved.

The third sign is when we are defensive about what we know is absolutely true. "We are true men, thy servants are no spies." After all, these ten brothers were true sons, yet before Joseph they were having to defend their position, though it was something that was so obvious it should not need a defense. When the Lord begins to deal with us we get edgy, defensive, and touchy.

The fourth sign is when we are forced to think about, if not refer to, that covered sin. "Thy servants are twelve brethren, the sons of one man in the land of Canaan; and, behold, the youngest [Benjamin] is this day with our father, and *one is not*" (Gen. 42:13, italics mine). They were having to refer to the sin that they had covered up. Joseph knew what they meant. But they used language that glossed over what had actually happened.

God has a way of showing us precisely what he is doing. Sooner or later we are going to come across it. Sometimes we manage to forget it. There is a defense mechanism called repression: we deny what we think; we push it down into our subconscious. We sometimes do it voluntarily, but more often than not we do it involuntarily. Why? Because it is so painful. We just dismiss it. We dare not think about it. But God has a way of bringing that sin back to us.

The fifth sign emerges when God directly puts his finger on the very matter we know to be most painful. Now what would be most painful for the brothers? It would be to have to tell Jacob that the governor of Egypt wanted to see Benjamin. Benjamin was the second son of Rachel, Joseph's mother, and he had taken the place of Joseph in Jacob's affection. Joseph told them to go back to Jacob and say, "There will be no corn unless we bring Benjamin."

How could this governor of Egypt know what is most hurtful? they would have thought. How can the Holy Spirit know the real "sore" spot? Of course he knows—far more perfectly than Joseph knew his brothers' fears.

The sixth sign is when he puts the hard proposal before us—demanding what appears to be unfair punishment. He does this to show how serious he is about sin. Joseph said, "Send one of you, and let him fetch your brother, and ye shall be kept in prison, that your words may be proved, whether there be any truth in you: or else by the life of Pharaoh surely ye are spies" (Gen. 42:16). The hard proposal was that all of them would be put in prison. Only one of them was to go back to Canaan to get Benjamin. God does this as his way of bringing home to us the seriousness of our offense. Joseph's proposal seemed beyond the bounds of fairness—especially as the accusation was not based on truth. After all, they did have a brother back in Canaan. Moreover, they most certainly were not spies. And yet, unfair though this seemed, it was hardly the punishment they really deserved.

The seventh sign that God is about to discover our sin is when he shuts us up for a while—when there is nothing to do but think: "And he put them all together into ward three days" (Gen. 42:17). All they could do was look at each other. We know what they eventually said to each other: "We are verily guilty concerning our brother, in that we saw the anguish of his soul, when he besought us, and we would not hear; therefore is this distress come upon us" (Gen. 42:21). Joseph gave them three days to think and they concluded: "God has done this. Our sin has been discovered."

The eighth sign is that God provides an alternative punishment. Joseph now said, "This do, and live; for I fear God: If ye be true men, let one of your brethren be bound in the house of your prison: go ye, carry corn for the famine of your houses" (Gen. 42:18-19). Joseph provided an alternative punishment. And this is the way God works. He first offers the hard proposal; in the words of John the Baptist, "Flee from the wrath to come" (Matt.

3:7). But then he offers an alternative punishment; he offers a substitute—One who bore our hell. And so Joseph virtually said, "Let one of your brethren be bound and he will take the place of the rest of you and you can go." This is what happened when Jesus died on the cross.

The ninth and final sign that God has truly dealt with us is that we come to terms with the fact that what God wanted once he still wants. Joseph wanted Benjamin. Nothing changed that. "But bring your youngest brother unto me" (Gen. 42:20). We may think that we can get out of God's original orders. God said to Jonah, "Go to Nineveh." After being in the great fish for three days, then being ejected on dry land, Jonah had to learn that God had not changed his mind. The message to Jonah was the same: "Go to Nineveh." God means what he says. His word is true.

The proof that we are true sons is that we are ready to prove our own sonship. The ten brothers had to accept Joseph's word: "This do, and live." We must accept God's word as final and infallible.

Prove that you are a child of God. First, accept what God has said. Second, accept God's alternative offer—his substitute for you. Third, accept totally the guilt of your own sin. "We are verily guilty concerning our brother." Are you ready to do that? Don't blame anybody else any more—your parents, society, the government, the world, or God. Blame yourself. And thank him for finding you out.

TWENTY-ONE
GOING
BY THE RULES

At this stage, the ten brothers didn't know it was Joseph they were having to face in order to buy food. Joseph was twenty-two years older, dressed in Egyptian garb, the governor of Egypt, and speaking through an interpreter. The time has not yet come for him to reveal himself. He was no doubt tempted to do it, but he had to restrain himself.

Joseph emerges again as a type of Christ. We can see from this how Jesus now relates to us though he is in heaven, at the right hand of God.

Now Joseph could not yet reveal himself to his brothers. He was determined to get the whole family down to Egypt—that was his goal. He knew this was why God had permitted everything. He was far beyond the stage of holding any grudge. He only wanted to do everything that God wanted; he could see that there was a plan in everything that happened. God wanted the family in Egypt, and Joseph must not do anything to abort that process.

Benjamin, Joseph's little brother, had not accompanied the ten who came to Egypt. But Benjamin was the key. "This do, and live . . . let one of your brethren be bound in the house of your prison: go ye, carry corn for the famine of your houses: but *bring your youngest brother* unto me; so shall your words be verified, and ye shall not die" (Gen. 42:18-20, italics mine). The ten brothers accepted Joseph's proposition. Simeon was left behind in their place.

141

He was the guarantee that Benjamin would be brought back to Egypt.

"This do, and live." One cannot but be aware that these very words sum up all of the law of Moses. "This do, and live" (see Lev. 18:5; Deut. 30:16). It is the sum of the law—the works of the law. There are two types of righteousness from Genesis to Revelation. One is legal righteousness. This reflects the Mosaic Law, which demands perfection. Paul sums it up in Galatians 3:10: "For as many as are of the works of the law are under the curse: for it is written, Cursed is every one that continueth not in all things which are written in the book of the law to do them."

In the Law, God demands 100 percent perfection—in thought, in word and deed—sixty seconds a minute, sixty minutes an hour, twenty-four hours a day, every day of your life. So if you want to be saved by your works, you have your work cut out for you. But I can tell you something that will save a lot of time and trouble. Paul said, "By the deeds of the law there shall no flesh be justified in his sight" (Rom. 3:20). This was Paul's way of saying that nobody is ever good enough.

But there is a second kind of righteousness: the righteousness of God which is by faith (Rom. 3:22). God sent his Son. He was a substitute, God's offering. He did everything that the Law demanded. He did what no other human being had ever done. Jesus kept the Law perfectly and on the cross cried out, "It is finished." Our debt was paid. This is called gospel righteousness. You believe the gospel and are saved.

Joseph listened to a conversation led by Reuben, the firstborn of Jacob, thus the oldest in the family. He wanted to say, "I told you so." He became the moralizing elder brother: "Spake I not unto you, saying, Do not sin against the child; and ye would not hear? therefore, behold, also his blood is required" (Gen. 42:22). Was that going to make them feel any better? No. Did it do any good? No. But there are some of us who develop into a Reuben. We pile guilt on a person who already knows he's guilty. And we do it out of a self-justifying spirit. Was Reuben without sin? What was it that Reuben had wanted to do? He had said, "Shed no blood, but cast him into this pit" (Gen. 37:22). But how much better off would Joseph have been? Joseph wouldn't have been standing before them right then if they had listened to Reuben. Self-righteousness always compares itself to another kind of sin which we

142

take to be not as bad. Had Reuben got his way, Joseph would have died. But you couldn't tell Reuben that.

But now look at Joseph, a type of Christ at God's right hand. This is so beautiful. What can be said about Jesus as the right hand of God? Jesus listens to all that we are saying. He hears all, sees all, even though he doesn't come forward and say, "I heard you say that." "They knew not that Joseph understood them" (Gen. 42:23). This is a reminder that our conversation is heard in heaven. Everything we say is picked up by Jesus. If we were conscious that every word we were saying was being monitored by Jesus, it would likely make a difference to our conversation!

So what is our Lord's reaction to what he hears? He weeps. Joseph "turned himself about from them, and wept." It must break our Lord's heart when he has to listen to the Church in division and see one moralizing, self-righteous Christian laying a guilt trip on another. Would it change your conversation if Jesus physically walked up when you were talking?

Jesus at the right hand of God also speaks through an interpreter. The ten brothers did not know that Joseph understood them, "for he spake unto them by an interpreter" (v. 23). I know of nothing more sobering, more grave, more scary than this. Every servant of Christ is his interpreter. I am Jesus' interpreter. All I am trying to say now is what I heard him say. The difficulty is that if I say it wrong, he doesn't stop me. If Joseph's own interpreter had repeated something wrong, Joseph couldn't say, "Don't say that," because it would have revealed that he knew what they were saying. I can make mistakes, and the Lord will not interrupt me. It is such a responsibility.

Joseph hid himself from them. To me this is a most gripping, tender moment. Joseph was tempted to break in and let them know who he was, but he turned away from them and wept. That is the sweetest hint that I get that my Lord feels things that he would love to say to me. But it is not the time. All things are on schedule. God has something in mind for us, and he cannot intervene until the right moment. The shortest verse in the Bible is two words long: "Jesus wept" (John 11:35). And the glorified Lord still weeps with us. He still feels. Jesus *is* touched with the feeling of our infirmities—not was—is.

Joseph wept, then returned to them again, "and communed with them." So with Jesus. Without telling us all he knows, he shows his face. He communes with us, leading us one step at a time according to the Father's will. Painful though this was for Joseph, all was going according to a perfect purpose and plan. Joseph did what he had to do. That is the way Jesus responds to us from God's right hand. He listens but goes by the rules. Even he cannot bend them.

TWENTY-TWO
THE TESTIMONY OF
A TROUBLED
CONSCIENCE

Everybody has a conscience, the reflective part of the mind. It has largely to do with the past, but it can deal with the future in that we may project how we would feel if we do this or that. But mainly the conscience reflects over the past. When all is said and done, our conscience is responsible for our happiness or unhappiness. For in the end, each person has to live with himself.

When someone gives in to temptation, he often represses his conscience. He refuses to consider how he will feel later but becomes preoccupied with immediate gratification. Then he may resort to drink, drugs, sex, or any pleasure that will get his mind off his conscience. But eventually he has to live with himself, and the conscience will not go away. Simeon had been held behind as the guarantee that the brothers would return with Benjamin. He emerges as a type of Christ here because he was their substitute: he took their place. He was the basis of the alternative punishment. Joseph had first said that he intended to keep all the brothers bound, but he offered an alternative punishment: Simeon would stay behind and the rest could go. He was a ransom, prefiguring our Lord Jesus Christ who "gave his life a ransom for many" (Matt. 20:28). The message of redemption is seen right through the Bible. Picture a scarlet thread attached to a strong needle; push the needle right through the Bible so that as you open it you see that scarlet thread, symbolic of the blood of Jesus, on every page.

These brothers found that their trip to Egypt had been quite an ordeal. They had thought it would be an uneventful trip, merely going to Egypt to buy corn. They hadn't thought about Joseph for twenty-two years, but they were thinking about him now. Some people go longer than that before being troubled with a conscience. Some go thirty years, some forty years. Some go to their deaths with covered sin, hoping that their sin will not find them out. "Be sure your sin will find you out." Why is it that not everyone's sin catches up with him in his lifetime? Some manage to go to death and don't have to face their sin until they stand before God. But some find out that their sin has caught up with them before they die.

So it was with Joseph's brothers. They were having to reckon with their own sin. They didn't know Joseph could understand them. And here they were, speaking in Hebrew, with Joseph listening to every word. "We are verily guilty concerning our brother, in that we saw the anguish of his soul, when he besought us, and we would not hear; therefore is this distress come upon us" (Gen. 42:21). I wonder how Joseph felt when he heard firsthand his brothers talking like this about him. Sometimes God brings someone right to the brink of vindication to test whether he will be quiet and let God continue with the whole enterprise of bringing things out.

What determines, then, whether a man's sin catches up with him in his own lifetime? The answer is, it depends whether God chooses to deal with that person. If God chooses to deal with us now, it means it won't come out at the Judgment (1 Cor. 11:32). Better now than then. If we think that it will be agony to confess our sins now, there is no way to calculate the agony, the sorrow, the bitterness, the woeful feeling we will have at the Judgment. Therefore, if our conscience is troubled now, blessed are we! It is wonderful! It means that God is dealing with us now.

The troubled conscience—how does it work? What are the signs? The first is the revival of memory, then fear. Here were nine brothers returning to Canaan, smarting under their load of guilt. Their deepest fears were beginning to be fulfilled. They were beginning to feel the pressure of the past. Things were moving quickly. They were wondering, "What next?" The one thing they didn't want known was what they had done with Joseph. And the one person they didn't want to find out was their father. They couldn't bear that.

What is your greatest fear? You will likely want to keep it to yourself.

"Joseph commanded to fill their sacks with corn, and to restore every man's money into his sack, and to give them provision for the way" (Gen. 42:25). Why did Joseph do that? He loved them. He didn't want to hurt them or to take their money. Had Joseph wanted to hurt them, he would have aborted the entire process of God's vindication right then and there. The governor of Egypt had the power to vindicate himself on the spot. But had he got personally and emotionally involved, the same God who had been with him up to then would have turned right on Joseph. Joseph could not bend the rules merely because God was with him. Vindicating oneself is something God will not tolerate.

If you vindicate yourself and get away with it, it is not a good sign; it suggests that God isn't dealing with you.

Joseph could have had a police escort back to Canaan. He could have faced Jacob and said, "I'm Joseph. Here's what your sons did to me." Joseph could easily have done that.

Sometimes God puts the servant he wants to use within human grasp of his own vindication as a test to see whether or not he will still let God do it. Do you want to be vindicated? Remember these two things: first, "Vengeance is mine . . . saith the Lord" (Rom. 12:19); second, be like Jesus (1 Pet. 2:21-23). That is the way God wants you to be. "Dearly beloved, avenge not yourselves, but rather give place unto wrath: for it is written, Vengeance is mine; I will repay, saith the Lord. Therefore if thine enemy hunger, feed him; if he thirst, give him drink: for in so doing thou shalt heap coals of fire on his head" (Rom. 12:19-20). Joseph fed them. He commanded that their sacks be filled with corn, their money be restored.

We have at this stage a classic case of a troubled conscience bearing witness. What ought to have been good news was regarded as bad news. On the first evening of their return journey to Canaan the nine discovered that their money was in their sacks. They should have been pleased. It would have been good news if they had good consciences. They would have said, "Isn't that nice?" But that isn't what happened. When they saw the money "their heart failed them" (Gen. 42:28). It brought them right down. If someone responds negatively to what is normally good news, it shows he has a troubled conscience. Good news ought to make us happy. "Their heart failed them, and they were afraid." Unconfessed sin breeds constant fear. "He that covereth his sins shall not prosper: but whoso confesseth and forsaketh them shall have mercy" (Prov. 28:13). "Perfect love casteth out fear" (1 John 4:18). God doesn't want us to be afraid. Jesus said, "Let not your heart be troubled, neither let it be afraid" (John 14:27).

The nine brothers now concluded that *God* was the only explanation for this strange series of events. "What is it that God hath done unto us?" (Gen. 42:28). Their awesome conclusion was that God must be doing this. They knew that if it truly was God, then they were getting closer and closer to having their sin finally exposed. It would only be a matter of time. The sooner God chooses to deal with us, the better. And remember that if God begins to deal with us, it is because he loves us. Much better now than at the judgment: "Wherefore doth a living man complain, a man for the punishment of his sins?" (Lam. 3:39).

The nine brothers arrived home. Perhaps they had a chat among themselves: "Who's going to do the talking? We must tell our father that we can't return to Egypt without Benjamin." It is interesting to see how events are worded here. The brothers reported to Jacob what had happened, carefully revealing only what they had to reveal: "The man, who is the lord of the land, spake roughly to us, and took us for spies of the country. And we said unto him, We are true men, we are no spies" (v. 30-31). And you know what this man said? "Bring your youngest brother unto me: then shall I know that ye are no spies" (v. 34).

They were getting closer and closer to the fulfillment of their worst fear—that their father might learn the truth. And yet if it hadn't been for Simeon left behind, they wouldn't even have said as much as they did. God has a way of forcing us to admit certain things. But now for the worst thing. They had to say, "Benjamin must go to Egypt." They didn't want to reveal even this but they had to.

It is a most painful thing to be boxed in. "I am the man that hath seen affliction by the rod of his wrath" (Lam. 3:1). When we know in our hearts that God is seeking us, we do better to come clean at once. He will win in any case. But when we know that it is a loving God who is seeking us, a God who accepts us, then this is the course of real peace. David said, "Let us fall now into the hand of the Lord; for his mercies are great: and let me not fall into the hand of man" (2 Sam. 24:14). "For whom the Lord loveth he chasteneth" (Heb. 12:6).

TWENTY-THREE
THE FOLLY OF
SELF-PITY

The central figure in this chapter is Jacob, the father of Joseph. What emerges now is a classic demonstration of self-pity. Who among us has not at some time given in to it?

Is there a cure for self-pity? The person who is given to this is an extremely hard person to reach. The irony is that although it is a very real condition, it never has a valid basis in fact. Jacob provides us with an example of self-pity. He also shows that self-pity is unjustifiable. There was no reason for him to be filled with self-pity, for Joseph was still alive. Of course, he didn't know that; but he also had no real proof that Joseph was dead.

Jacob became united with his nine sons on the basis of one thing—fear. "When both they and their father saw the bundles of money, they were afraid" (Gen. 42:35). The root cause of self-pity is fear. Whenever a person is filled with self-pity we can trace the cause to fear. An essential characteristic of fear, moreover, is that we want punishment. There is an interesting verse in 1 John: "fear hath torment" (1 John 4:18). The original Greek reads: "Fear has to do with punishment." When a person is filled with fear, the inevitable temptation is to punish—either to punish himself or punish somebody else.

Jacob wanted to hurt someone. "Me have ye bereaved" (Gen. 42:36). He put a guilt trip on his children. Self-pity and the desire to strike out at someone are defense mechanisms to bolster our self-esteem when we feel helpless. So Jacob's reaction to the news of his nine sons was partly one of a troubled conscience, yes, but also of self-pity.

The first thing that indicates self-pity is that one blames others. Jacob immediately said, "Me have ye bereaved of my children." He did it because he was upset with himself. For in one sense he was the cause of the whole situation. Jacob had not hidden the fact that Joseph had been his favorite son. That is what had made these brothers jealous. The old man was now having to pay for being partial. He was afraid, so he struck out and blamed them. It never does any good when we blame another person; we only condemn ourselves. Jacob ought to have realized that "the buck stops here" and accepted his own responsibility.

But he didn't do that. "Joseph is not, and Simeon is not, and ye will take Benjamin away." Jacob protected himself by fearing the worst. He read more into the situation than was there. Jacob had decided that he was not ever going to see Simeon any more. Self-pity jumps to bad conclusions without evidence. It plays into a syndrome of pessimism, feeding itself on the assumption of more bad news. A person like this wants bad news. He doesn't want to be contradicted. He is so sure that things are going to be bad that he almost resents it when one says, "It may not be that bad." "Oh, yes it is; yes it is," he answers. The person filled with self-pity is looking forward only to saying, "I told you so." You can see how nonproductive this is.

Self-pity wants sympathy. "All these things are against me" (v. 36). Jacob wanted sympathy, which is why we say, "Nothing is going right for me, everything has gone wrong. No one likes me; everything is against me." I once knew a sweet, old lady from Kentucky who had this habit of wanting to upstage me on any particular ailment I had. One could go to her and say, "I've got a pain in my side." But before you could finish she would say, "I've had a pain on my side for a week." Or someone might say, "I didn't sleep very well last night." She would say, "I haven't slept a wink for two nights." Or if one said, "I've got an upset stomach." She would say, "I haven't been able to hold any food down for a week." It didn't matter what trouble anyone had, she too had it, only worse. But all she wanted was sympathy.

Self-pity can even become borderline paranoia. Paranoia is a very serious mental illness in which someone is detached from reality. He withdraws into himself, often has delusions and seldom trusts anybody: "Everything and everyone is against me." I am not saying that self-pity always leads to psychosis, but it is pointing in that direction. If it isn't checked, it can become very serious, and, if you are a Christian, the devil will play into that feeling of self-pity so that you become suspicious of everybody; no matter what anybody does you begin to suspect their motives. Paranoia might be described in some cases as an extreme case of self-pity.

Another aspect of self-pity is that the person often refuses to accept simple advice. Reuben said to his father, "Slay my two sons, if I bring him [Benjamin] not to thee: deliver him into my hand, and I will bring him to thee again" (v. 37). But Jacob would not listen. He said, "My son shall not go down with you" (v. 38). Jacob could not bring himself to listen.

Self-pity also breeds insensitivity to another's feelings. "My son shall not go down with you; for his brother is dead, and he is left alone" (v. 38). "He is the only one left" (NIV). How do you suppose that made Reuben feel? Reuben was Jacob's first born son. Reuben could say, "I'm a son. What about Judah? What about Asher? What about Levi? We are all your sons." Jacob couldn't see how insensitive this remark was, but self-pity is like that. We become absorbed with ourselves and our own feelings. We don't realize we are hurting people.

This shows how counterproductive self-pity is, for when a person is filled with self-pity, he is making no real progress. Something has got to happen to pull him out of it.

Self-pity is the sort of thing that makes us feel all right at the time. We get hurt and begin to think about that hurt; the more we think about it the more we say, "I ought to feel this way." And then we begin to get angry. But when this is happening, we are really the ones who are impoverished. I can safely say there is nothing at all good about self-pity.

Moreover, Jacob was repeating his old mistake. You would have thought by now that he would have learned. It was because he had favored Joseph that all this had come about in the first place. Yet here he was, doing the same thing with Benjamin. Apparently, he hadn't learned a thing.

Self-pity even threatens others with greater guilt. "If mischief befall him by the way in which ye go, *then shall ye bring down my grey hairs with sorrow to the grave*" (v. 38, italics mine). Jacob now anticipated a punitive measure that he could hang over their heads. He was already paving the way: "If I were ever to do that, I want you to know what you are going to do to me"—making them feel all the more guilty. Self-pity always tries to make another person feel guilty. Do you get pleasure out of trying to make another person feel guilty? It is a way of trying to punish others.

What makes a person do what he once said he would never do? Jacob would have to eat his words. He had said, "My son shall not go down with you." That is pretty strong, isn't it? But eventually we find him having to change his mind. It doesn't mean he had been delivered from self-pity. But he was having to say, "All right, I guess I am going to let you all do what you say." What changed him? The hard realities of life. "The famine was sore in the land. And it came to pass, when they had eaten up the corn which they had brought out of Egypt, their father said to them, Go again, buy us a little food" (Gen. 43:1-2). They had no choice.

God can use the hard facts of life to bring a person to do what he said he would never do. This is the way God sometimes deals with someone to bring him to a knowledge of Jesus Christ. He just makes him face up to harsh reality. What do you know for sure about yourself? Well, you know you are going to die some day. You are now closer to death than you ever were. The only thing that brings some to their senses is the awareness that they are going to die. For when we die, we are going to face God and we are going to give an account of our life—how we have lived, and, in particular, what we did in the light of God's Word.

Jacob now said to his sons, "Go again, buy us a little food." He knew what he was asking. He knew what their reaction would be. And yet, though Jacob had changed his mind, he was not going to admit it openly yet. He just wanted to be talked into it. He wanted them to know he meant everything he had said at first. We all want to save face, don't we? Well, so did Jacob.

Then another son of Jacob entered into the picture—Judah. We have heard from Reuben. We know about Simeon. But now look at Judah. Judah is a type of Christ in a most wonderful way. For one thing, our Lord Jesus Christ was born of the tribe of Judah. "The Lion of the tribe of Judah, the Root of David, hath prevailed to open the book, and to loose the seven seals thereof" (Rev. 5:5).

"Our Lord sprang out of Judah" (Heb. 7:14). Jesus' ancestry is traced through Judah (Luke 3:33).

In what way was Judah a type of Christ? First, he gave a realistic picture of the situation. Judah said, "The man did solemnly protest unto us, saying, Ye shall not see my face, except your brother be with you" (Gen. 43:3). Second, Judah faithfully reported what he knew to be true. That is what Jesus did the whole time he was on the earth. "My Father worketh hitherto, and I work. . . . Verily, verily, I say unto you, The Son can do nothing of himself, but what he seeth the Father do: for what things soever he doeth, these also doeth the Son likewise" (John 5:17, 19). Third, Judah presented an uncompromising condition. "If thou wilt send our brother with us, we will go down and buy thee food: but if thou wilt not send him, we will not go down: for the man said unto us, Ye shall not see my face, except your brother be with you" (Gen 43:4-5). Fourth, he asked to be trusted. "Send the lad with me" (v. 8). "Trust me," Judah was saying in effect. Finally, some of the most moving words in all Holy Scripture are these: "I will be surety for him" (v. 9). This is where Judah was, most of all, a type of Christ. Jesus was "made a surety of a better testament" (Heb. 7:22).

> Before the throne my surety stands,
> My name is written on His hands.

Jesus not only says, "Trust me," but he has laid down his life. His death on the cross is our guarantee that when it is time for us to die, we may know we are going to heaven. Judah wasn't finished. He said in effect, "While we are talking we are wasting time." "For except we had lingered, surely now we had returned this second time" (v. 10). "Do it now," says Judah. "Tarry no longer."

Jacob finally gave in. Self-pity is essentially governed by self-righteousness, however, for Jacob said, "Take of the best fruits in the land in your vessels, and carry down the man a present, a little balm, and a little honey, spices, and myrrh, nuts, and almonds: and take double money" (vv. 11-12). In other words he didn't think that Judah was quite enough surety. He wanted to add things. Whereas Judah said, "I will be the guarantee," Jacob said, "All right, but do this—take the best fruits."

This chapter ends on a bittersweet note. The good note is that Jacob capitulated. But the note of self-pity lingered. Jacob's farewell to them was, "If I be bereaved of my children, I am bereaved" (v. 14). But God overruled. That is the only cure for self-pity.

TWENTY-FOUR
THE FORGIVING
GRACE OF GOD

It is a thing most wonderful,
Almost too wonderful to be,
That God's own Son should come from heaven,
And die to save a child like me.

—W. W. How

Ten scared men, including Benjamin, were heading for Egypt. Recent times had been traumatic for nine of them, not the least because they had been made to think about their sin. They had managed to sweep under the carpet all that they had done to their brother Joseph twenty-two years before, but of late, curious events had forced them to ponder matters they hadn't thought about for a long time.

What they didn't know was that all that was happening was traceable to a certain fact—a forgiving God was seeking them.

Have you had the experience of strange coincidences, curious events, shaping up in such a way that you began to reflect on things you hadn't thought about before, or had perhaps once dismissed as nonsense, so that you asked what was going on? The explanation to everything can be traced to this one fact—a forgiving God is seeking you. He is trying to get your attention, and he has to do it in such a way that you will be made to call on his name. When it is over, and we have called on the name of God, we look back and see what it took to make us do it. Then we blush and think, *Why did God stay with me so long?* He loves us so much that he won't take no for an answer. He stays with us. "The wrath of man worketh not the righteousness of God" (James 1:20).

We see in this particular episode man's predictable reaction to being utterly, completely, and totally forgiven. When God forgives us, we don't know how to react. It seems so strange that God should just wipe the slate clean. But in everything he does he is trying to show us how much he loves us. We often react negatively. We react in fear. We ask, "What's going on?" These ten brothers of Joseph were forgiven, but they couldn't believe it yet.

Why were they forgiven? It has to do with their meeting an inflexible condition that the governor of Egypt had imposed on them. He told them not to come back to Egypt unless they had Benjamin with them. At the time, it seemed unthinkable, the worst thing they could have been faced with. But Joseph had said, "Don't come back without Benjamin." The men took the gifts that Jacob had sent. "They took double money in their hand . . . and Benjamin" (Gen. 43:15). They would learn later that Joseph wasn't the slightest bit interested in their money. They thought, *This time we had better return the money and have twice as much to pay for more food.* How wrong they were! "Ho, every one that thirsteth, come ye to the waters, and he that hath no money; come ye, buy, and eat; yea, come, buy wine and milk without money and without price" (Isa. 55:1).

Joseph wasn't interested in their money but he was interested in seeing Benjamin. And so it is with God; the God who made us has put before us an inflexible, unchanging condition. "Jesus said, I am the way, the truth and the life: no man cometh unto the Father, but by me" (John 14:6). "Neither is there salvation in any other: for there is none other name under heaven given among men, whereby we must be saved" (Acts 4:12). We cannot be saved unless we call upon his name. We cannot bypass the blood of Jesus Christ and be forgiven.

The ten brothers presented themselves to the governor's office. They probably didn't see the governor himself at first. But Joseph was watching the whole thing. Joseph eyed his ten brothers, really looking for one person. He found him: Benjamin. When he saw Benjamin, he gave orders behind the scenes: "Bring these men home, and slay, and make ready; for these men shall dine with me at noon" (Gen. 43:16).

This is the way God dispatches angels to do his work. Angels are ministering spirits sent forth to minister to them "who *shall* be heirs of salvation" (Heb. 1:14, italics mine). In other words, God's angels start dealing with us before we are ever saved. When we have put our trust in Jesus and look back, we may begin to trace the different things that happened. We will say, "I believe God has been caring for me for a long time; he's been after me; he's been doing things for me."

The ten came to dinner. What was their reaction to all this? "The men were afraid" (Gen. 43:18). Often one's initial reaction to any work of God is fear. When good things are happening to us, or strange coincidences, are we afraid? We may say to ourselves, "There's an unseen, higher power at work here." The fear of God makes us reflect on our lives.

The men were afraid because they were unexpectedly brought into Joseph's house. They decided that the reason they were in Joseph's house was because Joseph had not been paid for the first transaction. They thought that he was going to get even with them. They were wrong, of course.

There is an important but delicate lesson to be grasped here. The brothers of Joseph were afraid. And God *was* at work. But it is not God's fault that they came to some hasty conclusions. I say this because many people never bother to examine their own fears. The delicate principle that needs to be grasped is that just because God's fear may be the cause of the way we are feeling and reacting, it does not necessarily follow that all the conclusions we jump to are right.

We can come to a false conclusion because we go further than God intended. Through fear, Martin Luther cried out in a thunderstorm, "Help me, St. Anne, and I will become a monk." People do things through fear that they are not really required to do. A guilty conscience rather than the fear of God can be the cause of a precipitous action. I suspect that some people don't become Christians because they put on themselves more than God himself is requiring, and they miss the simplicity of the gospel. And these brothers thought that money was the problem.

The truth is, Joseph wanted one thing—Benjamin. It could be

that because God *is* dealing with you (and you have a guilty conscience), you have begun to turn over a new leaf. You may think that is going to count for something. You might have given more money to the church or to some charity. When people are feeling guilty, they start doing all kinds of crazy things. They will make pilgrimages, they will go to a particular shrine or kiss a statue of the Virgin Mary. Some fancy that things like that matter. What a joy it was when Martin Luther discovered the truth of salvation by faith alone! When he saw this, his world was turned upside down—and eventually the world itself. He saw that faith alone satisfied the justice of God.

Like the brothers in Joseph's house, people often imagine that God is trying to get even with them. "We are brought here because this governor will seek occasion against us." That is the way many people react. They think God is out to get them. So they try to do particular things to avoid his punishment. Do you really think God will be satisfied if he punishes you? What satisfied God's justice? One thing: the death of his Son. Once the Lord had laid on Jesus the iniquity of us all—once God had punished his Son—his justice was satisfied. It's really a vain, presumptuous thing to think that God's trying to punish you.

Benjamin was what Joseph wanted. Nothing else would do. It wasn't the money. It wasn't anything else. He just wanted to see Benjamin. They had even imagined that Joseph wanted their donkeys (v. 18). What on earth would Joseph want with their donkeys? They thought, *He's really out to get us. He's going to steal this from us.* Yet we are talking about the wealthiest man in Egypt—second only to the Pharaoh. In just the same way, some people imagine that God wants these little things from us. God owns the cattle on a thousand hills.

Like the Prodigal Son, who had probably rehearsed his speech a thousand times, these brothers had come up with a little speech. They had it all ready. On the way to Egypt they had prepared it. One brother would have turned to Levi and said, "Levi, let's hear you say it." And he would have said, "Well, what I will say is, when we opened up our sacks we found this money, and we don't know how it got there. But we have got more money." And Reuben would have said, "Here's what I would say. . . ." We don't know which brother was the spokesman. They came to Joseph's house and talked with the steward. Somebody spoke up. Here is the way the speech went. "O sir, we came indeed down at the first time to buy food: And it came to pass, when we came to the inn, that we opened our sacks, and, behold, every man's money was in the mouth of his sack, our money in full weight: and we have brought it again in our hand" (vv. 20-21). They were scared to death.

What was the answer they received? The steward said, "Peace be to you" (v. 23). Peace. That is God's word to every troubled soul. Jesus went into the room and faced those troubled disciples who had fled. Simon Peter had denied him. They feared what Jesus would say. And what did he say? "Peace" (John 20:19). Peace. Are you troubled? Are you sorry? Do you feel awful inside? Have you been rehearsing what you would say to God? I can tell you his response to you: Peace. And by the way, you never get into trouble with God for making an honest confession.

To their astonishment, the steward said, "Peace be to you, fear not: your God, and the God of your father, hath given you treasure in your sacks: I had your money." The ten brothers were in *Egypt*. They looked at each other. Fancy hearing that kind of talk in Egypt! "Your God, the God of your father!"

When you become a Christian, you will recognize a certain language, the language of Zion. "The God of your father hath given you the treasure in your sacks. I had your money." Thus the money was returned on purpose. "I had your money. It's all right. I'm the one that did that. Don't worry about it. Oh, by the way, you have a brother here. Simeon, come on out." Simeon appeared before them, just as they had been promised.

They began to realize that they were being treated with unusual dignity. The steward brought them into Joseph's house. Picture these ten men from Canaan—Hebrews—in the prime minister's house. They couldn't get over this kind of treatment. The steward gave them water, washed their feet, and gave fodder to their donkeys. Imagine these ten brothers having servants washing their feet! They were looking at each other and saying, "What on earth is going on?"

Why was it happening like this? It was because they were forgiven men. Joseph had utterly, completely, and totally forgiven them. He wanted them treated with the greatest dignity. And it was Joseph himself who was going to serve them.

TWENTY-FIVE
OUR LORD'S CARE
FOR HIS OWN

How much does Jesus love us? There now emerges a moving account of how Joseph is a type of Jesus in heaven at the right hand of God. The eleven brothers are a type of the Church; indeed a type of the one who has come to Jesus. Here is a picture of how the Lord cares for his own, how he serves us. If we could see how much the Lord loves us—and truly feel it—none of us would be the same again.

If you have just "tasted" of the Lord, you know that he is gracious (1 Pet. 2:3). Jesus said that the kingdom of heaven was "like unto a merchant man seeking goodly pearls: who, when he had found one pearl of great price, went and sold all that he had, and bought it" (Matt. 13:45-46). That is the effect of seeing our Lord's love for us. If you have the *taste* of the Lord, and see how much he really loves you, I predict you will become totally different.

Jesus died on the cross. He was raised from the dead. He ascended to heaven, to God's right hand. That is where Jesus is now. And yet the Bible says that we are seated together with him "in heavenly places" (Eph. 2:6). That means that if we could *see* what is truly there, should the veil be lifted, every one of us would see Jesus. We now see through a glass darkly, however (1 Cor. 13:12). We don't see him with our physical eyes, but he is there.

Joseph's brothers were joined by Benjamin and Simeon. They came to Joseph's house and bowed themselves before him to the ground. That is the symbol of conversion, because the first thing we have to do when we come to Jesus is bow down to him. On the Day of Pentecost Peter said, "God hath made that same Jesus, whom ye have crucified, both Lord and Christ" (Acts 2:36). We must bow down to our sovereign Lord. That means repentance, admitting we have been wrong—wrong about Jesus, wrong about God, and wrong about ourselves. God says we are guilty. Repentance is agreeing with God that it is our sins that crucified Jesus. It will have an effect on us; we will be sorry that we have been wrong all these years. Repentance is raising the white flag of surrender and bowing down to him.

Joseph had been told by the Lord that some day his eleven brothers would bow down to him. He had waited no fewer than twenty-two years for that. This ought to encourage us. God's promises to us may be delayed for many years, but God keeps his Word.

We can see at this stage what one might call the unexpected benefits of becoming a Christian. I would even call it "fringe benefits" because the main benefit is that we are going to heaven. That is what it is really all about. But what about *on the way* to heaven? The Lord may not come this year. We may not die soon; we may live for a while. I hope we do! What about in the meantime?

The Lord cares about our welfare. After they bowed down to him, Joseph asked them "of their welfare" (Gen. 43:27). How are you doing? How are you getting on? God is interested in you as a person. He is concerned about your financial problems. He is concerned about your physical problems. He is concerned about any emotional problem you may have. God cares about material things. And I cannot exaggerate this: he feels more deeply about it than you do. Joseph's first question dealt with their state of affairs.

God is interested in your loved ones. Joseph then asked, "Is your father well, the old man of whom ye spake? Is he yet alive?" This was not a perfunctory question. He really wanted to know. Joseph was more interested in that matter than they could have known at the time. This story is so written that we can see how Joseph felt. He was totally interested in everything about them.

The only problem Joseph had was in refraining from telling them everything he knew. It was taking considerable discipline.

They may have thought *they* needed discipline to act properly in the presence of the governor. What they didn't know was that Joseph was having to hold back. He cared so much! That is the picture we have here. If we could realize how much God cares, I suspect that we would quit worrying. We would say, "I didn't know it was like that. I didn't know he cared that much." God cares about even the tiniest details—our slightest hurt, the most sensitive feeling. When we get our feelings hurt, don't tell anybody that this or that bothered us (they will only say, "Oh, quit worrying about that"); instead we can talk to Jesus. He cares.

Joseph was looking at these eleven brothers with such intensity, watching their every move. He studied the expression in their eyes a thousand times more closely than they looked at him. So is our Lord right now. He doesn't even need us to tell him. It's good to tell him because this is what the Bible tells us to do. "In every thing by prayer and supplication with thanksgiving let your requests be made known unto God" (Phil. 4:6). But he already knows everything. He knows it perfectly, backwards and forwards. He knows how it got to be where it is. "Surely goodness and mercy shall follow me all the days of my life" (Psa. 23:6).

They were not at ease in Joseph's presence at first. But before it was over with, they were. Look at the end of the occasion. "They drank, and were merry with him" (Gen. 43:34). When we first become Christians, we are not exactly at ease. It is new, a new discovery; it's a new world out there. And when we start to pray, we are not sure that we are going to say it right. We are a bit nervous. It is kind of a scary thing. The brothers were feeling uneasy at first. But the Christian life enables us to get more relaxed in the Lord's presence. So before it was over with they were merry with him.

The goal of Christian life and of Christian living is that we might have the joy of being at rest in God. Jesus said to Peter, "I am going to wash your feet." And Peter said to Jesus, "Oh no, you're not going to wash my feet!" Why did Peter say that to Jesus? Because he was too proud to let Jesus do it. So Peter said, "I'll wash yours, but you're not going to wash mine!"

But Jesus said to Peter, "If I wash thee not, thou hast no part with me." Simon Peter replied, "Lord, not my feet only, but also my hands and my head" (John 13:8-9).

Our problem is that we don't like to think that the Lord is serving *us* like that. Our pride is at stake. He has taken us on board totally, and it is his delight to serve us completely and utterly.

We see now an even more intimate glimpse into how much Christ loves us. The eleven answered, "Our father is in good health, he is yet alive." They again bowed their heads and made obeisance. Then Joseph "lifted up his eyes, and saw his brother Benjamin, his mother's son." He said (as if he didn't know), "Is this your younger brother, of whom ye spake unto me?" He looked at Benjamin and said, "God be gracious unto thee, my son" (Gen. 43:29). Joseph singled out Benjamin, his full brother. Benjamin was his "complete" brother, and that is the position of all of us in the family of God. If we are sons (or daughters) of God that means we are heirs; "heirs of God, and joint-heirs with Christ" (Rom. 8:17). And that means that Jesus is our elder brother and we are Jesus' little brothers and sisters. Jesus is our "full brother." We are his full brothers and sisters, and we have equal inheritance with him in our relationship with God since we are "joint-heirs" with him.

By the way, if anybody ever comes along to you and says that there is a chance that you might lose your salvation, ask them this question: is there any chance that Jesus could lose his place with the Father? Ask them: could Jesus be dislodged from the Godhead? Is there any way that Jesus could be disenfranchised by his Father? "Oh no," they will surely say. Then remind them that every Christian is made a joint-heir with Christ, and we are as secure in his grace as Jesus himself is in the Godhead. That is precisely what our relationship in the family is.

Joseph thus looked at Benjamin, his full brother. He had to exercise discipline *not to reveal all he knew.* Joseph was forced to treat Benjamin in a detached, objective manner. You would not have known at the time that Benjamin was that much different from the rest. And so our Lord is forced to deal with us in a particular manner as we begin to grow, and often our attitude will be, "Lord, why don't you just reveal your full glory right now?" Have you ever felt like that? You are talking to the Lord and you say, "God, show me your face, please. Why can't you? Why can't you just let me see you?" Moses felt the same way. He said, "I beseech thee, shew me your glory" (Exod. 33:18). It is the most natural feeling of every serious Christian. For this reason the Apostle Paul said, "We ourselves groan within ourselves, waiting for the adoption, to wit, the redemption of the body" (Rom. 8:23). He said, "We groan, earnestly desiring to be clothed upon with our house which is from heaven" (2 Cor. 5:2).

But there was nothing but love spilling over on to Benjamin, even if he didn't sense it then. What Joseph felt was total and purest love. He loved Benjamin, and yet he had to act in a particular manner. And so it is, if we only knew it, when we are saying to the Lord, "Why don't you just show me?" Remember, he wants to. He feels it. He loves you. But at the time what he is doing is right. It is good. It is the only way that he can be at that particular time. All of God's actions toward us are in purest love: "For whom the Lord loveth he chasteneth, and scourgeth every son whom he receiveth" (Heb. 12:6). There are certain things that Jesus would like to do for us, more than we ourselves may want. But he must wait, even as we must wait. Our Lord has bound himself to certain laws and principles. It requires time before everything that we wish to take place will be realized. Our Lord has to wait just as we have to wait. Moreover, it is more painful for him than it is for us.

What *did* Joseph give to Benjamin? He gave him his word: "God be gracious to you, my son." That is what every Christian has. You have God's Word. You have the Bible. If you really want to please the Lord, if you really want to follow him and do everything he wants you to do, and you want him to speak to you so much, then read and obey his Word. That is what shows that you really care. I remember how I used to call on Dr. Lloyd-Jones and have those precious conversations with him. But I proved my love for him not by calling on him at home but by reading his books. So when I called upon him we could just clarify things. A lot of people wouldn't bother to read a book. They would rather go and meet the man and say, "What do you believe about this?" Many of us are like that with the Lord. We say, "Lord, tell me this." The hymn answers:

> *What more can He say than to you He hath said,*
> *To you who for refuge to Jesus have fled.*

Joseph gave Benjamin his word. That is what we have. It is our task to learn it and apply it.

"And Joseph made haste." He was deeply moved. His whole being yearned for his brother; and he looked for a place to weep. But Benjamin didn't know that. Jesus was told that his friend Lazarus was sick. Our natural reaction would be, if Jesus really did care for Lazarus he would drop everything and go straight to Lazarus and heal him. But Jesus stayed where he was for two days. When he later showed up, Mary and Martha, Lazarus's sisters, were perplexed: "Lord, if you had been here, our brother wouldn't have died." Do you think that Jesus didn't love them? But he acted in this way so that the will of God might be manifested. In the end the glory of the Lord was revealed (John 11:44).

God feels a thousand times more deeply than we do for ourselves. This is the way Jesus feels behind the scenes. "We have not an high priest which cannot be touched with the feeling of our infirmities; but was in all points tempted like as we are, yet without sin" (Heb. 4:15). Our Lord is touched with the feeling of our weaknesses. It doesn't only mean that he used to be touched when he was on earth, as if that was the only time he could sympathize. It describes how Jesus feels right now. He yearns to reveal himself now. And yet he is bound to certain principles. One of those principles is described in Acts 14:22, "We must through much tribulation enter into the kingdom of God." But in the meantime he feels what we feel—only a thousand times more. Our Lord weeps with us now. He weeps because of what he sees that we don't see; for he has much more to feel deeply about than we have.

> *Standing somewhere in the shadows you'll find Jesus,*
> *He's the Friend who always cares and understands.*
> *Standing somewhere in the shadows you will find Him,*
> *And you'll know Him by the nailprints in His hands.*

What is the Lord doing when he hides his face? He is looking for a chamber in which to weep. He will not show you what he is thinking. He cannot at the moment. When he's hiding his face, you think he doesn't care. The opposite is true. He is looking for a chamber in which to weep, and when he reappears, it is to serve us.

"He [Joseph] washed his face, and went out, and refrained himself, and said, Set on bread" (Gen. 43:31). The bread that we are given by our Lord is but a taste of what he will give us in heaven. Jesus said, "Behold, I stand at the door, and knock: if any man hear my voice, and open the door, I will come in to him, and will sup with him, and he with me" (Rev. 3:20). The bread the Lord will give us is what will keep us going in the meantime. Between now and the time we see our Lord face to face, there is indeed a gap—one that keeps us from seeing him physically and literally. There is that veil over our eyes. But it is a gap that will be closed one day. Some day we will see Jesus.

That gap is revealed in this story. Joseph said, "Set on bread." And they served Joseph by himself and the eleven by themselves. They were separated. At one table there were the Hebrews, and there was Joseph the Egyptian by himself. Joseph was required to do that at this particular time. But his heart was at the other table with them. It is the gap that our Lord Jesus Christ endures until the day he can reveal his glory. However much we may wish that Jesus would come again, that he would come right now, I cannot began to tell how much more he wants to come! He also wants to clear his name before a godless world. But he must wait. In the meantime we see through a glass darkly, but then "face to face" (1 Cor. 13:12).

How well does our Lord know us in the meantime? "They sat before him, the firstborn according to his birthright, the youngest according to his youth: and the men marveled one at another" (Gen. 43:33). Apparently there must have been something like a nameplate in writing at each place where they were to eat. Judah would have said, "I'm supposed to sit here."

Simeon said, "Well, here's where I'm supposed to sit."

Dan said, "I'm going to sit here. Levi, where are you sitting?"

"I'm looking for my place. Here it is."

So they all sat down, and they looked at each other and realized that every one had been seated according to his birthright. They surely thought, *What on earth is going on?*

Our Lord knows the details. He knows everything. The way he guides our lives, the way he intervenes, proves it. We may sometimes ask, "Does Jesus care?" He does. He sees and knows me. He may let something happen which I didn't understand at the time. But eventually I see why. God deals with us a step at a time, knowing the details perfectly.

The last little point of interest was that Benjamin's portion of food was five times as much as the rest. This points to the Lord's care for those who are in the immediate family. What had Benjamin done to deserve this? Not a thing. He received the extra food just by being Benjamin. Why is God good to us? Because of who we are: full members of his immediate family. "For by grace are ye saved through faith; and that not of yourselves" (Eph. 2:8). I love the little chorus,

> *God is so good,*
> *God is so good,*
> *God is so good,*
> *He's so good to me.*

TWENTY-SIX
FORGIVING
OURSELVES

I used to think that the episode to follow was an unnecessary part of the story. I now think it is one of the most important parts of all. What do you feel about Joseph secretly putting his cup in Benjamin's bag? At first glance it is a very curious thing to do. Did Joseph do this to play a kind of game with his brothers? At this juncture Joseph had not yet told his brothers who he was, although he had been deeply moved by seeing them and had to go into another room to cry in secret. But the time had not yet come for him to reveal himself to his brothers.

They had dinner together, all seated according to their birthright. After dinner Joseph commanded the steward to fill their sacks with food—as much as they could carry. He also secretly returned their money: this was the second time their money had been returned. But then Joseph said, "Put my cup in the bag of the youngest."

At daybreak the next day they all left. But after a short time Joseph turned to his steward and said, "Go after them and say, " 'Why have you rewarded evil for good?' "

The steward immediately left and soon overtook them, repeating those words. The eleven brothers were dumbfounded. They said, "We wouldn't do that. We even returned the money. Why would we do it?" And so they started at the oldest, coming down, one at a time, until they found—lo, and behold—Joseph's cup in Benjamin's bag. There it was!

Why did Joseph do this? Was Joseph being naughty? Was he trying to vindicate himself? Was he getting all his anger out and really "sticking the knife in"? Is this what was happening?

This may surprise you. What Joseph did was the most loving and kind act yet done to them. Here again Joseph is to be seen as a type of Christ. Putting his cup in Benjamin's bag did not give Joseph the slightest pleasure. If anything, he was very anxious indeed how it was going to turn out. For what he did he did with great pain because he wasn't absolutely sure what they would do. And yet it was something he had to do—for their sake.

Joseph did this to test the depth and the sincerity of their repentance. These men had shown themselves repentant—that is, up to a point. When they had seen what was happening early on, they immediately saw that God was catching up with them. "We are verily guilty concerning our brother, in that we saw the anguish of his soul, when he besought us, and we would not hear; therefore is this distress come upon us" (Gen. 42:21). God had already stepped in. Events took shape in such a way that immediately they thought of their own sin. They hadn't had occasion to think of their sin for a long time. It had probably bothered them at first, but after a while they had managed to live with themselves.

The Bible talks about having a conscience "seared with a hot iron" (1 Tim. 4:2). Eventually a person can apparently live with his sin; he sweeps the dirt right under the carpet, as it were, and doesn't let things bother him any more. For years these brothers hadn't thought about Joseph, but now things were happening.

There are two kinds of repentance. One is being sorry because we got caught. We have all been like that. The second kind of repentance is a real change of mind. This Joseph needed to see. He knew that they were sorry: he had overheard their conversation. But what Joseph didn't know was whether they would do the same thing again.

So Joseph gave them the opportunity to do away with Benjamin—just as they had done away with him. *He would know by how they reacted to this opportunity whether or not a real repentance had set in.* Joseph did the kindest, most loving thing of all. He gave them a chance to save face—with him and with themselves, not to mention with their father. I must admit that I used to think that Joseph had put his cup in Benjamin's bag to have some fun with them before it was all over with. But I was smitten when I saw how wrong I was. If Joseph had wanted to hurt these men, it would have been the easiest thing in the world. With the power he had in Egypt he could have sent for old Jacob, or just have escorted them all back to face the old man. But he did want to see whether or not they had truly repented, and he was giving them a chance to see for themselves whether they had changed.

Have you ever wanted to know for yourself that you have really changed, that you are really different from the way you once were? I doubt whether a more relevant word is to be found in this book than this. Most people I run into—even Christians—have enormous problems with guilt. They are so sorry for the things they have done. Even though they know the Lord has forgiven them, they cannot forgive themselves. This very word can help anyone feeling guilty.

What is your guilt based upon? Something you have done (perhaps a skeleton in your closet)? We have all done things we wish we hadn't done. We have all done things we hope nobody finds out about. Perhaps we made a decision once but have seen how wrong it was. Possibly it is the way we brought up our children. All of us parents have guilt feelings. "If only I had done this differently." Have you done something recently, or a year ago, or maybe twenty years ago, for which you still have a sense of guilt? I can promise this. The kindest thing that could ever happen is to discover that you *wouldn't* do it again.

I think people feel bad not only because they cannot forgive themselves for what they did, but also because they know that the same vulnerability is there. If they could see for themselves that they *wouldn't* do it again, they could now live with themselves. They could begin to forgive themselves for what they have done. They could say, "I'm not what I was." When somebody can truthfully say that, he is beginning to come to terms with himself. The guilt that has plagued him, crippled him, and paralyzed him goes away, and he becomes free. For it is one thing to accept God's forgiveness, another to be able to forgive yourself.

Joseph could see that his brothers were feeling guilty. They had managed to repress the guilt. But no longer. And he gave them a chance to forgive themselves and see that they really had

173

changed. Benjamin's life was handed to them on a silver platter.

Here is the story. The steward accused them, "Why have you done this?"

They answered, "Why would we be so foolish? We would never steal the governor's cup." Then they fell into the trap Joseph had set for them. They protested like this: "With whomsoever of thy servants it be found, both *let him die,* and we also will be my lord's *bondmen*" (Gen. 44:9, italics mine). They were that sure they were innocent. They meant it, but they also didn't think it was anything they were going to have to fulfill.

So the steward said, "All right. I'm going to take you seriously." "Let it be according unto your words: he with whom it is found shall be my servant; and ye shall be blameless."

They were very confident. They all got down from their donkeys. Reuben got his bag out, then Judah, Levi, and all of them. Reuben said, "I'm clean." Judah did the same thing. One by one— Asher, Naphtali, and all of them. There was but one left: Benjamin. And there it was—Joseph's cup—in Benjamin's bag!

They didn't know it at the time, but here was their chance to prove that they had changed. Perhaps they were not even that conscious of a change. It would have been so easy for them to do away with Benjamin. They could truthfully go right back to Jacob and just say, "Well, here's what happened. The governor's cup was in Benjamin's bag, and we agreed that whoever had it should die. We are sorry to report that it was in Benjamin's bag!" That is what they could have done. They could have gotten away with everything, though it would have come out later, of course. The one thing that these men needed in order to forgive themselves was to see whether they would repeat virtually the same old sin.

And that is just what God does with us. Are you feeling guilty about anything in your past? Maybe there is something that haunts you. And you feel so rotten. You often weep. All due to guilt. Ask yourself this question: What would I do if I had the equivalent opportunity handed to me again? You may say to yourself, "If I had my life to live over, I would never do what I did." But you can't have your life to live over again. What is done is done. Even the blood of Jesus cannot undo the past. It can forgive the past. It can make you accept the fact that God accepts you. But you can't undo the past. So, one of the happiest things that can ever come your way would be for God to give you a second chance, as it were, by presenting an equivalent situation. Then you can discover for yourself whether you have changed.

The scary thing is that we don't detect it at first. God often comes along at an unexpected moment and puts Joseph's cup in Benjamin's bag. It is disguised. We don't at first realize that God is testing us to see if we really have repented.

Would the brothers pass the test? That is the question. And what did they do? "Then they rent their clothes." Now even that isn't enough. That just means they were sorry. But here is where the true repentance was proved: ". . . and laded *every man* his ass, and returned to the city" (v. 13, italics mine). All of them. They didn't say, "Good-bye, Benjamin. Tough luck, but good-bye." No. They all went back. Repentance had truly taken place.

Oh, what a sight it was for Joseph when they all came! That is what he wanted. He had had to do it. He had to know. Had they really changed? Were they truly sorry? He hadn't known for sure what they would do. When temptation comes to you, or the trial, or the equivalent circumstance—will you cover your sin the second time? That is the question. Are you so anxious to prove that you have really changed? Consider this proposition: the next time something inexplicable happens, it could be Joseph's cup in Benjamin's bag. You might find yourself reacting exactly as you did the first time. Or it may be that this time you just do what is right. Then you will see upon reflection that it shows you are not what you used to be.

We can see now that it was a kindness of Joseph. He was just letting these men see a change in themselves. After all, they were going to have a hard time later believing that Joseph had forgiven them. Joseph was making it easier for them to see that he really did forgive them. Joseph would later say, "You meant it for evil, but God meant it for good."

The past cannot be relived. What is done is done. Even God won't change what has happened. But when he grants us true repentance, he promises to "shape" the past so that it looks good. Eventually the *whole* past will "work together for good" (Rom. 8:28).

TWENTY-SEVEN
THE JUSTICE OF
GOD'S MERCY

We have before us another remarkable outline of the gospel. It centers on the intercessory work of Christ at God's right hand. Joseph had sent his brothers away, put his cup in Benjamin's bag, and then sent his servant after them. They discovered, to their horror, that Benjamin's bag contained Joseph's cup.

Here is an illustration of people with no bargaining power, the position we are all in before God. These eleven brothers acknowledged that the cup was indeed in Benjamin's bag; "the goods" were on him. They couldn't say, "It's not so." There it was, before their eyes. When they returned to the governor, it would do them no good to say, "We're innocent." So it is with us. Before we will ever be saved we have got to understand that we have no bargaining power.

What is it that keeps people from being saved? Essentially it is their self-righteousness. The kindest thing that God ever does to us is to knock out from under us our self-righteous props. Sometimes it takes a new development to remind us of our old sin. Putting his cup in Benjamin's bag was Joseph's test to see whether or not his brothers had truly repented. They could have sent Benjamin right on back, letting him take the blame, but they all came back. They weren't going to repeat the old sin.

The eleven brothers coming back was a good sign. But a sign was not enough. Joseph needed to know how deep their repentance was. Repentance is a change of mind; it is agreeing with

God; it is saying, "I was wrong." It is an essential ingredient in saving faith, which is the only kind of faith that assures of heaven.

What are the ingredients of true repentance? First, it is treating the one you have sinned against with deepest respect. The eleven brothers came into Joseph's house, and "they fell before him on the ground" (Gen. 44:14). Second, it is admitting that you have no bargaining power. You acknowledge your sin. Judah said, "What shall we say unto my lord? what shall we speak? or how shall we clear ourselves? God hath found out the iniquity of thy servants" (v. 16). Third, true repentance is submitting yourself as a servant to the one you have sinned against. "Behold, we are my lord's servants, both we, and he also with whom the cup is found" (v. 16). That is to say to God, "You can have my life." If you are ever going to confess Jesus Christ as your Savior, you must confess him as Lord because you can't have him as Savior and not as Lord. That means that he owns you, that you are not your own, you are bought with a price (1 Cor. 6:20).

At this point, Joseph turned to them and ordered that only Benjamin be kept behind. "The rest of you haven't done wrong," he virtually said. "I want only the one who stole my cup" (Gen. 44:17). The rest were free to return to Canaan.

There is now one of the most moving accounts of pleading for mercy in all Holy Writ. Whereas we have usually seen Joseph as a type of Christ, in this case it is Judah again. Judah was prepared to put his own life on the line and do everything he could to persuade the governor not to punish Benjamin. Benjamin was in real trouble, and Judah had an almost impossible task on his hands—to persuade the governor not to punish Benjamin. It is a picture of the way Jesus intercedes before the Father.

On October 31, 1955, I was driving in my car from Palmer, Tennessee, on my way to Nashville, at about half-past seven in the morning. I had been driving for perhaps an hour. Unexpectedly, the presence of the Lord came into my automobile. It lasted for maybe half an hour. I often wonder how I was even able to drive the car. I became literally a spectator—witnessing something that I had never seen before. I saw how real the intercessory work of Jesus is at the right hand of God. I had of course read in the Bible that Jesus is at the right hand of God. I had somewhere heard also of Jesus being our elder brother. But what I hadn't experienced was that he *really is there* and that he absolutely cared for me more than I cared for myself. I was given to see that Jesus was putting himself on the line before the Father, as if to say, "You take care of his need or blame me." I have never got over that. It has affected my interpretation of Scripture. It followed me all the way to Oxford. I have no doubt that it colored my research as I uncovered Calvin's position on the intercessory work of Christ. It has shaped my understanding of Galatians 2:20. Instead of looking at all my shame, the Father's gaze is truly turned to Christ.

Judah knew what it would mean if they had to go back to Canaan and face their father without Benjamin. The thought of that was something none of them could bear. Judah stepped forward. He made the most tearful plea you could ever imagine. The first thing he sought to do was turn Joseph's wrath away from Benjamin. "Judah came near unto him, and said, Oh my lord, let thy servant, I pray thee, speak a word in my lord's ears, and *let not thine anger burn against thy servant:* for thou art even as Pharaoh" (v. 18, italics mine). Judah's aim was to persuade the governor not to be angry with Benjamin. He said in effect, "Turn to me, blame me."

Judah then reminded the governor of certain indisputable facts as he told the governor all that had happened. The intercession of Christ is reminding God of his own word. Judah continued, "Thou saidst unto thy servants, Except your youngest brother come down with you, ye shall see my face no more" (v. 23). Here Judah was saying, "It's your word that has brought us this far. We have obeyed your word." Judah reminded Joseph again of the family situation and how their father Jacob had only one fear—that something might happen to Benjamin.

Judah's motive, then, was to move the heart of the governor to show pity. "Therefore when I come to thy servant my father, and the lad be not with us; seeing that his life is bound up in the lad's life; it shall come to pass, when he seeth that the lad is not with us, that he will die: and thy servants shall bring down the gray hairs of thy servant our father with sorrow to the grave" (vv. 30-31). Judah says in effect, "If you have got a heart, don't you see what this is going to do? We simply cannot go back and face our father without Benjamin."

That is what an intercessor does. We can never be saved unless we have somebody going before the Father on our behalf, caring for us just like that. That is what Jesus does for those who come to God by him (Heb. 7:25). We must see Jesus as our guarantee—as our surety—putting himself on the line without regard to the cost to himself. Judah continued, "Thy servant became surety for the lad unto my father, saying, If I bring him not unto thee, *then I shall bear the blame* to my father for ever" (v. 32, italics mine). A surety is always offered as a substitute payment. So Judah went on, "Now therefore, I pray thee, let thy servant abide instead of the lad a bondman to my lord" (v. 33). In other words, Judah was saying, "I'll stay. Blame me. Let Benjamin go. I'll be your servant." That is what Jesus is doing at the right hand of God. He is saying, "I died. Turn your gaze away from the sin and look at me."

An effectual intercessor also demonstrates that sheer justice would be done by punishing a substitute instead. This is what Judah was ultimately asking for. As we have seen, Judah could not bear returning to Canaan without Benjamin. He insisted that Joseph would be *just* by showing mercy to the accused and letting himself stand in his place. It is as though Judah argued, "If it's justice you want, here it is. Take me, punish me, keep me here. But please let Benjamin go."

The gospel of Jesus Christ can be summed up like this: God has found a way whereby he can be merciful to us and be absolutely just in doing so. If we see that we don't deserve mercy but are guilty, and also that someone else took our place, God can be merciful to us. He would be true to his justice. Sin must be punished, but the justice of God's mercy is that Jesus bore our punishment. He took upon himself all of our sins, thus freeing God to show mercy to us. God can do it because his justice has been satisfied.

TWENTY-EIGHT
INTERCESSORY
PRAYER

The ten brothers were changed men. We know this because they came back with Benjamin, although the governor's cup was in his bag. They might have deserted him. But they *all* came back. And Judah, one of the ten, gave a most impassioned plea for Benjamin's release. Judah's speech is an example of intercessory prayer, a practice too little known today, I fear. His intercession shows the grace of God at work in a forgiven man.

Intercessory prayer is almost always used by God to precede true revival—if not any good thing that comes to us. God's mighty acts in history tend to follow prayer. Jesus prayed all night before he chose the twelve. The 120 who were filled with the Spirit on the Day of Pentecost had tarried for ten days doing little but praying and waiting before God. There was a time when the Spirit came down in power and the place was shaken. There was a trembling (Acts 4:31). But that followed intercessory prayer. Peter was in prison, and an angel came and delivered him miraculously. But prayer had been made "without ceasing" for him (Acts 12:5). God's mighty acts tend to follow prayer.

What do you know about intercessory prayer? Do you know what it is to intervene for another person in prayer as though he or she were your own concern? That is what intercessory prayer is. It is pleading to God on behalf of another. It is stepping into the gap between the hidden God and helpless man—intervening for another with all the power at your disposal. I hope you will be involved many times in intercessory prayer.

Intercessory praying is what Christ does for those who come to God by him so that he gets personally involved in our case and totally identifies with us before the Father. That, moreover, is our promise: "Wherefore he is able also to save them to the uttermost that come unto God by him, seeing he ever liveth to make intercession for them" (Heb. 7:25).

Now Judah's plea to Joseph gives us some principles for effective intercessory prayer. The first principle of intercessory prayer is the assumption that we who intercede are not worthy in ourselves. This is not true of Christ at God's right hand, of course, for he never sinned. But in our case, we must acknowledge our own unworthiness. "What can we say?" Judah begins. "How can we prove our innocence? God has uncovered your servants' guilt" (Gen. 44:16, NIV). When we engage in intercessory prayer, we must never imagine that our prayer will be heard because of any worthiness on our part.

Second, we must acknowledge our servitude to God. "We are now my lord's slaves." We will not be effectual in prayer when we are not also Christ's bond slaves—in the way the Apostle Paul saw himself (Phil. 1:1). Our confession of unworthiness is to be matched by a total resignation to Christ's sovereign will.

Third, though the initial stages of praying often meet with no success, we must pray on. Joseph appeared to be utterly uninterested in Judah's concern. The governor insisted that Benjamin alone must pay for his crime; the rest could return to their father Jacob (v. 17). But Judah didn't give up. "Oh my Lord, let thy servant, I pray thee, speak a word in my lord's ears, and let not thine anger burn against thy servant" (v. 18). One of the best examples of this kind of persistence is found in Jacob's plea when he wrestled with the angel: "I will not let thee go, except thou bless me" (Gen. 32:26).

Fourth, we must acknowledge the sovereign authority of God to do what he pleases—and always be right. "For thou art even as Pharaoh" (Gen. 44:18). What the Sovereign chooses to do is absolutely right. His wisdom must not be questioned. "But our God is in the heavens: he hath done whatsoever he hath pleased" (Psa. 115:3).

Fifth, we must remind God of certain facts. Of course he already knows everything: "Your Father knoweth what things ye have need of, before ye ask him" (Matt. 6:8). This is important. Many fail here because they are too sophisticated to be simple. "If God already knows, why should I tell him?" is their reasoning. But effectual praying always rehearses the facts to God *as though* he did not know. This is seen in the intercessory prayer in Acts 4:24-30. Thus Judah proceeded to remind Joseph of all that had happened (Gen. 44:19ff.). But the governor knew everything.

Sixth, our hearts must be rid of all resentment. Judah's plea discloses that they had come to terms with the bitterness that had originally led them to get rid of Joseph. They had been jealous of their father's partiality to Joseph. Twenty-two years later found their father having transferred his affection to Benjamin. The ten brothers knew this full well. But they weren't bitter about it. Judah acknowledged that their father's life "is bound up with the lad's life" (Gen. 44:30). They had accepted this as a fact—but there was no bitterness. When Jesus demonstrated the possibility of praying in faith that we have already received what we asked for, our Lord immediately added: "And when ye stand praying, forgive" (Mark 11:25). Bitterness cannot mix with effectual intercessory praying.

Seventh, we must seek to move God's very heart. We must appeal to God's feelings. Childlike praying will do precisely this. Judah thought that if the governor had any heart at all he would not want to hurt their father. "It shall come to pass, when he (our father) seeth that the lad is not with us, that he will die: and thy servants shall bring down the gray hairs of thy servant our father with sorrow to the grave" (Gen. 44:31). The early church, faced with severe persecution, prayed, "Lord behold their threatenings" (Acts 4:29).

Finally, effectual intercessory praying will be devoid of any selfish concern. Judah was concerned not for himself but for the feelings of his father. It was for his father that he put his own life on the line in order that Benjamin might be released. "Let thy servant abide instead of the lad" (v. 33). Paul even said, "I could wish that I myself were cursed and cut off from Christ for the sake of my brothers" (Rom. 9:3, NIV). In essence, intercessory praying is standing in the gap between the pending threat to the glory of God and the sovereign will of God. It must be a selfless concern that governs intercessory prayer: the glory of God must be preeminent.

God also chooses to bind himself to conditions that will precipitate intercessory prayer. God can do anything, of course. Absolutely. But there is a sense in which God voluntarily binds himself to wait for his time.

We may ask why God doesn't step in the first time we ask for something. Why is it that we earnestly pray and there seems to be no answer? There is always a good reason for the delay. By and by we will understand. It is not that God is being an enemy to us. When he doesn't answer our prayer, it is because he has bound himself to certain conditions. It is not that God doesn't want to act sooner. He even waits on us. It is for our own sakes that he is waiting.

God brings about conditions that will precipitate intercessory prayer in order to give us a taste of his own love. It is a marvelous phenomenon, possibly not as frequent an occurrence as one might tend to think. For intercessory prayer is usually not for oneself but for another person or situation. Nonetheless, you get deeply involved in it—I will even call it emotional involvement. You feel another's hurt as though it were yours. It is like the church that prayed without ceasing for Peter. The church desperately needed Peter, and they prayed. When we pray for another like this, we also enter into the sufferings of Jesus. We will begin to feel what he felt—and feels. When we begin to be concerned for another person as though that other person's problems were our own, we are beginning to pray unselfishly. We are literally praying *for* another person.

That is the way Jesus is all the time. He didn't die on the cross for himself. He was without sin. He lived a perfect, sinless life. He died on the cross for our sins. And at the right hand of God he is not praying for himself but for those who come to God by him. Intercessory praying, then, is tasting God's love and experiencing how Jesus feels.

Intercessory prayer brings us face to face with the hidden God. God often seems hidden from us in intercessory prayer if only because we cannot be sure what his will is or what he is thinking. His mind is kept hidden from us. Even to the last minute, it may seem that God is taking no notice of our plea. All appearances would indicate that Judah's plea for Benjamin was in vain. Joseph's thoughts were hidden from Judah. And yet it is no less true that intercessory praying brings us *face to face* with God. Paradoxically, it is as though we are on God's level.

When we continue to intercede like Judah, we are eventually lifted up into a spiritual realm. We begin to say things to God that, were it not for the fact that we are being guided by the Spirit, could lead people to accuse us of impertinence. Though speaking to one who owes us nothing, we actually ask for things with boldness. For here was Judah having the impertinence to say, "Let Benjamin go and keep me instead." He was pleading unashamedly, with all his heart. But boldly. Intercessory prayer must continue even when God appears to be utterly unconcerned. The indication may be that he is going to do the very opposite of what you want!

What are the ingredients of intercessory prayer? First, carrying the burden. I suspect this is possibly why there is so little intercessory prayer. We don't like the burden, the pain. Imagine the pain of knowing that something is about to happen unless God steps in soon. Judah could see Benjamin was to be kept behind. He might have refused to get involved in order to avoid the ordeal of putting himself on the line and being rejected. We don't like the pain of pouring out our feelings, especially when it looks as though our prayer might not be answered. None of us naturally wants the pain of praying in vain. In our prayer life we often set a standard that we think we can easily reach, then pray for it. This way we are not going to be disappointed. We don't even like the pain of striving for a goal that seems unreachable. But intercessory prayer presupposes a burden.

Thus the second ingredient of intercessory prayer is that we must become vulnerable. We must put our deepest feelings on the line. We may have to say things to God that normally we would be too embarrassed or too proud to say. Judah admitted to Joseph that he had said to his father, "If I bring him not unto thee, then I shall bear the blame to my father for ever" (Gen. 44:32). Here was Judah conceding all that was at stake.

Intercessory prayer often operates best when it is almost a matter of life or death. And when that happens, we just speak what is on our mind. There is no playing games in intercessory prayer. We reveal our heart. But it means becoming vulnerable.

The third ingredient in intercessory prayer is the willingness to become expendable. Not just vulnerable, but expendable. Paul could say, "I could wish myself accursed." So with Judah. He was willing never to see Canaan again. He put Benjamin first. Not only was he willing to be the servant of Joseph in Egypt for the rest of his life, but he would be glad to be! "Just let me stay. Let Benjamin go."

Judah didn't know whether what he said was really making sense to Joseph. He hoped that what he was saying was reasonable. So he continued. But he had no assurance that we know of. He ended his plea by saying, "How shall I go up to my father, and the lad be not with me?" (v. 34). Judah was probably asking himself, "What's this man thinking? What's on his mind?"

The answer almost always comes unexpectedly—we don't know if God is going to act or not. But God had more in mind for Benjamin and those ten brothers than Judah ever prayed for. When God's time has come, he will show his glory, his power, and his greatness "exceeding abundantly above all that we ask or think" (Eph. 3:20). And yet God may remain hidden up to the very last moment. There may not be a single clue that he is about to intervene. For one thing, if we got that clue, we wouldn't pray as hard. We would relax. So God often hides his face right up to the last minute.

But when God's time has come, it will, if anything, bring more joy to him than to us who were so afraid that he wasn't going to act. For when Judah finished speaking—having used all the power, rhetoric, eloquence, passion, and emotion he ever had—not knowing whether he was making any impression or not, it was Joseph, the governor, who broke down. "Then Joseph could not refrain himself" (Gen. 45:1). He cried, "Cause every man to go out from me." No one was with Joseph when he made himself known to his brothers. "And he wept aloud." He cried so loudly that the Egyptians heard him, including everyone in Pharaoh's house.

What Judah and his brothers couldn't have known was that behind that ornate garb that the governor was wearing was a man who cared more than they did. Behind that officious, harsh voice there was a man with a heart.

Joseph had long dreamed of such a day as this. The day had finally come. What would it be like? Would there be vengeance?

Here was justice handed to him on a silver platter. Joseph could go for them. But he burst into tears. Joseph, the man, won out over Joseph, the governor. Joseph, the brother, won out over Joseph, the judge. Joseph, the man of love and forgiveness, won out over Joseph, the man of hate and vengeance. Tears were streaming down his face. Speaking emotionally in Egyptian he ordered, "Everybody out. All of you. Out."

Bewildered Egyptians, the civil servants, and even his interpreter, began filing out of the room. This governor began sobbing, his shoulders quaking and his voice reaching a high trembling, quivering pitch.

But Joseph wasn't embarrassed. He wasn't ashamed. This was the happiest day he had known in twenty-two years. In seconds the secret would be out. Joseph waited for that last Egyptian to get out of the room. He waited for the door to be firmly shut. His brothers wondered what was going on. Now the moment had come. His tongue did not break the silence in the Egyptian language. He spoke Hebrew. The language of Canaan. "I am Joseph! Is my father still living?"

In a stunned silence the brothers backed away. They were terrified. They couldn't answer.

Joseph could see they were afraid. He said, "Come close. I'm Joseph, the one you sold to slavery. But it's all right. God did it. Don't be angry with yourselves. God did it."

God is not mocked. Intercessory prayer is an enterprise which heaven honors. "Do not be deceived: God cannot be mocked. A man reaps what he sows. The one who sows to please his sinful nature, from that nature will reap destruction; the one who sows to please the Spirit, from the Spirit will reap eternal life. Let us not become weary in doing good, for *at the proper time we will reap a harvest if we do not give up*" (Gal. 6:7-9, NIV, italics mine).

One last thing. What happened in the end was what Joseph had wanted all along, however detached from Judah's plea he had seemed. So it is with God's dealings with us. When God responds to intercessory prayer, it is what he wanted to do all along. I do not claim to understand this. It is a great mystery indeed. But John said we receive when we ask "according to his will" (1 John 5:14). On one occasion Daniel prayed and fasted for three weeks after which God said in effect. "I heard you the first day" (Dan. 10:12). Why didn't God *answer* on the first day? I don't know. But I know this: "For since the beginning of the world men have not heard, nor perceived by the ear, neither hath the eye seen, O God, beside thee, what he hath *prepared* for him that *waiteth* for him" (Isa. 64:4, italics mine).

TWENTY-NINE
TOTAL
FORGIVENESS

Joseph now had a twofold task. First, to make his brothers see that he really was Joseph. Second, to show that he utterly forgave them for their sin of twenty-two years before, when they sold him into slavery. He needed to prove to them that he forgave them and that he forgave them totally. And so with our Lord Jesus Christ. He has a twofold task, to reveal who he is and that he utterly and totally forgives.

The one sin that God will not ever forgive is the blasphemy of the Holy Ghost (Mark 3:29). Many people have been genuinely worried that they have committed that sin. Many Christians struggle over their own assurance of salvation because they can recall something they have said or done—they may even have mocked God at some time—and they are afraid they can never be saved. But the blasphemy of the Holy Spirit is *not to believe that Jesus is the Son of God.* To show contempt for Jesus' deity is to sin against the Spirit because it is the Spirit's work to reveal who Jesus is. Therefore if we *now* believe that Jesus is God's one and only Son, we show infallibly that we most certainly have *not* blasphemed the Spirit. For no man can say that Jesus is the Lord (i.e., God in the flesh) but by the Holy Ghost (1 Cor. 12:3). The only way anybody will ever be saved is to believe that Jesus is *God in the flesh,* that he is alive right now, that he has been raised from the dead. For the resurrection of Jesus was a vindication of Jesus' claim to be the Son of God (Rom. 1:4).

Other than the blasphemy of the Spirit, then, "*All* manner of sin and blasphemy shall be forgiven unto men" (Matt. 12:31, italics mine). If we believe that Jesus is the Son of God and that he is alive, he offers us *total* forgiveness. The twofold task of the gospel is to convince us who Jesus is and that he completely forgives us.

Such knowledge seems incredible at first. Joseph's brothers were "troubled at his presence" (Gen. 45:3). To grasp that the one they had sinned against was truly alive and that he would actually forgive—and do so totally—was at first quite unbelievable.

All Joseph had put his brothers through in the recent days could now be clearly explained. He had been bringing them to the place where they would really believe and appreciate being forgiven. Total forgiveness had been more than Judah had bargained for when he had pleaded with the governor to let Benjamin go back. Receiving total forgiveness had not been in Judah's mind. He had merely wanted to remain in Egypt as Joseph's servant. But what Judah needed—along with the rest of the brothers—was forgiveness.

Could it be that we are trying to drive a bargain with God, but we haven't discovered our real need—the need to be forgiven of all of our sins? That is what the brothers needed. It was really what they *wanted!* But we couldn't have told them that—not at first. They hadn't even been thinking along those lines. We all tend to deny what we want because what we really want seems utterly out of reach: we just can't believe that God could be that good!

If we could have what we really want, what would it be? Most of us deny what we want because we think we can never have it. If we had told Joseph's brothers that (a) Joseph was alive, (b) Joseph *totally* forgave them, and (c) *God was behind all that had happened* over the previous twenty-two years, such knowledge would have seemed too wonderful. Not in their wildest fantasies had they conceived such a thought.

This is what conversion is. It is giving us more than we ever dreamed of. Perhaps we have been asking God for something. Or we have wished for something. But what God really offers is over and above anything that we have asked for. That is what conversion reveals.

"What if Jesus really is alive?" I asked that of an Israeli who sat next to me on a flight to Tel Aviv. His name was Boaz. I asked, "What would it do to you if you discovered that Jesus is really alive?"

He said, "That would change everything, and it would be wonderful."

There is no greater knowledge than this—that Jesus is alive and that he offers total forgiveness for all our sins. Boaz was staggered by this thought: Jesus' death on the cross was actually the punishment for our sins and says to us, "All is forgiven."

But that is not all. Jesus even says that all that has happened in our past is actually a part of God's plan. Can any news be more wonderful than that? How would that make us feel—to know that God says, "You are forgiven," and then says, "All that happened is in my will; it is what I have allowed for your life"? Absolutely nothing is more emancipating: we can feel the burden go. It seems entirely too good to be true, that God would offer me such forgiveness, wiping away the past, and then actually saying to me, "Look. This was what I had in mind because it is a part of my plan for your future."

That is *total* forgiveness. Total forgiveness is not only God saying, "I forgive" but proving how much he wants us to believe it. He wants to put the case before us so convincingly that we say, "He really *does* forgive me."

The only kind of forgiveness that is worth anything, in any case, is *total* forgiveness. After all, if God does not forgive me totally, I don't really want to be forgiven at all. Or I might say it like this: the only kind of forgiveness that I would want from *you* is total forgiveness. If I have offended and hurt you, and then you say that you forgive me, well, I would be glad to know that. But I might doubt that you really meant it. You would need to demonstrate to me that you really mean it. The only kind of forgiveness that would mean anything to me is total forgiveness.

What is total forgiveness? There are five principles, all of which come out of this story. First, total forgiveness is demonstrated to us when someone shows that he doesn't want anybody else to know what we have done to him. If, when you forgive me, you make it clear that you don't want anybody to know what I have done to you—that you are not ever going to let them find out—I would call that truly forgiving me.

What was the first thing that Joseph did? After Judah finished his speech, Joseph cried, "Cause every man to go out from me. And there stood no man with him" (Gen. 45:1). When Joseph made himself known unto his brethren, it was secret. Why did Joseph do that? He didn't want the Egyptians to know what his ten brothers had done to him. It was going to be a secret that would be buried for ever and ever.

Moreover, Joseph wanted those ten brothers (plus Benjamin and his father) to come there to live. He did not want a single person to know what those ten brothers had done. He didn't want them to get off to a bad start in Egypt. Otherwise there would be gossip in Egypt: "Do you know what those ten brothers did to Joseph? There goes Judah. Ah, there's Reuben. There's Gad. There's Naphtali. We know about them don't we?" The Egyptians would hiss at them. Joseph couldn't bear that.

It is the unforgiving spirit that wants to let the world know our own hurt. Love hides a multitude of sins. It is hate that wants to let the cat out of the bag. Hate wants everybody to know we have been hurt: "Here's what so and so did to me."

"Oh, did they do that to you?"

"Yes."

"Oh, that's awful."

"Yes it is. This is what they did to me."

Total forgiveness is when we protect the one we forgive.

So Joseph said, "Send everybody out." And this is the promise that we have in the gospel. "This is the covenant that I will make with the house of Israel after those days, saith the Lord; I will put my laws into their mind, and write them in their hearts: and I will be to them a God, and they shall be to me a people: and they shall not teach every man his neighbour, and every man his brother, saying, Know the Lord: for all shall know me, from the least to the greatest. For I will be merciful to their unrighteousness, and their sins and their iniquities *will I remember no more*" (Heb. 8:10-12, italics mine). That is the way God forgives.

Second, total forgiveness wants to make a person feel completely at ease. Joseph's brothers could not answer him, for they were "troubled at his presence" (Gen. 45:3). Therefore Joseph said to them, "Come near to me, I pray you." Why did he say that? He wanted them to be at ease in his presence. He wanted them to know by the look on his face that there was no hate whatever. In his eyes there was no feeling of vengeance—not the slightest desire to make them feel uneasy.

Hate hopes that another will feel uneasy. When we don't forgive, we want that other person to feel uncomfortable in our presence. We want to make him squirm! We hope he fully realizes what he has done! The look on our face tells it all—we don't forgive. Total forgiveness is not allowing them to feel uneasy. And this was Joseph. He wanted them to see the look in his eyes. "Come on, draw near, come close to me. I'm Joseph."

Third, total forgiveness will not even allow the person to feel bad or angry with himself. Joseph said, "I am Joseph your brother, whom ye sold into Egypt. Now therefore *be not grieved, nor angry with yourselves*" (v. 5, italics mine). That is our Joseph. He is saying, in effect, "Look. I know how you're going to react to this. Your immediate reaction is to feel awful. I don't want you to feel bad. Don't even feel angry with yourselves."

But how do most people tend to "forgive"? Sometimes we say, "Well, I forgive you, but I hope you realize what you've done. I hope you feel bad about it." When we really forgive another person, we want them to feel good. But if they think to themselves, *Why is it I don't feel good about it?* we haven't yet convinced them they are forgiven. Joseph knew their immediate reaction; he got right into their skin. He was feeling what they were feeling, and he was urging them, "Be not grieved, nor angry with yourselves."

Fourth, you make it *easy* for that person to forgive himself: we do it in such a way that it is obvious we really do forgive. This can be done. Joseph put it like this: "Be not grieved, nor angry with yourselves, that ye sold me hither: for God did send me before you to preserve life" (v. 5). In other words, *behind all that had happened* was a sovereign God looking out after *them*. And so Joseph said, "For these two years hath the famine been in the land: and yet there are five years [five years to come], in which there shall neither be earing nor harvest. And God sent me before you to preserve you a posterity in the earth, and to save your lives by a great deliverance" (vv. 6-7).

We now come to the most sublime statement in all the story of Joseph, "It was not you that sent me hither, but God" (v. 8; see Gen. 50:20). "It wasn't you. It was God."

How do you suppose that made them feel? I can tell you, it suddenly gave them a sense of dignity, a sense of worth, a way of saving face, a way of coping, a way of looking forward to the future. Such knowledge that *God* did it was almost too wonderful.

The proof of total forgiveness is this: we make it easy for the person to forgive himself. For the only forgiveness that is worth anything is that which makes it possible for us to forgive ourselves. It is one thing to say, "God forgives." It is another to forgive ourselves. There are many people walking around who claim to have God forgiving them of all their sins, yet they are not living in the present. They are living in the past. They cannot forgive themselves.

What is God saying to you? Forgive yourself. He's trying to show you *right now* how you can do it. Our gracious God comes from behind to *shape your past* so that, if you will believe him and give him time, you will come to see that his hand was with you even at your worst moment. Total forgiveness shows God's sovereign plan in everything. If you really do forgive someone, show that you mean it by bringing in God's total sovereignty. This will convince them.

And here was Joseph, saying all this to his brothers who had been so wicked. The principle is in Romans 8:28, my favorite verse in the Bible: "And we know that all things work together for good to them that love God, to them who are the called according to his purpose." Think of all that you have done that is wrong. All that is bad. All that is wicked. Can anything be better than this— that all things "work together" for good? This is what Joseph was saying to the very ones who had been so wicked, so jealous and so cowardly. "You didn't do it. God did it. It wasn't you that sent me here. God did it." Oh, the relief I feel—to think that God was with me in my worst moment! But this is the sovereign grace of God. Only a God like that can do it. He can shape your past and take your worst moment and, in time, so redeem your past that you can look back and not wish to change anything. This is the God of the Bible.

Finally, total forgiveness is demonstrated when we keep someone's sin hidden from the person who means most to him. Now what do you suppose the ten brothers feared most of all? It was

194

that Jacob their father would hear the truth. I suspect that these ten brothers could endure anything in the world but that. They would rather be shot—or hanged. They would prefer any kind of physical torture. They could have named anything in the world they would be willing to endure rather than that their father would learn what really happened.

Joseph knew all that. And so here is what Joseph said to them: "Say to him, God has made your son Joseph lord of all Egypt: come down and live in the land of Goshen." Those were the only instructions. Joseph might have said, "Go back to your father and my father, and come clean and tell him all that you've done." But he didn't do that. Total forgiveness is our not wanting the sin to be revealed where it would hurt most of all. We tend to threaten, don't we, and say, "Wait until so and so hears this." They say, "Oh, please, please; oh no, I can't bear that." And we hang that over their heads. Joseph had this option at his fingertips. If he had wanted vengeance, if he had wanted to make them squirm, if he had wanted to cut them and pour salt on the wound, he could have done it. But no. He said, "Go back and you say to our father, Joseph is alive. God made him governor of Egypt. That's all you need tell him."

The worst thing that can happen to us is to find out at the judgment of God that our sins are staring us in the face. But what Jesus does when he offers pardon is to assure us of total forgiveness. We forgive ourselves this way. We can start life anew. "As far as the east is from the west, so far hath he removed our transgressions from us" (Psa. 103:12). Our sins are washed away by the blood of Jesus.

God doesn't want us to feel sorry after he says, "I forgive you." But he only demonstrates his forgiveness when you are sorry. Joseph knew they were sorry. And when he saw they were sorry, he said, "That's enough. No more. I'm not going to let you feel bad." He just needed to know they were sorry. But once he saw it, he offered them total forgiveness. Never again were they even to think about it!

One more thing. The principle of Romans 8:28 is not set into operation as long as you feel a need to justify what you once did. If you have done something that was wrong but have stuck to your guns and justified it, the promise of Romans 8:28 will be postponed. But the moment you say, "I don't see how it could ever work together for good—what I have done is so bad," God steps in and says, "Leave the past to me."

Finally, God doesn't want our help in helping him to make things work together for good. As long as we meddle and try to do something that will help things, God won't do a thing. It will just get worse. But if we will take our hands off, God takes over. To show his power. And his love.

THIRTY
AFTER
FORGIVENESS,
WHAT?

Several things are implied and included when a person is converted to Jesus Christ. But the main thing is that he is given forgiveness of all of his sins. He is given eternal life and the hope of heaven; he knows that his sins will not be held against him. He has been given the righteousness of Jesus Christ—the "robe" of Christ's righteousness.

But is that the end? What happens next? Forgiveness of sin is only the beginning. God doesn't then forsake us. He doesn't forgive you to leave you. There is a life to be lived and a life to be lived to the full. You are not ready to live until you are ready to die.

Joseph had made himself known to his brothers who had sold him into slavery some twenty-two years before. They were horrified that the governor standing before them was Joseph. But Joseph was trying to get them to see that he forgave them. No strings were attached. He offered total, categorical, and immediate forgiveness. He forgave them right on the spot.

Let us be reminded of two things. The first is the importance of accepting God's forgiveness. For Joseph said to his brothers, "Now therefore be not grieved." When God offers us forgiveness for all our sins he wants us to accept this. We may say, "I am not worthy of it." But we must realize that when we continue pleading unworthiness, although understandable and in a real sense right, we show that there is still an element of self-righteousness in us.

God wants us to accept his acceptance of us; and if we don't *believe his word,* we are showing contempt for what he offers.

But the second thing is this: he wants us to forgive ourselves. This is the way Joseph put it. "Now therefore be not grieved, *nor angry with yourselves,* that ye sold me hither." Oftentimes the rub comes here. As we have seen, people often say, "I accept that God forgives me, but I cannot forgive myself." But I must repeat that not forgiving ourselves is not really accepting God's own forgiveness. For he *wants* us to forgive ourselves. In order to convince them how totally he forgave them, Joseph said, "It was not you that sent me here; it was God who did it. God did sent me before you to preserve life." Joseph made it easy for them to see that there was a sovereign purpose behind all that had happened. Therefore, not forgiving ourselves is really a form of self-pity.

What follows being forgiven? What was further required of these brothers? First, God wants us to believe his Word. This was the first test for the brothers. Joseph said to them in effect, "Believe what I say." And he put it like this: "For these two years hath the famine been in the land: and yet there are yet five years, in the which there shall neither be earing nor harvest" (Gen. 45:6). They had to trust what Joseph had to say about the future. So, too, with God. He wants us to believe his own word about our future. God has given us his Word—the Bible. Once we have become Christians, the Bible will become our most precious possession. It is the most valuable commodity there is. The Bible—God's infallible Word. It tells us how to live our lives. We must read it every day; we should also engage in Bible study, using the distilled wisdom of others who have gone before. We must not trust merely in our own natural ability to read the Bible. Now I say this guardedly because we must trust the Holy Spirit to guide us as we read. But we all need direction, and this is why we have preaching, teaching, and Bible study.

Joseph's brothers could have questioned him: "How do you know what the future is? How do you know it is going to be like that?" But Joseph was giving his eleven brothers an opportunity to believe his word and to redeem the time. One of the first reactions every Christian has after being saved is, "Why didn't I do it sooner?" And there is a subtle form of guilt that comes in through the back door. We may begin to feel so ashamed that we waited so long. This sense of shame is quite common. But God says, "There's time left. Where are you going from here?" After all, God has guided us up to now. "Through many dangers, toils and snares [you] have already come." God has led us to this point, and he will lead us on. So our next step is to accept God's purpose for our lives. Joseph said, "God sent me before you to preserve you a posterity in the earth, and to save your lives by a great deliverance" (v. 7). God has a plan for us. He has already thought it through! In heaven there is a blueprint with our name on it! Joseph shows us that God was interested in these brothers and in their futures.

Many of us sometimes begin to feel, "Maybe God hasn't thought everything through in my case. Surely God doesn't have an absolute plan for *my* life." But he does. God has a will for each of us. The most foolish thing we can do is to take our lives into our own hands, or to think that we can upstage God. Now if we think that we can do it better, that God ought to take one or two hints or instructions from us about how our life should be led, we are mistaken. God has a plan of his own, and the worst thing we can do is rush past it. For it is possible to become a Christian and then get in the flesh, taking things into our own hands and getting into all sorts of trouble. "Are ye so foolish? having begun in the Spirit, are ye now made perfect by the flesh?" (Gal. 3:3).

Joseph wanted his brothers to get acquainted with the *family secret*. Do you know what it is? It is that God was behind your own conversion, behind it completely and absolutely. Now some people tend at first to react negatively to the family secret. But listen: "It was not you that sent me hither, but God" (v. 8). That's what Joseph could say. "It wasn't you that did it." After all, they thought *they* had done it. They knew what they had done. But Joseph said, "Stop. Hold it. It wasn't you, it was God."

Many of us die hard at this point, especially when we struggled over the decision to become a Christian and died a thousand deaths in the process. Some have felt the force of their own strength and will, and when finally they made that step, it was as though they did it all themselves. Then after they are in the family, they learn the family secret—that it wasn't they who did it at all, it was God. Jesus put it like this: "Ye have not chosen me, but I have chosen you" (John 15:16). John writes: "We love him, because he first loved us" (1 John 4:19), and Paul said, "But we are bound to give thanks alway to God for you, brethren beloved of the Lord, because *God hath from the beginning chosen you* to salvation through sanctification of the Spirit and belief of the truth" (2 Thess. 2:13, italics mine).

I urge you to accept the truth about the sovereignty of God. It is a humbling thing to realize, however. The great C. H. Spurgeon tells the story of how he came to see the family secret. Mr. Spurgeon was converted in a Methodist church. Some time later he was sitting in church, feeling bored by the sermon. His mind began to wander and he began to ask himself, *Why am I a Christian?* He thought, *I'm a Christian because I heard the gospel. I'm a Christian because I believe.* But then he asked himself, *Why did I believe?* And he said, "At once, like a flash, God opened it up to me that God was at the bottom of it all and that it was totally by God's grace."

We should accept not only the sovereignty of God but the sovereignty of Christ. Listen to Joseph: "So now it was not you that sent me hither, but God: and *he hath made me a father to Pharaoh*" (v. 8). Imagine this! Joseph, the governor of Egypt, a young man, is called a father to Pharaoh! What an extraordinary statement.

Our Lord Jesus Christ is sovereign. He is sovereign over every nation, whether that nation recognizes his rule or not. But all the better if they do: "Blessed is the nation whose God is the Lord" (Psa. 33:12). All the better if that nation recognizes that "Righteousness exalteth a nation: but sin is a reproach to any people" (Prov. 14:34). "He hath made me a father to Pharaoh, and lord of all his house, and a ruler throughout all the land of Egypt."

But a caution is in order when learning the family secret. Do not let it lull you into a passive complacency. There is a danger when you learn the family secret. If you know that God is sovereign there is a tendency to say, "Well, there's nothing for me to do." I must confess that I once fell into this trap. Some of us have had such an unbalanced view of God's sovereignty and power that we have ended up doing almost nothing! We said, "God can do it."

But after having said, "It was not you that sent me but God," Joseph immediately added, *"Haste ye,* and go up to my father, and say unto him, Thus saith thy son Joseph, God hath made me lord of all Egypt: come down unto me, *tarry not*" (Gen. 45:9, italics mine). "Haste ye. Do it. Get on with it. Right now."

These men might have said, "Well, now that we have seen that God has done everything, let's just enjoy ourselves. Let's relax and do nothing."

God will not let us get away with that. I can tell you that the great men and women of God—those whom God has used the most—have been those who believed *simultaneously* in the absolute sovereignty of God on the one hand, and on the other, accepted their full responsibility as though it were utterly up to them. "Haste ye. Go up to my father." God doesn't reveal his power and glory to let us do nothing. He says, "Make haste. Move. Get on with it. Go. Do it now."

But there is more: begin now to tell the good news. What was the good news? They were to say to Jacob, "Joseph is alive and he's governor of Egypt." Can you imagine more dazzling words than that? Joseph is alive! He's alive! What greater news can we have than the message: "God offers you free forgiveness, for the resurrection of Jesus proves it"?

"Make haste. Tell the good news." Jesus said, "Go ye into all the world, and preach the gospel to every creature" (Mark 16:15).

What precisely do you tell others? You tell *them* not to delay as well! "Go up to my father, and say unto him, Thus saith thy son Joseph . . . come down unto me, *tarry not.*" In other words, they were to say to Jacob, "Do it now." And that is exactly what we do with those to whom we give the good news. We must say to them, "Receive the Lord right now." Right now. The content of the gospel demands urgency. "Today if ye will hear his voice, harden not your hearts."

Another thing that we need to learn after we have received God's forgiveness is about the conditional promises of the Bible. God's promises are subject to our *doing* what Christ says. I hinted at this above. We can become Christians, then rush past God's will for our lives and get our own lives into an awful mess. And this is where the conditional promises come in. For Joseph was now assuming that they would do as he said. And if they did? "Thou shalt dwell in the land of Goshen, and thou shalt be near unto me, thou, and thy children, and thy children's children, and thy flocks, and thy herds, and all that thou hast: and there will I nourish thee; for yet there are five years of famine" (Gen. 45:10-11).

Three things were promised if they obeyed and went to their

father. First, security. "Thou shalt dwell in the land of Goshen." If we keep God's Word, he will supply our need and we will want for nothing. Second, Joseph's own presence: "Thou shalt be near unto me." And that is exactly what is promised to those who obey the Lord. We will know the presence of Christ. He will be near us. Third, protection for our family. We all worry about our loved ones and our children. Joseph promised, "Thou, and thy children, and thy children's children." What a promise!

What if they didn't obey? The answer is here: "Lest thou, and thy household, and all that thou hast, come to poverty" (v. 11). He made it clear that if they *didn't* do what he said that was what was going to happen.

> *Trust and obey,*
> *For there's no other way,*
> *To be happy in Jesus,*
> *But to trust and obey.*
>
> —J. H. Sammis

God's way is best.

Finally, after we have received forgiveness, we need to go on to learn how real Jesus is. Joseph said, "Behold, your eyes see, and the eyes of my brother Benjamin, *that it is my mouth that speaketh unto you*" (v. 12, italics mine). How will Jesus be so real to us? By the Holy Spirit. Joseph said, "My mouth that speaketh." The same Holy Spirit that gave us the Bible will give us that inner peace and testimony of the Holy Spirit. By the Spirit Jesus will show us how much he loves us. For Joseph fell "upon his brother Benjamin's neck, and wept" (v. 14). He kissed all of his brethren, "and he wept upon them" (v. 15). That's how much he loved them.

If we will just listen to the Lord, we too will see that he loves us more than words can tell. He cares for every detail of our lives. He cares for our feelings. For, "after that his brethren talked with him" (v. 15). This points to communion in prayer. We talk to Jesus, he talks to us.

Talk to him, knowing that he is your God. Worship him. Praise him for his majesty and his glory. But know equally that you must worship him in the most intimate and sweet way as his Spirit enables you to say, "Abba, Father" (Gal. 4:6).

THIRTY-ONE
THE JOY OF
THE LORD

"The joy of the Lord is your strength" (Neh. 8:10). What is the "joy of the Lord"? Is it joy that comes *from* the Lord? Or is it the Lord's *own* joy?

Answer: it is both. It is how he feels in himself but also what we feel from him. But how can the Lord's own joy do anything for us? Some may ask, "What is God's happiness going to do for me?" The answer is that to the extent we can see how happy he is, we are happy. It is the joy he has *which we see* that gives us strength.

There are two principles to be grasped, and these emerge in the life of Joseph, as we will see below. The first is that the Lord is always happy with himself. Moreover, the Lord is happy with himself, whether we see it or not. "In thy presence is fulness of joy" (Psa. 16:11). God is a personal being. Now some think that he exists only for us and that he could not live without us. Not so. God is a triune God from all eternity who is happy in himself. He didn't have to make anything out of nothing. He is personal, a being independent of creation. He does not therefore need us to make him happy.

The second principle is that the only real happiness we have is when we see how happy he is. If God in his kindness will just give us the barest peep—just a glimpse—so that we can see how happy he is, we will find real happiness. Moreover, any happiness apart from his own joy is false. It is counterfeit and will not last.

The happiest being in the universe is the Lord Jesus Christ. And yet his happiness derives not only from who he is but also from what he has done and what he continues to do. For the joy of the Lord also has to do with his activity.

What happens, then, that makes the Lord happy? Here we again see Joseph as a type of Christ. Now Joseph has made himself known to his brothers. It has been disclosed that he is the head of state in this great land of Egypt. This revelation of himself to the eleven brothers gave Joseph unspeakable joy. Try to imagine what he was feeling! He could not restrain himself before all those present. He began to weep. Now when we cry, it may be because we have the greatest pain, but it is equally true that we cry when we have the greatest joy.

I never will forget a moment when I was ten years old. It was in August 1945. My mother was driving the car and she was crying. Tears were rolling down her cheeks until she was having trouble driving. And I said, "Why are you so sad? Why are you crying?"

But she said, "Oh no, I'm happy, I'm happy. The war is over, the war is over. Your daddy will not have to go into the military, and those daddies who are there will get to come home. I'm crying because I'm happy."

Joseph was feeling such happiness that the only way to express it was to weep. And he just let himself go.

There are four "sources" for our Lord's joy: (1) the joy he feels within himself because of who he is; (2) the joy he feels from his achievements; (3) the joy from knowing that his Father is pleased with him; and (4) the joy he has in seeing us happy. This becomes our joy and strength.

The "joy that was set before" Jesus (Heb. 12:2) is the joy that he now actually *has!* Jesus as a man endured certain things because he was promised a joy worth waiting for. He didn't enjoy the things that were happening to him much of the time. When people scoffed at him, spat on him, laughed at him—do you think he enjoyed that? When they made him a crown of thorns and pressed it down on his head—do you think he liked that? When they drove nails through his hands into a slab of wood, took his clothes off, then hoisted the cross to which he was nailed up into the air and dropped it into the ground—do you think he liked that? How do you think he felt? Then there was Mary Magdalene at the cross. Her heart was breaking. How do you suppose Jesus felt? But now we *look to Jesus* "the author and finisher of our faith; *who for the joy that was set before him* endured the cross, despising the shame, and is set down at the right hand of the throne of God" (Heb. 12:2, italics mine).

The joy of the Lord, then, is the joy that Jesus *now* has. It is the joy that had been set before him but which he now has. Having done everything that was required of him, he is now seated at the right hand of God. We are therefore talking about one who is happy! This is partly because he could look back over his thirty-three years on earth and not regret a thing. Can you say that? Can you say that you are happy about everything you have ever done? No, you can't. I can't. When I look back over any thirty day period or, if I were to be totally candid, any twenty-four hour period, I say, "Why did I say (or do) that?"

But here is Jesus. When he sat down at the right hand of God, he could look back over his life and have no regrets. None. He never sinned—not once. When enduring all of the scoffing, rudeness, humiliation, he was saying to himself, "It won't be much longer."

Joseph was the prime minister of Egypt. He was now happy in himself. He hadn't always been so happy. Do you think he liked it when he was sold into slavery? Do you think he liked it when he was lied about by Potiphar's wife? Did he enjoy it when he was put into a dungeon, then kept there when the butler could have cleared his name? What kept Joseph going? God had told him a long time ago that he would be vindicated one day. And Joseph believed that. He didn't know how it was going to happen. It didn't look possible, but he believed and waited. It was the joy that was set before him that kept him going. Joseph fell upon his brother Benjamin's neck and wept. He also kissed all of his brothers and wept on them. Why? Because he was so happy. The joy of the Lord, then, is his own joy.

Second, the joy of our Lord comes from knowing that the Father is pleased with him. At this point Pharaoh again becomes a type of the Father. Everything that Joseph desired for his brothers the Pharaoh ensured by absolute, irrevocable law. Joseph wanted them to come and live in Egypt. He wanted them to go back to Canaan, get old Jacob their father, and bring all the family to live in the land of Goshen. That is what Joseph wanted.

The news spread throughout Pharaoh's palace: "Joseph's brethren are come: and it pleased Pharaoh well" (Gen. 45:16). And Pharaoh said to Joseph, "Say unto thy brethren, This do ye; lade your beasts, and go, get you into the land of Canaan; and take your father and your households, and come unto me: and I will give you the good of the land of Egypt, and ye shall eat the fat of the land" (vv. 17-18). Pharaoh continued, "Now thou art commanded, this do ye." In other words, all that Joseph requested the Pharaoh made legal. It was an order. "This is what you are to do." That made it law.

This reminds us of the perfect unity in the Godhead. For there is no disagreement between the Father and the Son. Jesus put it like this:

> Verily, verily I say unto you, The Son can do nothing of himself, but what he seeth the Father do: for what things soever he doeth, these also doeth the Son likewise. For the Father loveth the Son, and sheweth him all things that himself doeth. (John 5:19-20)

Jesus also put it like this, "All things are delivered unto me of my Father: and no man knoweth the Son, but the Father; neither knoweth any man the Father, save the Son, and *he to whomsoever the Son will reveal* him" (Matt. 11:27, italics mine). When Jesus was talking to the Father he put it like this, "I pray for them [the disciples]: I pray not for the world, but for them which thou hast given me; for they are thine. And all mine are thine, and thine are mine; and I am glorified in them" (John 17:9-10).

Joseph had said earlier to his brothers, "You will dwell in the land of Goshen." But Joseph hadn't consulted with the Pharaoh when he promised this. But as soon as the Pharaoh heard of Joseph's wish, he ordered it at once—which made it final.

And what joy it gave to Joseph to know that everything that had happened pleased the Pharaoh. What joy it gave Jesus to know that while he was living his life, he was pleasing the Father. He was able to look to the Father from hour to hour as if to say, "How am I doing?" He didn't want to please himself. He was dedicated to pleasing the Father. Even at the age of twelve, he had said, "I must be about my Father's business" (Luke 2:49). He had endured suffering and had delivered the parables and the teaching concerning the kingdom of God, and he had done everything right. After all that, what joy it was on the cross to say, "It is finished" (John 19:30). He knew he had pleased the Father.

What joy was in the heart of Jesus when he was welcomed in heaven. Of course I don't know what it was like. But I love to imagine it. It could be that all heaven had come to a standstill, that they were counting the moments until Jesus came back to the Father. It had been forty days since the crucifixion. During those forty days Jesus had been raised from the dead and had appeared at various times to his disciples. All heaven was watching. Jesus gave his last words to the disciples in Acts 1:8. As he was saying good-bye to them, he knew that he was going back to heaven to be welcomed by the Father. What joy there must have been for Jesus, as he disappeared behind the cloud, to know that he was going to see the Father.

> *Look, ye saints! The sight is glorious:*
> *See the Man of Sorrows now,*
> *From the fight returned victorious,*
> *Every knee to Him shall bow.*
>
> —Thomas Kelly

He was welcomed by the angels. For all I know, Abraham, Isaac, and Jacob were given a special seat to behold Jesus coming back to heaven. I suspect that Elijah saw it. So did Isaiah and Jeremiah. John the Baptist was there and personally saw Jesus being welcomed back. What joy Jesus must have felt when the Father said, "Sit thou at my right hand, until I make thy foes thy footstool" (Acts 2:34-35). Jesus now intercedes for us at the right hand of God. And what Jesus asks for, the Father immediately commands. This is what is now happening. We have this promise that Jesus ever lives to make intercession for those who come to God by him (Heb. 7:25).

How long will Jesus be there? Until the last day. One morning the Father is going to say to Jesus, "Do you know what today is?" Perhaps Jesus will turn to the Father and say, "I think I know what you are getting ready to tell me to do." A day is coming when Jesus will stand up. Now he is seated, and, for all I know, it will be the first time he will have stood up since welcoming Stephen home to heaven. But there's coming a day when Jesus is going to stand up. And there will be the sound of a trumpet. The old Negroes in Alabama thought it would be Gabriel who would blow the trumpet. We don't know who will blow it. Some thought it was a silver trumpet. Perhaps! What we do know is that the Lord will descend, and there will be a shout, the voice of an archangel! "The dead in Christ shall rise first: then we which are alive and remain shall be caught up together with them . . . and so shall we ever be with the Lord" (1 Thess. 4:16-17).

The joy of the Lord consists, moreover, not only in that he has pleased his Father but in seeing his people made happy. If you think *you* are going to be happy when Jesus comes the second time, let me tell you that it will be but like crumbs from the table compared to the joy our Lord will have on that day. Parents, what makes you happy on Christmas Day? Is it not seeing your children happy? This is what makes Christmas Christmas, is it not? When I watch my son or daughter open a present that they had hoped for, and I see their joy, it is my joy. I delight in just seeing their faces. And that is what makes our Lord's joy complete. His joy comes not only from what he did or from pleasing his Father but also from seeing the expressions on our faces when we see him.

What was it like on Easter morning when Jesus first appeared to Mary Magdalene? Do you know why he appeared to her first? I suspect that Mary Magdalene took it the hardest when Jesus was betrayed and crucified. Oh, the joy Jesus felt when he could see her as she wrapped her arms around him. He had to say, "Stop clinging to me." There was the joy that Jesus felt when he could say to Peter, "It's all right." For Jesus knew how Peter felt when he wept his heart out (Matt. 26:75). Jesus wanted to go to Peter and say, "It's okay." There were those disciples in the upper room. They had forsaken the Lord in the last hour; now they heard that he was alive and they were so ashamed. But what joy Jesus had in going to the disciples to say, "Peace. Peace. It's all right. It's okay." And when *they* saw that Jesus meant it—that he held no grudges, but absolutely and totally forgave them—what joy they felt! What joy he felt in seeing them accept his forgiveness!

And so it was with Joseph. It had been his task to convince his brothers that he offered them total forgiveness. And they could see that Joseph forgave them. What joy Joseph got as he wept on their shoulders—knowing that they accepted his forgiveness.

The official order of Pharaoh was: "Regard not your stuff; for the good of all the land of Egypt is yours" (Gen. 45:20). For the Lord gets great joy in supplying our need. Is God hiding his face from you at the moment? Or are you in some financial difficulty? Perhaps the answer you have been waiting for is postponed. You may cry, "God, don't you care?" He cares. In the same way that Joseph had to wait for the right moment—being neither too late nor too early, so Jesus knows how much you can bear. And he knows just how long you can endure that difficulty. And when *that* day comes, he will supply that need. And when he sees what it does for you it gives him great joy! Joseph could look at his brothers and say, "Don't worry about a thing. You will have the best of the land. Everything is yours. Don't worry about your things. You shall eat of the fat of the land."

Then Joseph turned to Benjamin and gave him three hundred pieces of silver and five changes of raiment. As we have seen, the relationship that Joseph had to Benjamin is analogous to the relationship that Jesus has to us. Joseph and Benjamin were full brothers. The Apostle Paul wrote that we who are members of God's family have been adopted into that family. "The Spirit itself beareth witness with our spirit, that we are the children of God: and if children, then heirs; heirs of God, and *joint-heirs* with Christ" (Rom. 8:16-17, italics mine). We are full brothers, just like Joseph and Benjamin. A full relationship is what God offers to those who come to God by Jesus. Imagine this! An open invitation to become a member of the royal family: to be a *joint*-heir with the Son of God. "For I reckon that the sufferings of this present time are not worthy to be compared with the glory which shall be revealed in us" (Rom. 8:18). The Lord will get great joy from seeing his people happy.

The Day of Pentecost was a day toward which all history was moving. We often call it the birthday of the Church. But what joy the Lord felt in heaven when he sent the Holy Spirit on the 120! But was it joy in heaven only? There were sweet expressions on the faces of those in that upper room. And what love they felt! What oneness! And yet the joy they felt was but the overflow of the joy our Lord felt in seeing them filled with the Spirit. It was the day when all things came together for them: they now know why Jesus had died and risen from the dead.

"Eye hath not seen, nor ear heard, neither have entered into the heart of man, the things which God hath prepared for them that love him" (1 Cor. 2:9). Everything that gives us joy—whether it be as the Spirit unveils truth, or Christ's coming again—gives the Lord great joy. He knows what it does for us to see his glory. Furthermore, God does want us to be reunited with our saved loved ones. Of course the main thing will be seeing Jesus. Seeing him will make heaven heaven. But let us not underestimate this: we will be reunited with our saved loved ones. I've got a mother there. I'm looking forward to seeing her, and it will give the Lord joy to see us reunited.

What is happiness? It is the degree to which we see the Lord's own joy. Do you want to see the Lord's joy? Accept the total forgiveness that he offers you. Don't try to argue with him. Don't say, "I just can't cope with total forgiveness." If these brothers had said to Joseph, "From now on we are going to prove ourselves," it would have shown contempt for Joseph. Those brothers were forgiven men. So are we. This brings unspeakable joy. And strength.

THIRTY-TWO
LOST HOPE
REVIVED

In this chapter we turn from Joseph to Jacob, his father. Joseph had sent his brothers back to Canaan asking them to bring their father to Egypt. There would be five more years of the famine. There was no food anywhere else in the world.

It was the task of the brothers to tell their father the news. The grieved, old man had said, "I will go to my grave in mourning." And now Jacob was to be told that Joseph was alive and was governor of Egypt. There would be much for Jacob to absorb.

Two relevant things emerge from the taking of the news to Jacob. The first is how a person is brought to the knowledge of his salvation through Jesus Christ. We are brought to Jesus Christ by conversion. We have got to be changed. Something must happen to us so that we make a U-turn in our lives. It is the result of admitting that we have been wrong and of confessing that Jesus Christ is Savior and Lord. And it only happens by someone else telling us (Rom. 10:14). Somebody has got to tell us the good news. Whoever does that is simply the Lord's instrument "by whom ye believed" (1 Cor. 3:5).

Now can you imagine more startling news than this—old Jacob, who for twenty-two years has lived under the assumption that Joseph was dead, is told that he is alive and that he is governor of Egypt. The messengers, the instruments—none other than the sons of Jacob—were bringing good news to their father.

Dazzling news. Startling news. Shocking news. But wonderful news. Joseph was alive.

Remember that the brothers who took the news were *forgiven men*. If anybody was ever unworthy to carry news like that it was these ten brothers. What right had they got to be the bearers of news like that? But we are all like that. What right have I to share the news that Jesus Christ died on the cross? I'm the one that put him there. I'm the guilty one. Here I am coming and telling you this! But I am forgiven and God has commissioned me. Passing on the good news doesn't make me better than the other man. I am not. I come as a forgiven man.

There is one other thing that will bear our looking into. Joseph ordered his brothers to be loving. The last thing he said to them was, "See that you fall not out by the way" (Gen. 45:24). "Don't quarrel on the way" (NIV). This is important for anybody who is sharing the gospel. If he is to be effective, he must avoid any kind of quarrel. If I am not right in myself, if I have got any kind of grudge against anybody or am harboring the least hurt, I fear that God would not bless me. Here was Joseph sending his brothers on their way; they are going to give this extraordinary news, so he says, "Don't fall out with each other."

The second thing that emerges in this account is this: the grace of God revives forgotten hopes. There is a fresh burst of grace even to the Christian. God's grace brings to our memory things we had forgotten about. This is an essential characteristic of the work of the Holy Spirit. Jesus said that when the Spirit comes, he will bring to our remembrance the things that Jesus had taught (John 14:26). But many times, between those bursts of glory that come on the soul of the Christian, we tend to forget things; we tend to live by assumptions that may not be right. And then comes the Lord and stops hiding his face! He shows himself, and we see things that we had forgotten.

Have you give up hope? Have you give up hope that God would ever speak to you again in an undoubted manner? Have you an assumption that you have lived under for a long time, maybe twenty-two years, perhaps two years? You have taken it for granted that something has "got" to be true. Could it be that you came to a hasty conclusion on inadequate evidence and for years have assumed something? You saw certain evidence—like Jacob seeing Joseph's blood-soaked coat—and you said, "Ah, that means this," and you whipped into a depression from which you have not recovered. It could be that you have given up hope of being in the will of God, though you would give a million dollars to know that you are.

Perhaps you decided some time ago that the Bible is not really true, that it is a faulty document. You used to believe the Bible. But you came across some so-called evidence that convinced you that there is no way that the Bible could be God's infallible, inerrant Word. You sighed "Oh, well!" and you have been living under a cloud ever since. But if something could happen to make you see that the Bible really is true, you would be set afire! You could conquer a thousand worlds.

Perhaps you would like to believe that there really is a heaven. You used to think it might be true. But you have since wondered. Oh! The thought that there is a heaven! What it would do for you!

Perhaps you would like to think that you could be saved just by trusting what Jesus did on the cross. By believing what he did plus nothing else! Imagine believing that Jesus in his own body bore all of your sins on that cross and that God offers you a *free pardon.* You may say, "I would love to believe that."

What assumption have you been living under that you have not ever looked at again? You have assumed something for years. And yet, were you to look at it in a careful, objective way, you would have to admit that it was *inconclusive* evidence that led you to this assumption.

Could it be a case of unanswered prayer? Have you prayed for something that you quit praying about a long time ago? Do you not know that you only have to pray in the will of God one time for that prayer to be answered? "If we ask any thing according to his will, he heareth us" (1 John 5:14). If you have asked in God's will, he is going to answer it sooner or later. But maybe you have given up. One of these days God is going to answer your prayer, and you will be found blushing!

What plan have you envisaged for yourself that you once thought was God's will? Yet you have given up. Or perhaps you have had a conviction about something. Maybe you were alone in it. Maybe there were certain circumstances that didn't add up for others, and in the end you let go of it.

For twenty-two years Jacob had been satisfied that one thing was true: his son Joseph was dead. The ten brothers, who had just sold Joseph to the Ishmaelites, had taken that coat of many colors and dipped it in blood—the blood of a goat. Then they had come home to their father with the coat dipped in blood and laid it before Jacob. They didn't say a word. They let old Jacob do the talking. What did he say? "It is my son's coat; an evil beast hath devoured him; Joseph is without doubt rent in pieces" (Gen. 37:33).

That was Jacob's conclusion. But he was wrong. You couldn't have told him then that he was wrong. He had seen the coat. Blood was all over it. It was Joseph's coat all right. The evidence had satisfied Jacob that Joseph was dead.

Then came the brothers with the message: "Joseph is alive." Now we are not told the details of everything that was said. It is likely that the news was broken more carefully and slowly. I don't know. The way it reads here you are led to believe that they just came to their father and said, "Joseph is alive—he's governor of Egypt" (Gen. 45:26). But perhaps this is a summary of the message. Perhaps they said, "We've got some stunning news. We want you to sit down now. Just sit in your chair. We've got something to say to you that you're going to find a bit hard to believe. But we know that it is true. We don't know where to start. We don't know how to say it. But Joseph is still alive. And he's even the governor of Egypt."

And Jacob fainted! Verse 26 says, "For he believed them not." Now why this reaction? Well, it was a natural reaction, wasn't it? A natural reaction to overwhelming news. It touched on Jacob's most sensitive nerve—his son Joseph.

What if the most sensitive thing in *your* whole life were touched on, and you realized that you had lived under an assumption that was quite wrong? What would Jacob prefer to believe more than anything in the world? I suppose if you were to say to old Jacob, "Fantasize for a minute. What would you *like* to be true?" I doubt that Jacob would even think to say that he wished Joseph were alive because we all want to fantasize something within the circumference of at least a *remote* possibility. Could it be that what God wants to do with you, you couldn't even *think* about? There is a promise that God is "able to do exceeding abundantly above all that we ask or *think*" (Eph. 3:20, italics mine). Now that is the way God likes to work.

Jacob fainted because there was nothing he would rather believe! But he couldn't handle this kind of information. It was simply too good to be true. Now Jacob was partly to be blamed for his sorrow. He had accepted the verdict of Joseph being dead on insufficient evidence. It was conclusive to him, but he was wrong.

I fear there are many today in the Christian ministry who started out believing in the infallibility of Scripture. But they got under a professor either at seminary, Bible college, or university who showed them so-called "evidence" about the Bible. They said, "Look. You couldn't possibly believe that Moses wrote Genesis, Exodus, and Leviticus." Some of these young men go to college with heads like sponges, soaking up anything they are told. And now they preach but don't have any power because they don't believe the truth of the Bible. They turn to the "social gospel" or to politics, campaigning over issues like poverty or radical strife.

I can tell you this. The devil will take advantage of our listening to inconclusive evidence. He will have a field day with us and drive us into all kinds of despair, confusion, and sorrow.

Jacob no doubt blamed himself for much of what had happened. One could do a character study on old Jacob. He wasn't the perfect man. He had not always been a very nice man. I would predict that he began to blame himself: "God is punishing me." Perhaps he looked over his life and remembered how he had stolen the birthright from his brother, Esau. He had taken advantage of poor Esau. And it could be that Jacob was saying, "I can see now that I shouldn't have done that, and I'm going to my grave in sorrow. God is angry with me."

Perhaps you have been punishing yourself and assuming God was punishing you when that was not the case at all, but you had too hastily assumed something.

What a pity that Jacob hadn't held on to the feeling he had when he discerned that what Joseph said to his brothers was right and that God was going to use Joseph one day.

Jacob fainted. Sometimes we faint under *good* news. Sometimes we become so at home with our sorrow or with some impediment, fault, or particular life-style (though we didn't want it at first) that we get used to it and don't want it changed. A person can develop a physical problem and get so used to it that he likes it. I once had a filling in my tooth fall out. It didn't hurt and there were no nerves, so I could stick my tongue in that hole and I enjoyed it. The day came when I had to go to the dentist for something else. He said, "I must fix that hole." And I said, "No, don't fix that. I like it." We become so used to something that is bad at first that to have the opposite, though it is best for us, brings a negative reaction.

Neither do we like to admit that we have been living under a false assumption. How do you think this man Jacob felt when he realized that he had wasted twenty-two years, all because he had believed that Joseph was dead? Now he was having to cope with this and sort it out. Many people don't like the idea of becoming a Christian because they cannot bear to say, "I've been wrong." And often a backslider doesn't want to get right with God because he doesn't want to have to admit that he's wasted so many years.

Jacob had two things to absorb. First, that Joseph was alive. Second, that he was governor of Egypt. The gospel message is always twofold: general and particular. The general message is that Jesus Christ is alive and that he is at the right hand of God. But there must be a particular application: something has got to happen to you. It is not enough for me to say, "Jesus Christ is alive." You can just say, "Thank you very much, that's interesting." You are called upon to repent, to admit you've been wrong, to confess your sins, to believe in your heart that God raised Jesus from the dead and then confess him openly.

The immediate reaction to a general message is often negative. Something must also be brought home to you. Old Jacob heard the general message. He fainted. But then he was given more: "And they told him *all* the words of Joseph, which he had said unto them," (Gen. 45:27). Joseph had said to them, "Now therefore be not grieved, nor angry with yourselves, that ye sold me hither: for God did send me before you to preserve life" (Gen. 45:5).

When the brothers of Joseph told their father "all the words," they went through the hardest moment that they had ever had to experience for then they confessed their sin to Jacob their father. Joseph himself had gone to pains to protect them. He had even kept the Egyptians from hearing. He did not require that they tell their father. As far as Joseph was concerned, it need never be known. But they elected to tell Jacob anyway. They wanted to confess it all and get it off their chests.

It was at this moment that old Jacob began to believe that it might be true. It may be that they had to tell him this to get him to believe it. I don't know. When he first heard the words "Joseph is alive" he fainted. But when they told him *all* the words that Joseph had said to them: "and when he saw the wagons which Joseph had sent to carry him, the spirit of Jacob their father revived."

It was the news that he would see Joseph again that he needed. His spirit revived. Jacob said, "It is enough." It was his way of saying, "It's all right. I'm going to get to see Joseph again. I will see him before I die."

What else revived Jacob? The news meant that Joseph's dream had been right and that God had a plan for Israel. Old Jacob had these enormous guilt feelings for all that he had done. But he could now see that God hadn't left him. Malachi the prophet was going to come along later and say, "Jacob have I loved, Esau have I hated" (Mal. 1:2-3). Jacob was already getting the message that God did love him. Yes, there were twenty-two years of wasted sorrow. Yes, he saw what his sons had done to Joseph. But when he saw the wagons—infallible evidence—he said, "This *is* real. I am going to see Joseph. It is enough."

THIRTY-THREE
ACCEPTING
THE NEW
AND DIFFERENT

We will continue to look at Jacob and see things from his point of view. The father of the twelve, surnamed Israel, was undergoing one of the great traumas of his life. When they said, "Joseph is yet alive," Jacob's heart fainted. But the greatest trauma of his life had been when the ten brothers brought him the coat of many colors, which they had dipped in blood. On the evidence of the blood-soaked coat, Jacob concluded: "An evil beast hath devoured him; Joseph is dead." So for the next twenty-two years Jacob believed that Joseph had been killed by a wild beast.

But suddenly he heard news that Joseph was alive and was prime minister of Egypt! Obviously this was good news. But it was traumatic as well. He had to come to terms with twenty-two years of needless sorrow. He had said, "I shall go to my grave in mourning." And now he was having to sort this out and forgive himself for twenty-two years wasted—all because of living under this false assumption.

But there is still another reason why Jacob was undergoing a trauma: he was having to bid farewell to an old life-style and accept the new and different. The word came from his son Joseph, "Move to Egypt. Live with me. There are five years left of this famine, and I will give you the land of Goshen. You will have the fat of the land. Come. Bring everything—all that you have with all of the family." Jacob knew that this was the right thing to do. But he was having to bid farewell to familiar surroundings and ways, and it meant that he would have to leave Canaan for ever. This was particularly difficult for him for two reasons.

The first reason has to do with a very natural reaction. Jacob was by then a very old man—more than a hundred years old—and old people naturally find it more difficult to adjust to change. Yet Jacob was being asked to pull up stakes and face the unknown in a different country. Most of us are congenitally allergic to change. By nature we like things to continue as they are. Sometimes young people find it easier to accept change, but as they get older they, too, find themselves becoming entrenched in a way of thinking, and eventually find themselves unable to accept change after all. It is so easy for a young person to be critical of an older person and say, "Well, you are just set in your ways." If you are a young reader, in a few years you too will know what it's like to have to change. It can be painful. For very few of us really like change. We say, "Why can't it be as it was?" Here was a man more than a hundred years of age having to accept the new and different.

The second reason this was traumatic was because Joseph's message appeared to contradict God's word to his father and grandfather. It was *Canaan* that was to be the land of promise. This was what God had said to Abraham, Jacob's grandfather; it was what God said to his father, Isaac. And now Jacob was being told that he must *leave* Canaan.

How do you suppose that made him feel? Did he protest, "How can I leave? How can I do a thing like this?" He could argue, "I can't do this as it would go right against all that God had promised." But we read: "Israel took his journey with all that he had" (Gen. 46:1). What a move! What courage!

What is the relevance of all this for us? I think it is relevant primarily for those who are not Christians and have never come to believe in the power of the blood of Jesus Christ. Consider a phrase like that for the non-Christian: "believing in the power of the blood of Jesus Christ." I'm sure this strikes the non-Christian with a feeling of strangeness and unease. If you ever become a Christian, it will be because you trust that blood to save you. But at first it is something totally new and different.

But the call to Jacob to move to Egypt is also relevant for the Christian. It is a challenge to all of us to be willing to accept the new and the different. What is almost always forgotten is a motto of the great Reformation under Luther and Calvin: *the Church reformed but always reforming.* What often happens to a church is that it is reformed—period! Because we become opposed to change and will not accept the new and different, the Church becomes staid, cold, lifeless and (surprise, surprise) largely ineffective. Jonathan Edwards taught us that it is the task of every generation to discover in which direction the sovereign Redeemer is moving, and then to move in that direction.

But I think this also speaks to the backslider. Have you been running from God? Are you playing games with yourself and with God and with everybody you know? Perhaps you have been such a phony! God is putting his thumb in your back, despite your having become adjusted to the old world, and telling you to move on.

God in his mercy and kindness prepares all of us for the new and different. When God wants us to move to the new and different, how does he do it? Does he just say, "All right. Change. Right now. Change." Is that the way he does it? No. He has a way of preparing us. In this chapter I want us to see precisely how God prepares his own for the new and the different.

The first way God does it is by making the new and different an attractive alternative to a bleak and dismal past. Jacob's heart had fainted because "he believed them not." Then they told him "all the words" of Joseph. Those words included, "Be not grieved, nor angry with yourselves, that you sold me hither: for God did send me before you to preserve life." That was their way of saying to their father, "We are the ones who did it. Blame us." And then they showed Jacob the wagons Joseph had sent to carry him. Jacob put two and two together and knew they wouldn't tell a story like that if it weren't true. And then he said, "It is enough; Joseph my son is yet alive: I will go and see him before I die." So the new and different became an attractive alternative to all that Jacob had lived through.

For the past twenty-two years, Jacob was a man who had been preoccupied with himself—filled with sorrow and self-pity, operating totally in a sphere of the false and the counterfeit as a result of an assumption based upon inconclusive evidence. God blesses us only as we live in the sphere of *truth*. But Jacob had been living in the sphere of a lie. He had said, "Joseph my son is dead; I shall go to my grave in mourning."

Here is something very interesting and very sad. During these twenty-two years, as far as we know, Jacob had none of those sweet and precious experiences with the Lord. We are talking about a man who knew the Lord. He had known experiences with God that were quite extraordinary. Once, after leaving Beersheba, Jacob had dreamed:

> Behold a ladder set up on the earth, and the top of it reached to heaven: and behold the angels of God ascending and descending on it. And, behold, the Lord stood above it, and said, I am the Lord God of Abraham thy father, and the God of Isaac: the land whereon thou liest, to thee will I give it, and to thy seed; and thy seed shall be as the dust of the earth, and thou shalt spread abroad to the west, and to the east, and to the north, and to the south: and in thee and in thy seed shall all the families of the earth be blessed. And, behold, I am with thee, and will keep thee in all places whither thou goest, and will bring thee again into this land; for I will not leave thee, until I have done that which I have spoken to thee of. (Gen. 28:12-15)

This was indeed a precious, intimate experience with the Lord.

This was not the only time that happened to Jacob. On another occasion the Lord came to Jacob, and the angels of God met him. When Jacob saw the angels he said, "This is God's host" (Gen. 32:2). Later God gave Jacob one of the most extraordinary experiences that is recorded in all Holy Writ. Jacob wrestled with an angel until the breaking of the day, then said, "I will not let thee go, except thou bless me."

The angel asked, "What is thy name?"

"Jacob."

And the reply came, "Thy name shall be called no more Jacob, but Israel: for as a prince hast thou power with God and with men, and hast prevailed" (Gen. 32:24-28). What a wonderful thing to experience!

Can you recall a time when the Lord was real to you? Have you known precious experiences with God, but not lately? Why? Is it because you have been living under a false assumption? Have you based what you now believe on inconclusive evidence? Have you become virtually a counterfeit? Has your heart become cold? Is nothing like it was?

So here was Jacob, who used to know the Lord so intimately. But from the time he decided that Joseph was dead, Jacob knew nothing of God coming to him, showing his face, bestowing a wonderful sense of his presence. Jacob had known none of this for a long time.

How long has it been since the Lord has been real to you? It could be that God is saying something to you now. He wants you to turn your back on your present life-style and accept the new and the different.

If we accept as fact what was really a false conclusion based upon misleading evidence, we should not be surprised if God hides his face and there is little or no blessing. Moreover, when God hides his face, the old devil moves in. Satan will take full advantage of this and will sit alongside and accuse you. He will say, "You have never been saved. Those times you thought God was real were just psychological experiences. It just met a need at the time."

I'll tell you another thing that will happen if you believe what isn't true. All of the guilt feelings you ever had will flourish. Questionable things you have done will haunt you. When you are living where you ought to live with God, they don't bother you. But when your heart gets cold, a sense of guilt emerges and you feel so awful. Why? Because God works in the sphere of truth. The good news that Joseph was alive enabled Jacob to accept the new and different because it was an attractive alternative to all that he had been experiencing for twenty-two years.

Are you so opposed to change? Take a look at yourself. What are you really like now? Isn't God trying to say something to you? Are you in such a rut that you easily allow the devil to haunt you? But now Jacob could see something that he hadn't seen in years. All those experiences that he had with the Lord were coming back to him. Yes, he had so much to absorb when he heard the news "Joseph is alive." Jacob began to say to himself, "If Joseph is alive and has been exalted to this high position in Egypt and is now sending for us, it means that I wasn't cast off by God after all." He saw that all his guilt feelings were groundless. It turned out that God had owned everything that he had ever done—even his partiality to Joseph.

If you are a parent, I dare say that a sore spot in your life is your children. You feel that you have failed with them, that you have let them down, that you haven't been all that you ought to have been. Maybe you feel guilty because you loved the child too much. Or not enough. Or you over-protected that child. Or didn't take enough care. You look back and you think, *Oh, what have I done? If I could just go back. I wish that my child were just a baby. I could start again and see to it that his life turned out differently.*

I guarantee that when Jacob saw that blood-stained coat of many colors he blamed himself for all that happened. He hadn't been perfect—far from it. All that he had ever done was manipulate and connive. He was a very mischievous man. During these twenty-two years God had hid his face. All Jacob could think of was, "I'm going to my grave in mourning."

There may be one other thing that hit him. That great promise which God had made to Jacob a long time before actually said: "I am with thee, and *will keep thee in all places whither thou goest, and will bring thee again into this land.*" Now Jacob could happily reflect upon that promise. During all those years he may have wondered what it meant—"I will bring thee *again* to this land." "I'm in it now," he would have said to himself. "If I am brought *again* to this land, it means I have got to *leave* it."

Perhaps there is some verse the Lord made real to you a long time ago. But over the years you decided or feared that it was not coming to pass. Or there may be a particular Scripture that has puzzled you. There are difficult passages in the Bible. No Christian, minister, scholar, or theologian understands all of the Bible. There may well be verses that have particularly puzzled you, and God has withheld the meaning from you. But there may come a day when something happens. You will say, "Ah, *that* is the way it is to be understood!"

Jacob's mind began to work. "If Joseph is alive, it means that God hasn't forgotten me after all. It means all that he promised years ago is still valid." God had said, "I will never leave you. I will be with you always. My presence will go with you." And Jacob's heart revived. Accepting the new and different became such an attractive alternative. He knew that God was saying,

"Move on now, move on. Didn't I say I would bring you *back* to this land?"

Those in God's family have this guarantee: their grossest failures are turned into greatest successes. Why? Because you are God's child. You are a joint-heir with Jesus Christ. God is going to honor his Son—you can mark that down. God is determined to glorify his Son, and *you* are a joint-heir. That means that anything that touches your life—anything that happens to you—becomes God's problem.

> *When through the deep waters I call thee to go,*
> *The rivers of sorrow shall not overflow;*
> *For I will be with thee, thy trials to bless,*
> *And sanctify to thee thy deepest distress.*

But God further prepared Jacob for the new and different by doing something else. He restored to him those old experiences with God that he had once known. We read: "Israel took his journey with all that he had, and came to Beersheba, and offered sacrifices unto the God of his father Isaac." Now for the first time in twenty-two years, "God spake unto Israel in the visions of the night, and said, Jacob, Jacob. And he said Here am I. And he said, I am God, the God of thy father: fear not to go down into Egypt; for I will there make of thee a great nation: I will go down with thee into Egypt; and I will also surely bring thee up again: and Joseph shall put his hand upon thine eyes" (Gen. 46:1-4).

God prepared Jacob for the new and different by restoring the kind of communion with him that he had once known. Jacob knew what he wanted to do first. He wanted to go to Beersheba. Beersheba was a special place in his family history. It was one of the places where God met with his grandfather Abraham. It was a place where God met with Isaac. And it was right after he had left Beersheba that Jacob himself had that first great experience with God. Going to Beersheba would make everything seem exactly right. Why did he want to go there? To offer sacrifices unto the God of his father, Isaac. Why do that? Because he had no righteousness in himself. Jacob knew that a God who was this good would only be satisfied with a righteousness by substitution and sacrifice. After all, Jacob knew that he had done nothing to deserve that kind of attention from the Lord. Jacob could give you a thousand reasons why God should have forsaken him. God should have dropped him a long time ago. So when he discovered that God could be so kind and patient after all these years, it had to be because of a righteousness *outside* himself.

I referred above to the blood of Jesus. Why is that blood so precious? I only know this: God demands a righteousness that is outside sinful man. You cannot produce the standard of righteousness that God demands. I don't care how hard you try. You may try really hard for two days, and during those two days you may think you are not doing too badly. But even in those two days, were you to realize what sin is, you would know you had sinned from the first hour of the first day. For God demands perfect righteousness, and you can't produce it. What happened was that he sent his Son into the world. Jesus died on a cross and shed blood—blood from one who knew no sin. But he was made sin for us (2 Cor. 5:21). It is through the sacrifice of another, through Jesus Christ, that God is appeased. And that's the gospel.

Why did God say, "Fear not"? Jacob was an old man and he was afraid. Perhaps he had second thoughts about all that he was about to do. And God knew that. So God said to him, "Go down into Egypt; for I will there make of thee a great nation."

Why did he have to go to Egypt? Why not Canaan? Why couldn't he have stayed there? Why couldn't it have been arranged for Joseph to send food over the border for the next five years? Why is it that God makes us move when we are so comfortable where we are?

God does this. The task of every Christian is to be sensitive to the voice of God, who is always leading us to the new and to the different. It was a tremendous step of obedience for old Jacob to take at his age when he was set in his ways and most vulnerable. So God said, "I will be with thee."

Now there's one last thing. God said, "I will surely bring thee up again." This goes back to the original promise. Moreover, "I will bring you up again" refers to Jacob's death. It meant that he would die in Egypt but that his body would be brought back. After all, it is not where you are when you die that matters. It is who is there beside you when you die, and what happens after you die.

Sooner or later all of us must experience death—the inevitable new and different. But if in the meantime God has continually led us to the new and different, death will merely be one more experience of his faithfulness and presence. "Fear not to go down to Egypt . . . I will go down with thee."

THIRTY-FOUR
ANTICIPATING
THE NEW
AND DIFFERENT

When we speak the "language of Zion," using biblical images to express our thoughts, we describe a transition from the dismal to the glorious in terms of a journey from Egypt to Canaan.

But with Jacob it was the opposite. He was going from Canaan to Egypt, and it was no small thing for this elderly man to do. As we have seen, he was going right against all that he had always believed and all that his fathers had believed. They had believed that Canaan was to be the Promised Land. Yet, here he was having to say good-bye to Canaan, knowing full well he wouldn't come back alive.

Jacob was experiencing what everyone experiences whom God uses, the loneliness of doing what seems to everybody else to be utterly wrong. There is a verse in Lamentations: "It is good for a man that he bear the yoke in his youth" (Lam. 3:27). In other words, we normally think of God putting a younger person through trials in preparation for the future. But here was a man more than a hundred years old having to experience an enormous ordeal in old age. He was having to prepare for the new and different at a time when most people are in their sunset years and expecting to go to heaven any minute. But not Jacob. He knew that God had a plan for him in Egypt.

It would have been wrong for Abraham to go to Egypt. As a matter of fact, Abraham did go to Egypt and got into all kinds of trouble. And God had specifically said to Isaac, "Go not down into Egypt" (Gen. 26:2). Here was Jacob, having been brought up from his mother's knee to believe that Egypt was the worst place in the world to be, knowing what trouble his grandfather had gotten into when he went to Egypt, now accepting the fact he was to go there. He had the horrifying experience of realizing that what would have been wrong for Abraham and Isaac was right for him. Can you imagine some critic saying to Jacob, "You shouldn't do a thing like that. How do you suppose your father would feel? How do you suppose your grandfather would feel? Look at what you're doing. You surely know that Canaan is the land of promise." But Jacob said, "I believe it's right. I've got to go and I'm looking forward to it."

What made him look forward to going? Certain principles lay behind his looking forward to the new and to the different. The first principle is this: God leaves us with no viable alternative when he leads us to the new and different. We have already seen how God motivates us by making the new and different attractive. But there is more to it than that. Left to ourselves, we would still never move forward—unless God actually forces it upon us.

I have been thinking about my own life as I have been preparing this chapter. I think that, with one or two exceptions, every major decision I have ever made in my life has been forced on me; it has been as though I hadn't any choice. I have known what it is to want something really bad and not get it. But what *God* has wanted has more often than not been forced upon me. Now the main exception would be my choice of a wife. She didn't force herself on me; it was the other way around. I prayed a lot about it, but I worked at getting her as though I didn't believe in prayer. I just knew I had to have her. However, other major decisions in my life have been forced upon me.

Now why is this? As I have said, all of us are congenitally opposed to change. According to some psychologists, the most traumatic experience that anybody goes through is birth itself. A baby is born. He doesn't want to leave his mother's womb. And that is exactly what happens as we are born again—it is traumatic; we undergo turmoil, frustration, confusion, pain. We talk about a wrench. When God begins to work in us and we realize that something is happening—when we are now having to reexamine everything we ever believed in our life, it is truly traumatic. When we realize that there *is* a God in the heavens, that he is dealing with us and making us uncomfortable with our sins, what never bothered us before begins to bother us; we tremble as we begin to do things that previously have not bothered us at all.

There is a name for this: conviction of sin. This is God coming in. There is a sense in which we would have to say that he is forcing himself on us. Now I say that guardedly because there is a sense in which the opposite is true; God doesn't force himself in an obtrusive manner. And yet, as the Psalmist put it (Spurgeon was fond of quoting this): "Thy people shall be willing in the day of thy power" (Ps. 110:3).

I grew up in Ashland, Kentucky, and there is an old song that is sung back in the hills of Kentucky: "He doesn't compel us to go against our will; he just makes us willing to go." But the process is painful.

The new and different. All of us want to remain the same. Were it not for God just *stepping in,* sometimes like a bolt out of the blue, we would never change. He grabs us and says, "This is what you are going to do."

Jacob saw this. This is the thing that gave him such peace; it is the reason he was willing to go on to Egypt and was looking forward to it: he saw that God did it. He could only say to himself, "This is out of my hands. I didn't plan this. I didn't ask for this. This is something God has done." When we know God has done it, we have peace. We can face a thousand worlds. And so it is with our own conversion. Knowing that God did it keeps us when the going is rough.

The second principle is this: we will never look forward to the new and different until we get ourselves sorted out. For twenty-two years, Jacob had lived under a melancholy delusion: he had believed that Joseph was dead. He had lived under a cloud because he had accepted as "fact" what was not a fact at all. Very possibly he had even begun to doubt God's own love and forgiveness. But then when he saw the wagons and realized that Pharaoh had indeed sent for him—that Joseph was really alive—he took courage. He knew that not only was God alive but that all he said was absolutely true: "I am with thee, and will keep thee in all places whither thou goest, and will bring thee again into this land." He saw now that God was still with him, and he could also easily forgive his sons for what they had done to Joseph.

Moreover, what is equally important is that Jacob could now

forgive himself. It is very important to forgive ourselves because if we can't, God's forgiveness becomes almost meaningless. And what will help us forgive ourselves is to realize that God's purpose for us has not been thwarted, that he is still with us and is going to do everything that he promised.

Even if you have wandered from the Lord, even if you have not been living as you ought, God has not forsaken you. It is no accident that you are reading these lines right now. God is giving you a tap on the shoulder saying, "All right now. It's about time you get straightened out." There is no way that we can look forward to the new and different until we ourselves understand God's greater purpose for us.

But here's another principle. There will be no liberty to look forward to the new and different until we accept God's own good news as valid and then act upon it. The good news was that Joseph was alive. Jacob had to believe that and act on it. At first this good news was traumatic. His heart had fainted. But eventually Jacob accepted the good news: "It is enough; Joseph my son is yet alive: I will go and see him before I die." Then Israel "took his journey with all that he had"—he had to act.

Once you hear this gospel there comes a moment in time when you *commit* your life, including your whole future, to Jesus Christ. You must do it consciously and know what you are doing.

Many people will say, "I am not opposed to change; I just need to know that God's in it." How do we know whether God is in the new and different? First, it is not a divinely approved new and different if there is not also an undoubted continuity with the past. For the new and different can also be of the devil. Change for its own sake is utter folly. So how can we be sure that the new and different is of God? One way of knowing is if there is an undoubted continuity with the past—this shows that it is the *same God* who is leading you. God leads from A to B and B to C, each step linking up with past steps. And Israel took his journey with all that he had and came to Beersheba and offered sacrifices "unto the God of his father Isaac" (Gen. 46:1). It was Jacob's way of affirming the past and saying, "I'm going to accept the new and different, but it's the God of my father who is leading me and I will be safe." Remember that change for its own sake is foolishness. "Remove not the ancient landmark, which thy fathers have set" (Prov. 22:28). God soon spoke to Israel, "in the visions of the night, and said, Jacob, Jacob. And he said, Here am I. And he said, I am God, the God of thy father" (Gen. 46:2-3). So we can face the new and different and look forward to it when we see how it fits in with the past and know that it's the same God.

> *Through many dangers, toils, and snares*
> *I have already come;*
> *'Tis grace hath brought me safe thus far,*
> *And grace will lead me home.*

—John Newton

But there is also a sense in which there must be a clean break with the past. For Israel took his journey "with *all* that he had." This tells us that he left no deposit in Canaan. He knew he wasn't coming back. He might have said, "What about our possessions here in Canaan? Let's just take what we need and leave the rest. We're going down to Egypt for the five years left of the famine. I think this much will do for five years—we don't want to take everything." No. There was none of this. For you will never come to look forward to the new and different until there is an utter abandonment of your past. You leave nothing. You must know you are not turning back.

A further proof that God is in the new and different is that his own word is clarified. We have already looked at Jacob's old promise from God, "I will bring thee again into this land." Now you can be sure that for years Jacob wondered, "What on earth does that word *again* mean?" How many of us are aware of certain verses in the Bible that trouble us? We know they are there, but what do they mean? You will not know until you move from A to B, B to C. And the proof that the new and different really *is* of God is that there will be a sweet clarification of God's word to you. It will come home with such lucidity and power that you will know without doubt that God's hand is upon you. Doing God's will is the only thing that is going to unlock what you have been mystified about for a long time.

THIRTY-FIVE
THE GOD WHO
KEEPS HIS WORD

The forgotten men of the story are the brothers of Joseph. I will not call them unsung heroes, but in the end they were in fact trophies of divine grace—models of what God can do with those who have sinned grievously. These brothers had a deep hurt. Because of jealousy, they had conspired against their brother. At first they had been going to kill him outright. They had thought it over and decided they wouldn't do that. But they sold him to the Ishmaelites. They lost track of him and certainly never expected to see him again. It was a grievous sin that they committed.

Now we find them models of grace. Do you know what is one of the surest signs of grace? It is to remain unvindicated yourself and yet to harbor no bitterness against the one who is vindicated. These men were so sure Joseph deserved to be hurt and set permanently aside. They felt it wasn't fair that their father should single out Joseph and make him the favorite. They felt they had every right to feel hurt. They got carried away and sold Joseph into slavery.

Twenty-two years later, the brothers were found out and Joseph was exalted. An extraordinary aspect of the story—and it is often forgotten—is the attitude of the brothers now.

We can call these ten brothers trophies of grace because they swallowed their pride and came to live under Joseph's shadow in Egypt. They might have chosen to rebel in Canaan. After they had gone back to Canaan and announced to their father that

Joseph was alive they could have said, "But we're not going. We're not going to live under the shadow of that man." But they didn't split the family. We read in chapter 46:6-7: "They took their cattle, and their goods, which they had gotten in the land of Canaan, and came into Egypt, Jacob, *and all his seed with him:* his sons, and his sons' sons with him, his daughters, and his son's daughters, and all his seed brought he with him into Egypt" (italics mine).

They didn't rebel against Jacob, and they knew that Jacob still felt the same way about Joseph. Did some of them opt to stay back in Canaan? They were in a position to have done that. They were their own men. They could have stayed right where they were and said, "No, father, thank you very much; we will just say good-bye. If you want to go to Egypt to live, that is your privilege. But there is only so much we can bear. We aren't going to be around Joseph. We couldn't stand it. He's the governor of Egypt, and we know how you feel about him." But that wasn't the way they looked at it. They all came.

Why did they come? It was because they believed what Joseph had told them. Joseph had said, "Now therefore be not grieved, nor angry with yourselves, that ye sold me hither: for God did send me before you to preserve life." Joseph had made it clear that he forgave them totally. He had given them a way of saving face with themselves when he said, "You didn't do it. It was God who did it. God was behind the whole thing." Joseph forgave them but did that solve their problem? They had to *accept* his forgiveness.

These brothers accepted that they had been forgiven by the one they had sought to harm. Talk about swallowing your pride. Imagine accepting this forgiveness. The first thing that is required before we can ever be saved is to realize that we need to be forgiven, then we need to accept the forgiveness that is offered. These brothers also demonstrated that they had been changed; their lives were different. They were willing to live in Egypt without being resentful of Joseph's success—they were not coming to Egypt to eat sour grapes but to fit in. They were going to be those who could show that they were glad God had forgiven them. For what was at the bottom of all this was that they had sinned against God. It wasn't the matter of a relationship between themselves and Joseph; it was between themselves and God. They actually had to forgive God for choosing and vindicating Joseph. Joseph was born with a silver spoon in his mouth, and yet he was the one God used. And they forgave God for this. It is a sure sign of grace when you justify God for the instrument he has chosen.

Here also is a picture of how the Lord Jesus Christ is unashamed of his brethren. "For both he that sanctifieth and they who are sanctified are all of one: for which cause he [Jesus] is not ashamed to call them brethren" (Heb. 2:11). Joseph demonstrated how he in turn was unashamed of those who believed his word. He made his chariot ready. Yes, he was going to see his father Jacob. But he was also going to see the eleven brothers. Moreover, he let all Egypt know that he was heading for Goshen. You can be sure the rumors were out all over Egypt: the governor of Egypt has a father and eleven brothers from Canaan. Joseph might have said, "We want to keep this quiet. Let family matters be." No. He made his chariot ready. Openly. He demonstrated that he was not ashamed to welcome his brothers into Egypt.

Joseph was even unashamed to show his feelings and weep before all his family. He fell on his father's neck and "wept on his neck a good while" (Gen. 46:29). And that is what our Lord is like. One of the things so sweet and tender about Jesus is that he shares his feelings with us. How many friends have you got like that? Do they keep their opinions to themselves, or hide behind an image? They might nod or put on a fake smile. But you wonder, do they really know what I am trying to say? Do these people really care? Jesus was utterly free and void of fear. He was not in bondage to other people's opinions. When Jesus came to the tomb of Lazarus, he wept. Jesus is now at the right hand of God; and he still shows his feelings: he is touched with the *feeling* of our weaknesses (Heb. 4:15). He does not moralize or scold. He is touched. And he shows his feelings.

Joseph further showed that he was unashamed because he promised to intercede for them: "I will go up, and shew Pharaoh, and say unto him, My brethren, and my father's house, which were in the land of Canaan, are come unto me; and the men are shepherds, for their trade hath been to feed cattle; and they have brought their flocks, and their herds, and all that they have" (Gen.

46:31-32). That is what Jesus did. "And I will pray the Father, and he shall give you another Comforter [the Holy Spirit] that he may abide with you for ever" (John 14:16).

But Joseph told them what to say as well, "When you come and talk to the Pharaoh, he is going to ask you what job you do." Joseph was showing his brothers that he was not ashamed of them. God will teach you how to pray and give you words to say. Joseph showed further that he was unashamed of his brothers by giving responsibility to them. It is a wonderful thing that God entrusts us with a job to do. We don't feel that anybody really accepts us until he gives us responsibility. It shows that we are being trusted. It is an honor to think that we have been asked to do something.

Joseph was not ashamed of his brothers despite the way they would be looked at by the Egyptians. For shepherds were despised by them (v. 34). I find this so interesting. Joseph says, "Now look, I know the Pharaoh. I know how his mind works. He's going to ask you, 'What is your occupation?'" We might think that Joseph would hedge here. But no, "You say that you are shepherds. Just tell the truth to the Pharaoh. And say not only that you are shepherds but that is all you have ever been. That's what our father did, that's what our grandfather did. That's what we are—shepherds." A shepherd was an abomination to the Egyptian. That was the worst thing you could be. But Joseph showed that he was not ashamed of his own family though he was the prime minister of the strongest and most prestigious nation in the world.

Finally, Joseph proved beyond all doubt that he wasn't ashamed of his brothers by presenting them to the Pharaoh himself. Joseph said to Pharaoh, "My father and my brethren have all come." He then presented five of his brothers to the Pharaoh.

Jesus will present us to the Father. He will even tell you what to say to the Father: you must admit to what is abhorrent to his nature. For just as shepherds were an abomination to any Egyptian, sin is abhorrent before the face of the Father. I don't have the vocabulary to explain how much God hates sin. And yet the only way we will ever be saved is by admitting our sin. We must come clean and see what God does with us. Jesus will present us to the Father not only now but in the end. Jesus prayed, "Father, I will that they also, whom thou hast given me, be with me where I am" (John 17:24). That is a promise that we will be presented faultless to the Father some day before the presence of his glory. That means that we are going to go to heaven when we die.

It is really true. One day we are going to be there. We will not have any sin. We will not know tired bodies. We will not know the hurt from criticism. "And God shall wipe away all tears." We are going to heaven, that is, we are if we have come to the Father and admitted what we are.

From the life of Joseph we can see how God keeps his word. He does this, first, by not bringing up our past.

Have you got a skeleton in your cupboard? Are there sins that you have committed and which weigh heavily on you? Do you wish for the feeling that all the sins that you have committed could be washed away? Would you like to think the burden could go? It can. What Joseph put to the Pharaoh, the Pharaoh agreed to: "You can have it." Jesus by dying on the cross took your sin, and the promise is that "he ever liveth to make intercession" for those who come to God by him (Heb. 7:23).

> *Just as I am, without one plea,*
> *But that Thy blood was shed for me;*
> *And that Thou bidd'st me come to Thee,*
> *O Lamb of God, I come! I come!*
>
> —Charlotte Elliott

I can make you a promise. It is not really a promise—it is God's word. He will never bring up your past. He will wash your sins away by the blood of his Son. "As far as the east is from the west, so far hath he removed our transgressions from us" (Ps. 103:12). It's only the devil—never God—who will bring up your past. Pharaoh never knew about the awful past of the brothers because Joseph's love buried their past from him.

The second way Joseph demonstrates how God keeps his word is in the way he continued to care for his brothers after their arrival in Egypt. Here is what Pharaoh said: "The land of Egypt is before thee; in the best of the land make thy father and brethren to dwell" (Gen. 47:6). They would have the very best. That is the result of Joseph's care. His brothers would live in the middle of plenty while the rest of the world was in famine. No, they didn't drive Rolls Royces. They lived in tents. That was their life-style; it was what God ordained for them.

But they had glory. How do we know that? They had the ear of the king. They could go to the Pharaoh any time they wanted because they could do it through Joseph their brother. Who else in Egypt could do that? We too have this promise as God's children. We could call this a subsidiary benefit of being a Christian. Paul said, "But my God shall supply all your need according to his riches in glory by Christ Jesus" (Phil. 4:19).

THIRTY-SIX
LIVING IN THE OVERFLOW OF ANOTHER'S GLORY

Joseph was reunited with his father and eleven brothers in Egypt. Who would have dreamed that the young man, who had been given the coat of many colors, then sold by his brothers into slavery, would end up as the prime minister of the greatest nation in the world at the time? But as a consequence of Joseph's gift and his interpretation of Pharaoh's dream, we find him the head of this nation. He had prophesied that there would be seven years of plenty followed by seven years of famine. And everything was turning out exactly right. Two years into the time of famine, Joseph was reunited with his father and brothers. The famine was universal, so Joseph called for his father to come and live in Egypt. Had they stayed in Canaan they might have died. People were dying all over the world from lack of food and water, but not Jacob and his sons. For in Egypt they were going to eat well. They were going to have the best of the land and on top of that live in prestige, in glory, even having the ear of the king. Jacob and the eleven brothers had come to live in the overflow of Joseph's glory.

Now sometimes a person delights to live in the overflow of another's glory; sometimes he resents it. There are those who cannot bear the thought of not living in their own glory. Others are quite happy to live in the overflow of another's glory. Sometimes a wife will be quite willing to live in the overflow of her husband's glory, and once in a while we hear of a husband who

241

lives in the overflow of his wife's glory. I think the present husband of England's prime minister seems to be coping very well. Some years ago Billy Carter, a former U.S. president's brother, was living in the overflow of his brother's glory. But he wasn't handling it too well. And there are those who may do it not because of being related; the lady-in-waiting at Buckingham Palace is quite happy to live in the overflow of the glory of Her Majesty the queen. Possibly those on the staff at 10 Downing Street or in the White House, are quite happy that the pinnacle of their lives lies in being near somebody who is great. They have never themselves achieved greatness but live in the overflow of someone who has.

And yet that is not what I mean now. For it is one thing to jump at the chance to live in the overflow of another's glory and quite another to surrender voluntarily to it—when it takes great grace to do so. Bowing the knee to their brother Joseph was not what those brothers had wanted. They had wanted him dead— or at least out of the way. They sold Joseph to the Ishmaelites, never expecting to hear from him again. But he turned up as prime minister, and this was a humbling thing for them. They even had to forgive God for exalting Joseph. Why, they could ask, did God use that spoiled son of his father who had paraded his gift before them? Joseph had been so insensitive! But God selected Joseph to preserve them, and they had to come to terms with that. These brothers showed great grace because they became willing to say, "God, it was right for you to do this." They bowed the knee to Joseph, fulfilling his dream and prophecy—and they did so gladly. Now these brothers were going to spend the rest of their lives living in the overflow of their brother's glory.

Joseph emerged once more as a type of Christ. The first thing that he did was promise to intercede for them. Joseph showed that he was not ashamed of his family though they were shepherds and therefore an abomination to Egyptians. The highest compliment that our Lord can give us is to intercede for us, knowing *all* there is to know about us. Now it could be that you know people who can intercede for you, and they do it because they know it is going to help. Or they may do it because they *don't* know all that there is to know about you. And you don't want them to know because if they knew everything about you, they might back down and say, "We cannot intercede for you in the light of what we now know." But there was Joseph, promising to intercede to the Pharaoh, knowing *all* about his brothers. Joseph kept his word.

The overflow of Joseph's glory meant direct access into the presence of Pharaoh. "He took some of his brethren, even five men, and presented them unto Pharaoh" (Gen. 47:2). Why did he do that? He wanted them to talk to the Pharaoh themselves. And so with you; when you come into the presence of God you talk to him yourself. Do you know what it is to talk to God directly? You talk to God yourself because you are your own priest. Jesus said, "At that day ye shall ask in my name: and I say not unto you, that I will pray the Father for you" (John 16:26). It was our Lord's way of saying, "You will do the praying." Peter said, "Ye also, as lively stones, are built up a spiritual house . . . a chosen generation, a royal priesthood" (1 Pet. 2:5, 9).

Joseph brought five of his brothers and presented them to the Pharaoh. Why five? This is symbolic of a selection of some for a certain task. Paul said, "For the body is not one member, but many. If the foot shall say, Because I am not the hand, I am not of the body; is it therefore not of the body? And if the ear shall say, Because I am not the eye, I am not of the body; is it therefore not of the body?" (1 Cor. 12:14-16). For in the body of Christ there are certain things that must be done, and God has a work for each of us. For some he has a work that nobody else can do. Jesus said, "You have not chosen me, but I have chosen you" (John 15:16). "Unto whomsoever much is given, of him shall be much required" (Luke 12:48).

What do you say then when you go right into the presence of God? You tell him what he already knows. Now the Pharaoh knew who these eleven men were that had come from Canaan. Of course he knew. But he asked them, "What is your occupation?" And so they answered, "Thy servants are shepherds, both we, and also our fathers" (Gen. 47:3). This is a hint to us when it comes to our praying. You tell God what he already knows. Why do that? Because he asks you to.

The Pharaoh would know whether they were telling the truth. "All things are naked and opened unto the eyes of him with whom we have to do" (Heb. 4:13). And when you talk to God, nothing can be more foolish than to try to convince God of something about yourself, as though you were informing him. Or you might wish to pretend in God's presence. God knows whether you are telling the truth. Jesus said, "Your Father knoweth what things ye have need of, before ye ask him" (Matt. 6:8). And yet you ask him because you are opening your heart to him; you know that you are accepted for being you. Not having to pretend. Not having to say anything to make an impression on God.

What was their plea to Pharaoh? And were they going to talk for themselves? Keep in mind that a shepherd was an abomination to Egyptians. But here they were—shepherds, actually talking to the Pharaoh. How could they do this? It was because they were there through the authority of Joseph. Joseph's authority allowed these shepherds into the presence of the king. So we have at God's right hand a High Priest who is actually touched with the feeling of our weaknesses and has authority with the Father. We enter by a "new and living way"—the blood of Jesus (Heb. 10:20).

Joseph had told them what to say. They said to Pharaoh, "To sojourn in the land we are come." That is what Joseph told them to ask: "Tell Pharaoh that you want to stay here." And they did. That's not all. On top of that they admitted their helplessness. They went on to say, "To sojourn in the land are we come; for thy servants have no pasture for their flocks." Here they were, putting themselves on the line, admitting before the Pharaoh that they had nothing to give in exchange.

When you come into the presence of God, I can tell you what not to say. Do not try to impress him with your ability, or how lucky God would be if he had you, or how much better off he would be. If you have any idea that God needs you or that you are going to help his image in the world—don't talk to God. There is only one way for you to talk to him: tell the truth and don't hide anything. They admitted their helplessness and made themselves vulnerable. "For the famine is sore in the land of Canaan." They made the Pharaoh see that *they* knew how bad their plight was. And the Pharaoh listened. The Pharaoh knew they were in trouble. He knew about the famine in the world and that people were dying. Now how do you think the Pharaoh would react if they had hidden the truth and said, "We don't really need any help, but we would appreciate staying here a while."

Do you want to know what will move the heart of God? Confess it all. Don't hide a thing.

They came clean. "We want to live here. There's a famine in the world. We're in trouble." They made a plea that the Pharaoh would have mercy. And so they concluded: "We pray thee, let thy servants dwell in the land of Goshen" (Gen. 47:4). A plea for mercy. Have you ever asked anybody for mercy? Do you know what it is to ask for mercy? Whenever you ask for mercy, it will be because you have nothing to give in exchange. You have no bargaining power. As long as you think you have some leverage, you don't need to ask for mercy. Use another word. But when you are at rock bottom and have nothing to offer—no leverage—that is what moves God's heart.

Though they had the promise of the ear of Pharaoh, it did not follow that they stood in his presence without fear and trembling. The first thing that Joseph did was to make them respect the Pharaoh. He was the highest authority there was in the world at that time. These brothers knew that. As we come into the presence of the most High God we need to know something of the one by whose authority we come. They knew who Joseph was, and we must know who Jesus is. They believed that Joseph was telling them the truth. We must believe all that Jesus has told us. But they still had to ask for themselves. They had to discover for themselves whether Joseph did have the authority that he claimed.

When we come directly to God, trusting entirely that what Jesus said was true, the Father turns to the Son. The Pharaoh turned to Joseph. He didn't turn to them but to Joseph. It is the way the Godhead works. We have in this story an organizational chart that shows us something of the eternal Godhead; it shows us something of the relationship between the Father and the Son. Pharaoh spoke to Joseph, "Thy father and thy brethren are come unto thee" (v. 5). The simplicity of it. The Pharaoh acknowledged what is true. And the next thing was a reaffirmation of Joseph's preeminence in Egypt: "The land of Egypt is before thee." The Father turned to the Son, "Sit thou at my right hand, until I make thine enemies thy footstool" (Ps. 110:1). For God had said to the Son "Ask of me, and I shall give thee the heathen for thine inheritance, and the uttermost parts of the earth for thy possession" (Ps. 2:8).

The Pharaoh thus reasserted the authority of Joseph before those ten brothers. All that the Father ever does is with his own

Son's honor in mind. The Pharaoh had previously made a decree that everyone would have to bow the knee to Joseph. And so the first thing the Pharaoh did was turn to Joseph and reaffirm his authority—"The land of Egypt is before thee." All this was going on with the five brothers looking on; they observed for themselves how powerful Joseph really was. Once Jesus took Peter, James, and John into a mountain, and the glory of God came upon them; they were overshadowed by a cloud. At the end they heard a voice from heaven, "This is my beloved Son: hear him" (Mark 9:7). In all that the Father ever does he honors his Son.

But there is more: they got preferential treatment. "The land of Egypt is before thee; *in the best of the land* make thy father and brethren to dwell" (italics mine). God's people have a certain indemnity in a land of famine and wickedness. This kind of promise is built into your salvation once you honor the Son of God.

> He that dwelleth in the secret place of the most High shall abide under the shadow of the Almighty. I will say of the Lord, He is my refuge and my fortress: my God; in him will I trust. Surely he shall deliver thee from the snare of the fowler, and from the noisome pestilence. He shall cover thee with his feathers, and under his wings shalt thou trust: his truth shall be thy shield and buckler. Thou shalt not be afraid for the terror by night . . . nor for the destruction that wasteth at noonday. A thousand shall fall at thy side, and ten thousand at thy right hand; but it shall not come nigh thee. (Ps. 91:1-7)

All this comes from living in the overflow of Christ's glory.

THIRTY-SEVEN
GOD MEANT IT
FOR GOOD

> But as for you, ye thought evil against me; but God meant it unto good, to bring to pass, as it is this day, to save much people alive. Now therefore fear ye not: I will nourish you, and your little ones. And he comforted them, and spake kindly unto them. (Gen. 50:20-21)

These words explain the greatness of Joseph. If we want to know why God exalted Joseph to the lofty position of prime minister of Egypt, it is because he learned how to forgive. In a word: he learned to love.

The hardest lesson in the world we have to learn as Christians is how to love. None of us comes by love naturally. I am not talking about physical love, sexual love, love for nature, love for family, or love for your hobby. I am talking about a level of love that is exceedingly rare. Before he could ever be used, Joseph had to come to the place *where he loved, where he totally forgave.*

Perhaps you have never ever had the experience of having to forgive somebody who has done something bad to you. If you haven't, this chapter won't mean quite so much to you. But you may need it later. If you are a Christian, there will come a day—it may be soon—when the unexpected, the unthinkable happens to you. Your immediate question will be "God, why did you let this happen?" The temptation will be to let yourself be filled with bitterness, hatred, and desire for revenge.

Joseph had been sold into slavery by his brothers. And yet he had been given a promise from God that he was going to be used. After he arrived in Egypt, he was landed with a very good job. He became the high man in the household of Potiphar, an officer of rank and stature in Pharaoh's government. Then Joseph was falsely accused and was put in prison. While in prison he had what appeared to be an opportunity to get out but it didn't work. I can tell you what happened in that prison; I'm as sure of this as I am sure of anything—God did not exalt Joseph until he became willing in his heart totally to forgive his brothers.

Many years have now passed. Joseph's father, Jacob, has died, and the ten brothers are fearful that, with the old man no longer there, Joseph would want revenge at last. And they come to him. They are scared. Trembling. What would he do to them now? And what did Joseph say? "You meant it for evil, God meant it for good." These words are proof of a godly man.

What is even more amazing is that Joseph could talk like this when, in a sense, he had nothing more to live for. He had had his success. He, too, was shortly going to die. He had made it. There was no need to show love in order to be used by God in the future. What he *could* have done was get vengeance on those brothers. He could have said to himself, "Well, I've done everything right up to now. There's nothing more God can do for me because I've reached the top. I'm as high as you can get. I'm prime minister. Up till now, I've kept my covenant with the Lord. I've forgiven my brothers. But I don't have to now. My father's gone; he won't know about it." Joseph could have gone after them. But here is a man who did the very opposite.

Equally interesting, the brothers of Joseph should actually have mistrusted Joseph. They came to him; in my opinion they manufactured a message. You might differ with me. It could be that Jacob *did* leave a message before he died. That is possible. But I suspect that Jacob didn't ever say this. They say that Jacob had said it; they thought that this might carry some weight with Joseph. And so they came to him and said in effect, "We just thought you would like to know that before Dad died he wanted us to tell you that you should be merciful to us."

When Joseph heard the message, he wept. I believe he wept because he was so hurt that they had thought that he would want to hurt them. The fact that they would send a message like that suggests that is what *they* would have done had they been in Joseph's shoes. They judged Joseph by their own standard, disclosing unwittingly how much was still wrong with them. What made Joseph weep was that he could say to himself, "Do you really think that I've been a hypocrite for seventeen years? Do you really think that the whole time you have been living here in Goshen I've been putting on a big act? That I didn't mean it the first time when I said 'God meant it for good' ?"

Joseph was now having even to forgive them for what they had just done. And he said to them, "You did think evil." Now they had made him say that. They put it right in his lap. As if to say, "All right, yes, you did think evil—but wait a minute, *God meant it for good.*"

Joseph demonstrated that he had forgiven them all along. But for those seventeen years the ten brothers had lived under the fear that perhaps they weren't really forgiven. Perhaps you have received the Lord—it may have been seventeen years ago, but you can't really believe that God has forgiven you. Well, he has! Why do you have those thoughts? Are you not judging God by your own standard? The reason you are having so much difficulty accepting God's forgiveness is possibly because you are having difficulty forgiving another person. You then project that feeling upon God and conclude, "I don't believe God has really forgiven me."

It is a most startling discovery for a good number of Christians—it has happened to some who have been saved for years—to realize what they should have known all along: that God really *did* forgive them, that all sin was completely washed away. Forgiven! Forgotten! Never will your sin be held against you. For if you have asked God to wash away your sins by the blood of Jesus, they are gone.

Of course, the brothers of Joseph acknowledged what they did. Sometimes, however, we are called upon to forgive people who refuse to acknowledge that they have even done anything wrong. And there are those who don't think they have done anything wrong. But you have got to forgive them, too—they are the hardest people to forgive.

There are ways that we can know whether or not we have really forgiven another person. It is one thing to say, "I have forgiven him for what he did"—we can say it and think we mean it—but it is another thing to truly and *totally* forgive.

There are four proofs of total forgiveness. The first is that you don't want the other person to be afraid. Joseph said unto them, "Fear not: for am I in the place of God?" (Gen. 50:19). When you have totally forgiven another person, you don't want them to be afraid of you. Do you know the feeling of wanting another person to be just a little bit afraid of you? You refuse to be very friendly so that they remain worried whether or not you have forgiven them. Perhaps you give them the ever-so-slight cold shoulder—the type of thing that another couldn't be absolutely sure about. We are all experts at this, aren't we? Or we act as though we don't see them; or we say all the right words—we even put on a smile—but we convey an unloving feeling so that the other person still feels unforgiven, because that is what we want them to feel. We have all done that, haven't we? Why? We want to control them so that they will be afraid of us.

"Fear has to do with punishment" (1 John 4:18, NIV). When you haven't forgiven another person you want to punish. You punish that person by saying something not very nice—just to hurt him a bit—anything, any innuendo, you just stick the knife in to put them in their place. But *you* are the one that is afraid when you do that. "He that feareth is not made perfect in love" (1 John 4:18). When you want another person to be afraid not only have you not truly forgiven them but you are really afraid of them.

The second way of knowing that you have really forgiven someone is that you refuse to take advantage of any superior position you might be in. Joseph said, "Am I in the place of God?" Now he could have used his position to make them afraid of him. Sometimes this is the only way a person can get respect from another. This is the reason policemen wear uniforms. Joseph refused to use his official position to get their respect. He wanted to be transparently open with them. He wanted them to see and respect *him*—a man who had forgiven them. He didn't want them to be afraid of him in his position.

You are really putting yourself in the place of God if you *force* another to respect you. You do it because you haven't really forgiven them. You *have* forgiven when you refuse to let another person even think that you are something special. The proof of forgiveness is shown in your refusal to take advantage of your own position or any situation in order to make them look up to you. You must want them to feel that there is nothing special about you at all. When they feel that they know that you really *do* forgive them, and this is an extraordinary experience for both of you.

"As for you, ye thought evil." Joseph had to say that because they had just acknowledged that they had done evil. He would not have said a word about that had they not forced him to mention it. And yet by admitting what they had done, they had made Joseph's task somewhat easier. I repeat, it is harder to forgive the one who thinks he has done no wrong.

To be able to say "God meant it for good" is an *attitude*. It is an attitude we must feel toward those who will not admit they intended to harm us. After all, what does it matter whether or not they admit it? We ought to be able to see the hidden hand of God in *anything*. Why should it matter whether they come clean? It doesn't matter. If you see the hidden hand of God, that matters. When you know that all things work together for good, that God has got your life in his hands, and that whatever affects you affects him, you are beginning to get free. Moreover, when he sees your hurt, he feeds that into his infallible computer and says, "I'm going to make that situation work out for good in such a way that, if my child will just wait and let me handle it, he will see it."

It doesn't matter, then, whether anybody admits to what they have done. In a way, it is better if they don't. For that gives you a greater test, a greater victory. Because what you want to see is that God *is* in it for good. The Christian is a person who has the opportunity to show that he sees God's hidden purpose in evil. It is something that the non-Christian cannot see. When the non-Christian sees evil, what is his reaction? He wants to shake his fist heavenward. Sometimes he will actually say, "If there's a God, I hate him. God, if you are there, I hate you." The Christian *sees* the same thing, the same malady, and all the bad that has happened. But he says, "Just wait." There's an expression, "Don't tell the score in the middle of the game." The non-Christian hastily tells the score—whether it be from an airplane disaster, a tornado, poverty, losing her job, losing a loved one, or having a friend desert him. The non-Christian tells the score, shakes his fist, and says, "This is it, this is final." The Christian says, "It's not over yet. Give God a little time."

The third proof that you really have forgiven another person is that you bind up the wound so completely that you show that all that happened really was *meant to be*. Now Joseph had already said, "Be not grieved, nor angry with yourselves, that ye sold me hither: for *God* did send me before you *to preserve life*" (Gen. 45:5, italics mine). More than anything else, this helps the other person save face.

On Good Friday "it pleased the Lord to bruise him" (Isa. 53:10). The mystery of mysteries is that God punished Jesus for *our* sins. I don't know whether this has ever hit you, but it is an awesome thing to realize that *we* were the ones who crucified Jesus. And yet Jesus was the Lamb slain from the foundation of the world, so that God could say, "I did it." Crucifying Jesus was a wicked act, yet it all happened "by the determinate counsel and foreknowledge of God" (Acts 2:23).

Everything that happens to us who are God's children is for good. Those whom God adopts into his family are often brought to him through tragedy. It is sometimes God's way of luring us into his family. It may be that adversity has driven us to our knees. It may be that we blush to think that the only time we sought God was when something bad happened. We are all like that, but in the kindness of God he lets us save face and says, "It all happened because I was behind the whole thing."

Joseph's brothers knew they were totally forgiven because Joseph was saying, "This was meant to be." And when they could see that he *really* thought that, it freed them.

The final proof that you have really forgiven the other person is that you keep on forgiving them. It is one thing to do it once. And mean it. But you are not finished. How do you know you have *really* forgiven them? And the answer is: you keep on doing it.

What did Joseph say? "God meant it for good. Don't be afraid." "I will nourish you and your little ones." That was how long it was going to last. "And he comforted them, and spake kindly unto them" (Gen. 50:20). Thus, all that he said to them proved his forgiving them—not only that day but the next day and the day after that. You know you really *have* forgiven and that it is not just a burst of emotional feeling because you keep on doing it. Total forgiveness holds two months later. Six months later. Two years later. Forever.

That is the way it is with God. He gives us a pardon once and for all. Once saved, always saved. He gives us an eternal security the moment we are converted. God would never ask us to forgive another when he himself wouldn't do the same with us.

The most natural thing in the world is to want vengeance. Joseph had a chance to have the last word before he died: the opportunity to take personal vengeance was handed to him on a silver platter. Why didn't he take it? Because he had his eyes on another world. The writer of Hebrews selected one moment, out of many possible moments, in Joseph's life to show that he had faith. What event did he pick? "By faith Joseph, when he died, made mention of the departing of the children of Israel; and gave commandment concerning his bones" (Heb. 11:22). Why that? Joseph was thinking about life beyond the grave. His affection lay beyond anything that he could see. His attachment was for that Promised Land. Abraham, his great-grandfather, had gone about looking for a city whose builder and maker is God (Heb. 11:10). Joseph wanted to be identified with heaven, not Egypt. Do you think that Joseph would want to have a blemish on his life now? Here he was, getting ready to die. And to think of getting vengeance? No. He was going to heaven.

For Joseph to say "God meant it for good" was the easiest thing he ever did. He had forgiven them long, long before. What is more, Joseph was thinking beyond the sphere of this present, earthly journey. When we become enamored with heaven, there is no place for holding a grudge. What is more, it was true: God *meant* it for good. Joseph was only telling them the truth. "And we know that all things work together for *good* to them that love God, to them who are the called according to his purpose" (Rom. 8:28, italics mine).

How good is "good"? Is there good, better, and best in God's scheme of things? All I know for sure is this: at the beginning of the Book of Genesis, God looked over his unfallen creation and said, "It's good." Over the next forty-nine chapters every evil under the sun transpired, not the least of which was the story of Jacob and his sons. But at the very end of it all God could use that word *good* to describe what happened to Israel, the product of fallen nature.

Therefore, when I read that "all things work together for good," then learn what God can call "good," I am content with the word *good*. For what God calls good is good enough.